Spiral to Infinity Steve Allen

"Fractal images are often made up of small images-within-images, constantly repeating and going smaller and smaller."— **Steve Allen**

Investigations

IN NUMBER, DATA, AND SPACE®

Student Activity Book

Common Core Edition

PEARSON

Glenview, Illinois • Boston, Massachusetts
Chandler, Arizona • Upper Saddle River, New Jersey

T E R C

The Investigations curriculum was developed by TERC, Cambridge, MA.

NSF

This material is based on work supported by the National Science Foundation
("NSF") under Grant No.ESI-0095450. Any opinions, findings, and conclusions or
recommendations expressed in this material are those of the author(s) and do not
necessarily reflect the views of the National Science Foundation.

ISBN-13: 978-0-328-69752-6

ISBN-10: 0-328-69752-4

6 7 8 9 10 V011 15 14 13 12

Spiral to Infinity Steve Allen

"Fractal images are often made up of small images-within-images, constantly repeating and going smaller and smaller." — **Steve Allen**

Investigations
IN NUMBER, DATA, AND SPACE®

How Many of Each?

Investigation 4

Where Does It Go?

In which bin would you put each shape?

Write the letter of the bin under the shape.

NOTE Students sort the following mathematical materials: (a) **connecting cubes,** which are multicolored plastic cubes that snap together; (b) **pattern blocks,** which consist of six shapes: hexagons, trapezoids, triangles, squares, and rhombuses; and (c) **Geoblocks,** which are three-dimensional shapes.

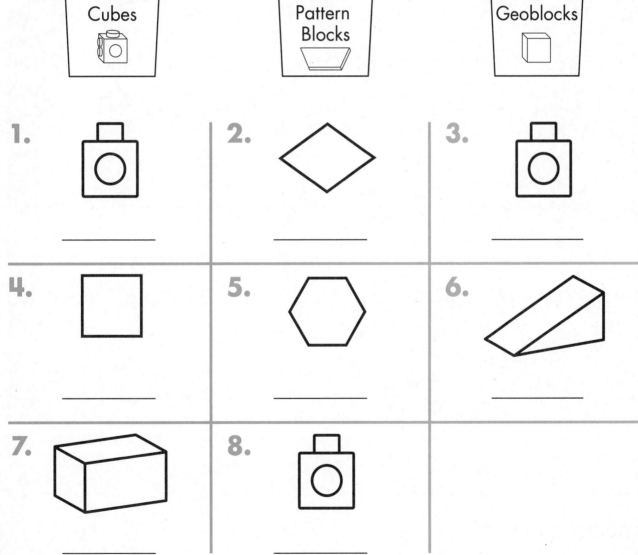

1.

2.

3.

4.

5.

6.

7.

8.

Using a Calendar

Here is a calendar for you. Fill in the month and dates.

Then find a place to hang it at home.

NOTE Students practice recording dates and creating, reading, and using a calendar as a tool for keeping track of time.

SMH 17, 18, 19

Name of Month

Sunday	Monday	Tuesday	Wednesday	Thursday	Friday	Saturday

Special Days

_____   _____

How Many Apples?

There were 7 apples on each tree. Some fell off. Write how many apples are still on the tree and how many fell off.

NOTE Students practice counting and breaking a number into two parts (e.g., 7 = 4 + 3).

1.

On _____   Off _____

2.

On _____   Off _____

3.

On _____   Off _____

4.

On _____   Off _____

5.

On _____   Off _____

6.

On _____   Off _____

Counting 20

1. Color 20 cubes.

NOTE Students count different groups of objects up to 20.

SMH 21–23

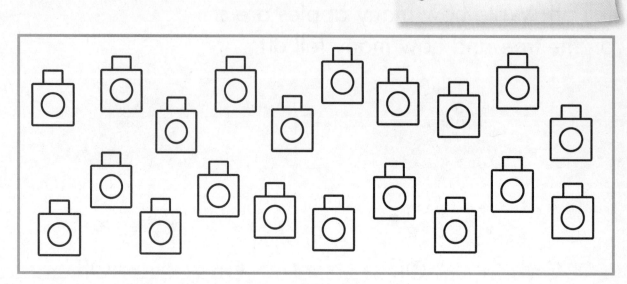

2. How many flowers are there?

There are _____ flowers.

Ongoing Review

3. Look at the pattern. How many white counters are there?

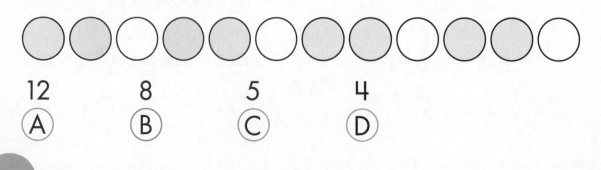

12   8   5   4
Ⓐ   Ⓑ   Ⓒ   Ⓓ

What Is It?

Connect the cubes.
Count from 1 to 20.

NOTE Students practice counting and identifying numbers 1 to 20.

SMH **6–8, 21**

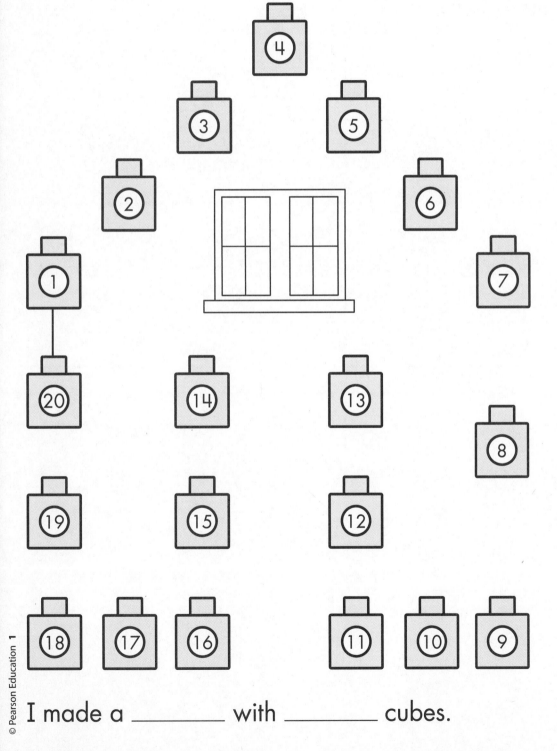

I made a _____ with _____ cubes.

Which Number Is Greater?

Circle the clown in each picture who is balancing more balls.

NOTE Students compare two numbers and identify the greater.

SMH 6–7, 21–23

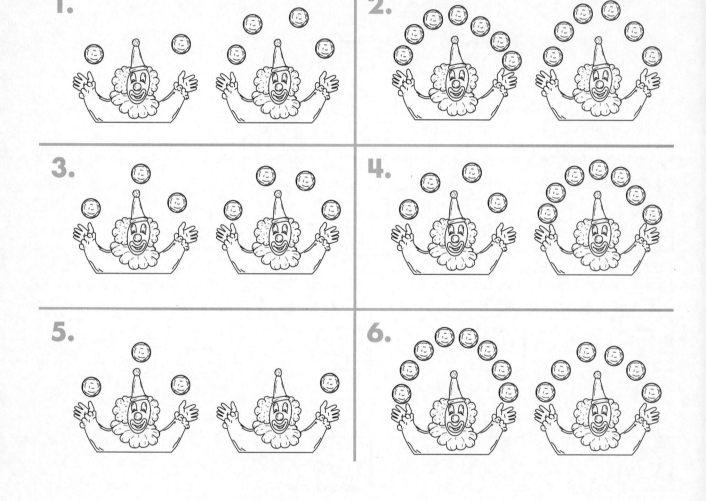

1.

2.

3.

4.

5.

6.

Mystery Boxes

Choose a Mystery Box. Count the objects inside.

I counted the things in

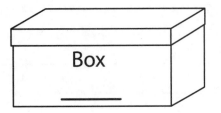

Here is what I found.

Make a Staircase

Color squares to make a staircase.
Then turn this page upside down.
What do you see?

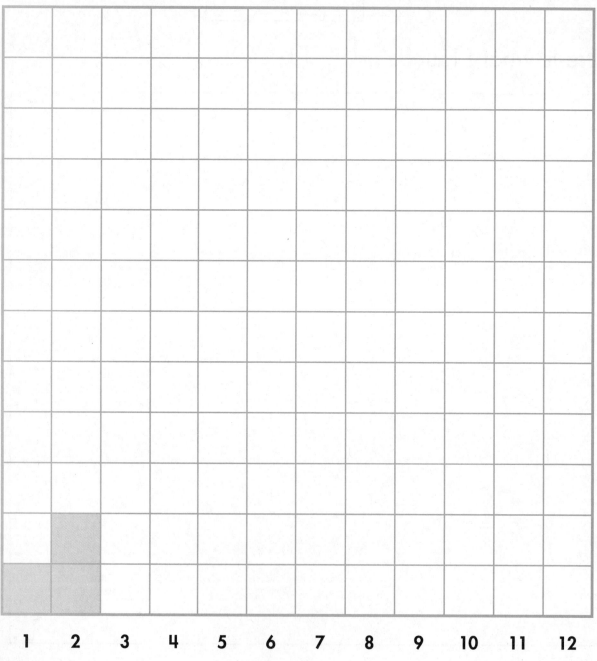

1   2   3   4   5   6   7   8   9   10   11   12

Compare

Pretend that you are playing the game *Compare*.

Circle the card that has more.

NOTE Students compare two numbers and figure out which amount is greater.

SMH **G2**

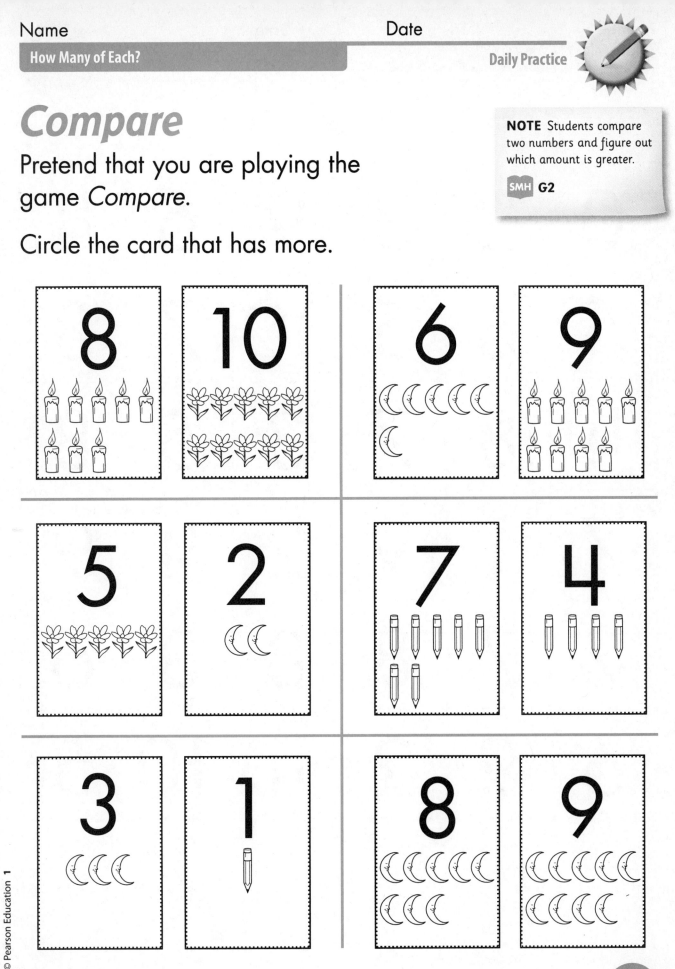

Plus or Minus 1 BINGO Gameboard

0	2	3	9	6	4
5	6	5	10	7	3
4	8	7	3	5	8
7	1	9	2	4	9
2	7	8	8	3	6
6	9	2	4	10	5

Plus or Minus 1

NOTE Students add and subtract 1.

SMH 44–45

Add 1.

1. $6 + 1 =$ _____

2. $9 + 1 =$ _____

3. $1 + 2 =$ _____

4. $1 + 1 =$ _____

Subtract 1.

5. $8 - 1 =$ _____

6. $3 - 1 =$ _____

7. $5 - 1 =$ _____

8. $7 - 1 =$ _____

More Spots

Circle the puppy on the right that has more spots than the puppy on the left.

NOTE Students compare quantities to decide which is more.

SMH 21–23

1. (2) | (1) | (3)

2. (8) | (10) | (6)

3. (4) | (5) | (0)

Ongoing Review

4. Which picture shows 5 crayons in all?

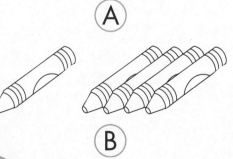

Ⓐ

Ⓒ

Ⓑ

Ⓓ

Play *Compare* at Home 1 (page 1 of 2)

Play *Compare* with someone at home. You and your partner each turn over a card. Write the numbers. Circle the card with the larger number. The first cards show what to do.

NOTE Your child brought home materials to play a game with someone at home. Encourage your child to explain how to play the game. Please help your child fill out and return this sheet.

SMH G2, 21–23

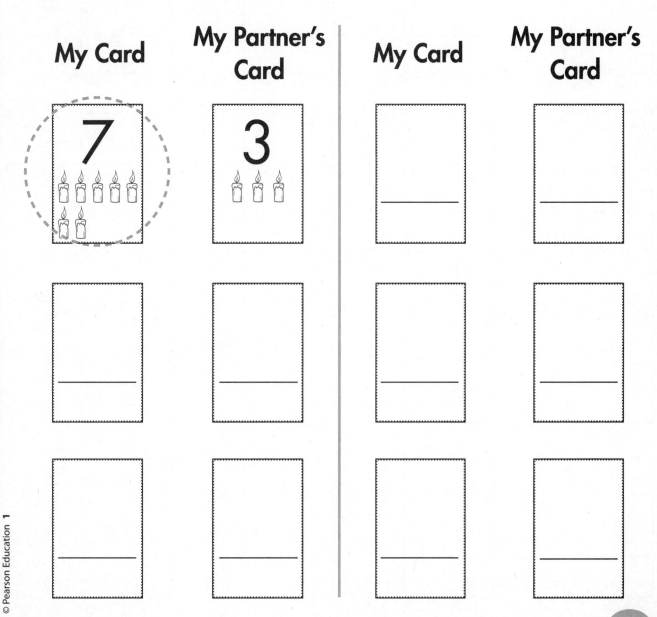

My Card	My Partner's Card	My Card	My Partner's Card
7	3		

© Pearson Education 1

Play *Compare* at Home 1 (page 2 of 2)

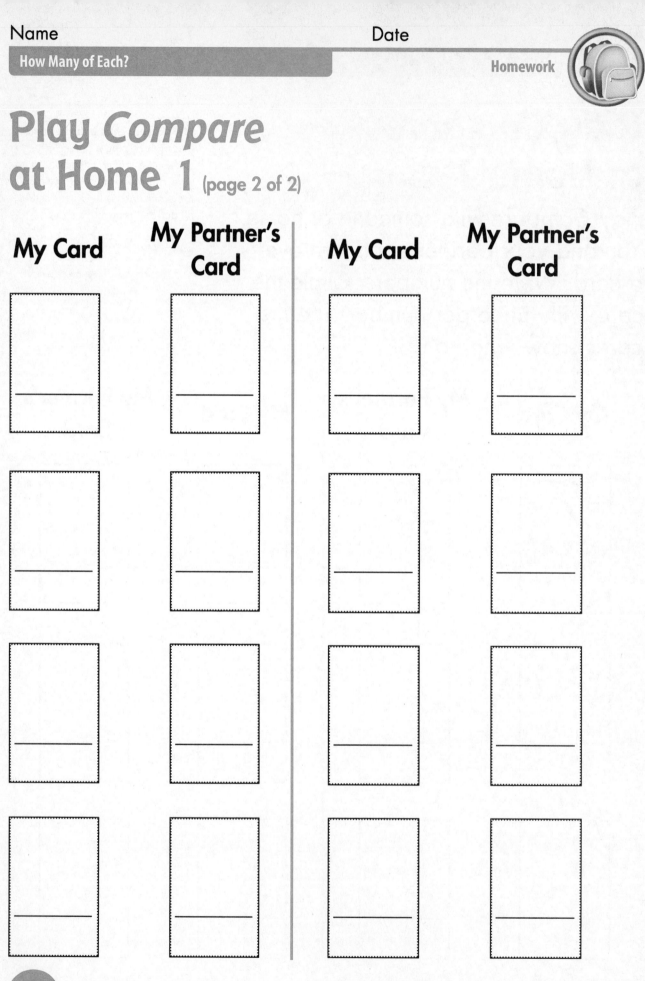

My Card

My Partner's Card

My Card

My Partner's Card

Start With/Get To

Write the missing numbers on the number line.

Here is an example.

NOTE Students practice writing numbers and counting.

SMH 26, 31

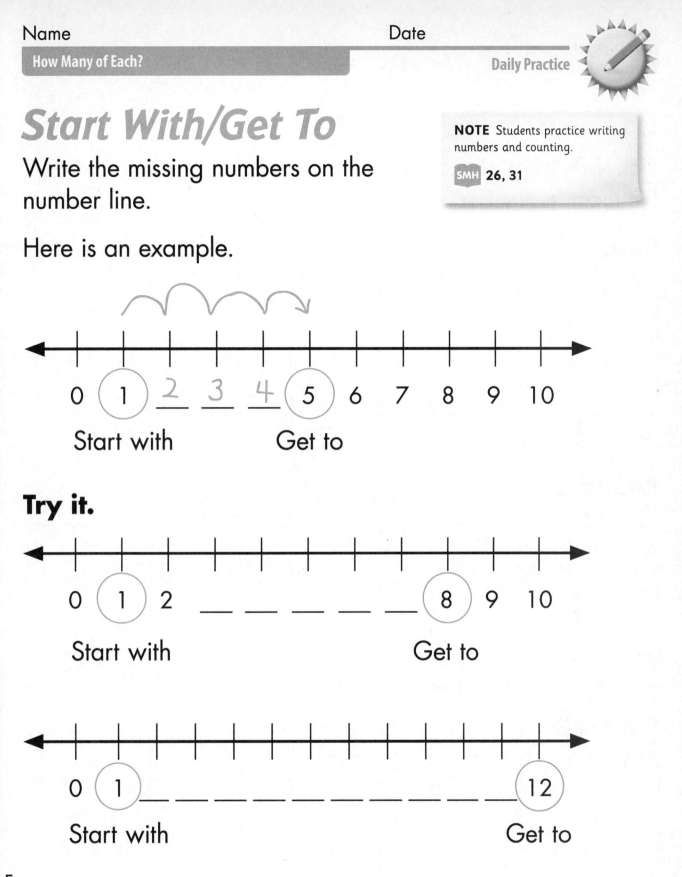

Try it.

Ordering Numbers

Pick 4 Primary Number cards from a deck.
Put them in number order.

Round 1

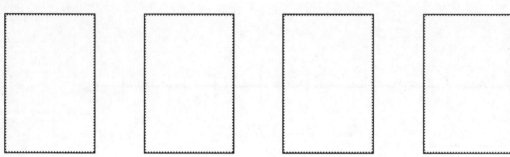

Round 2

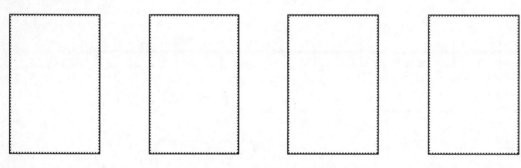

Round 3

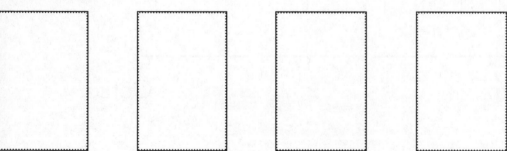

Order, Please!

NOTE Students practice writing and ordering numbers. They also count sets of cubes and identify the numbers that represent these amounts.

SMH 6–7, 21–23

1. Write the numbers to put the cards in order.

   Then connect the towers of cubes to the right number.

11	9	6	3	8	1	12	2	5	10	4	7
1											

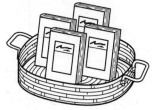

Ongoing Review

2. Which basket has the same number of books as the one shown below?

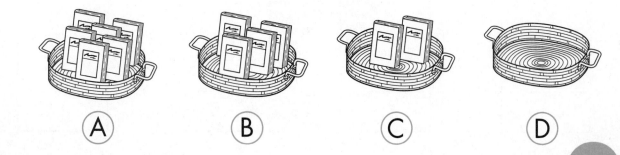

A B C D

Play *Compare* at Home 2

Play *Compare* with someone at home. You and your partner each turn over a card. Write the numbers. Circle the card with the larger number. The first cards show what to do.

NOTE For homework, your child will play a game with someone at home. The materials should be at home from a previous homework assignment. Encourage your child to explain how he or she compared numbers by asking questions such as this: How do you know that 7 is more than 3? Please help your child complete and return this sheet.

SMH **G2, 21–23**

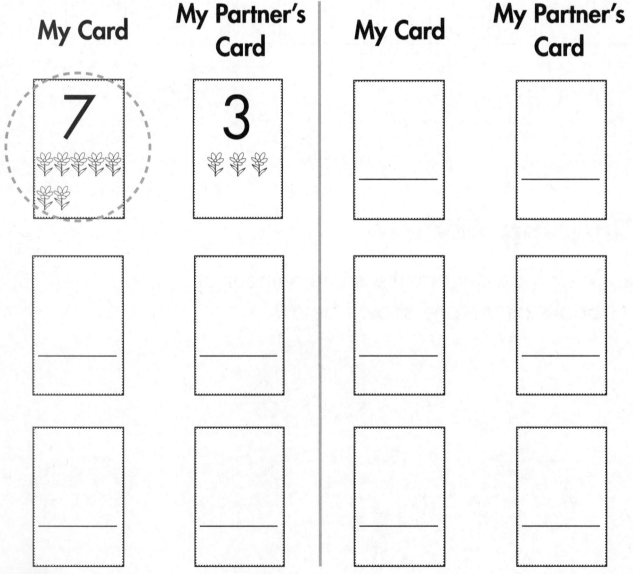

My Card	My Partner's Card	My Card	My Partner's Card
7	3	___	___

Compare Numbers

Circle the card that shows the larger number.

NOTE Students compare two numbers and identify which is larger. They also determine which of two totals is larger.

SMH 21–23, G2, G6

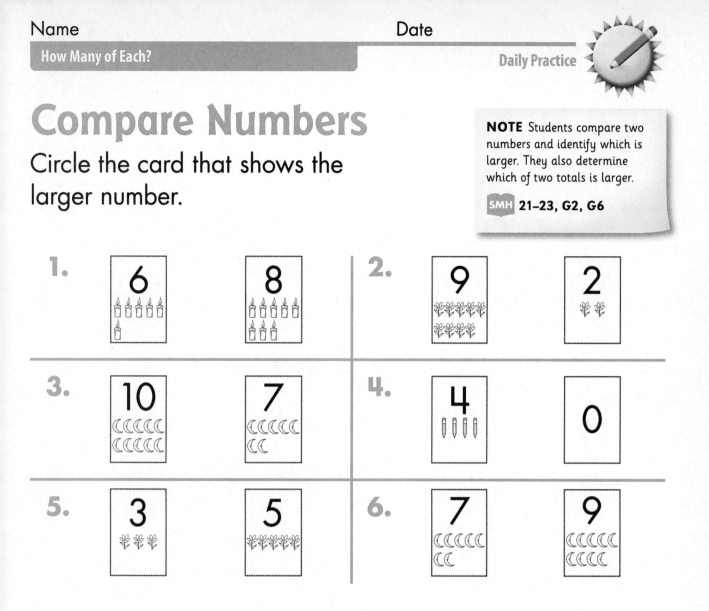

Circle the **pair** of cards that shows the larger total.

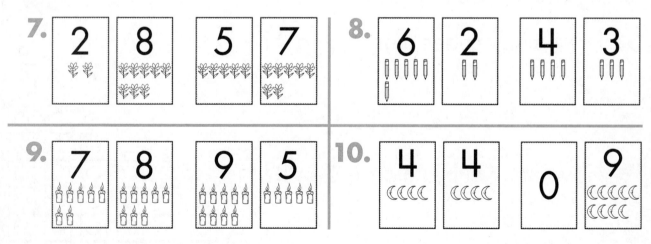

How Many?

NOTE Students practice counting.

SMH 21–23

1. How many students do you count?

_____

2. How many students do you count? _____

Ongoing Review

3. How many cubes high is step A?

2   3   5   7
Ⓐ   Ⓑ   Ⓒ   Ⓓ

4. How many cubes high is step B?

7   6   4   3
Ⓐ   Ⓑ   Ⓒ   Ⓓ

© Pearson Education 1

Play *Double Compare* at Home 1
(page 1 of 2)

Play *Double Compare* with someone at home.

NOTE Your child will play a game with someone at home. The materials should be at home from a previous homework assignment. Encourage your child to explain how to play the game. Please help your child complete and return this sheet.

SMH **G6**

You and your partner each turn over two cards. Write the numbers. Circle the pair of cards that shows more.

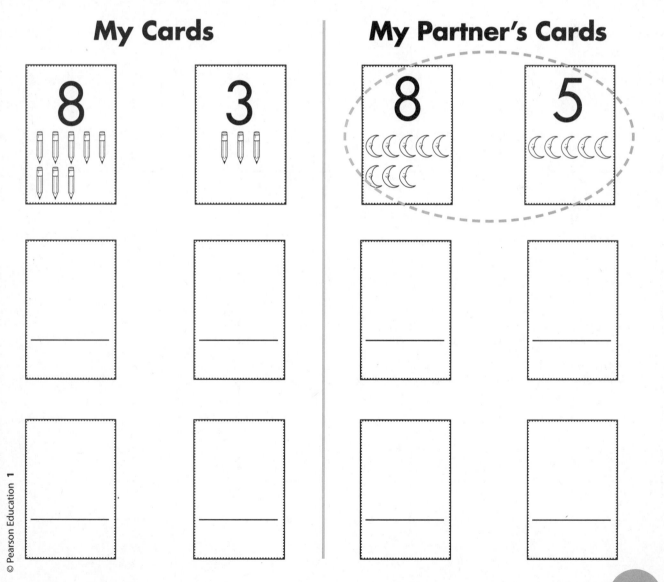

My Cards

My Partner's Cards

Play *Double Compare* at Home 1 (page 2 of 2)

My Cards   ## My Partner's Cards

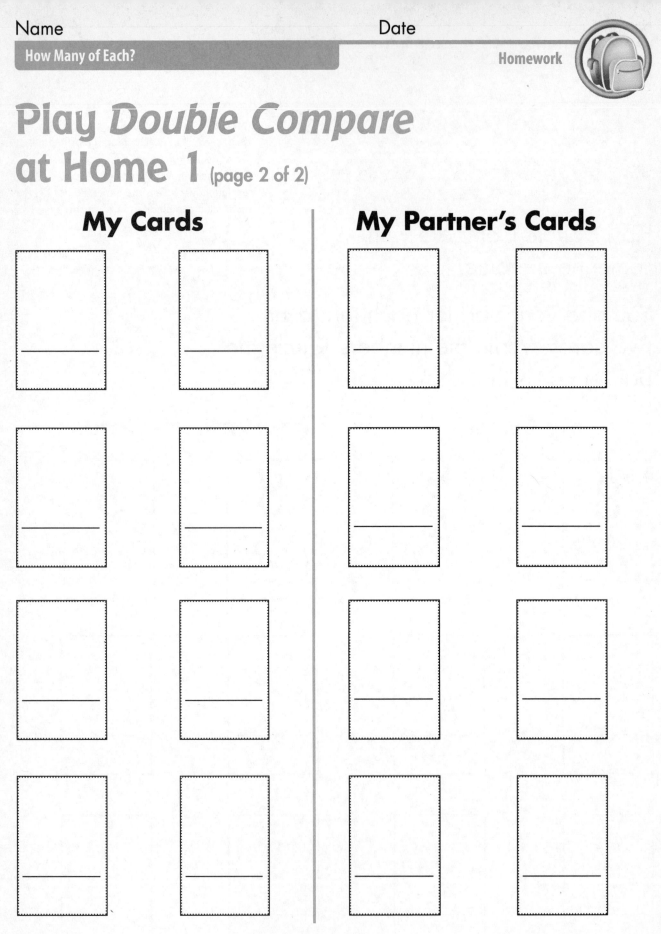

How Many Pencils?

Solve the problem. Show your work.

I was cleaning the classroom.
I found 5 pencils on the floor.
I found 6 pencils under the window.
How many pencils did I find?

Story Problem 1

Solve the problem. Show your work.

Sam went to the zoo.
He saw 3 monkeys in a tree.
He saw 6 more monkeys on the ground.
How many monkeys did Sam see?

NOTE Students combine two quantities to solve a story problem.

SMH 33–37

Roll and Record Recording Sheet

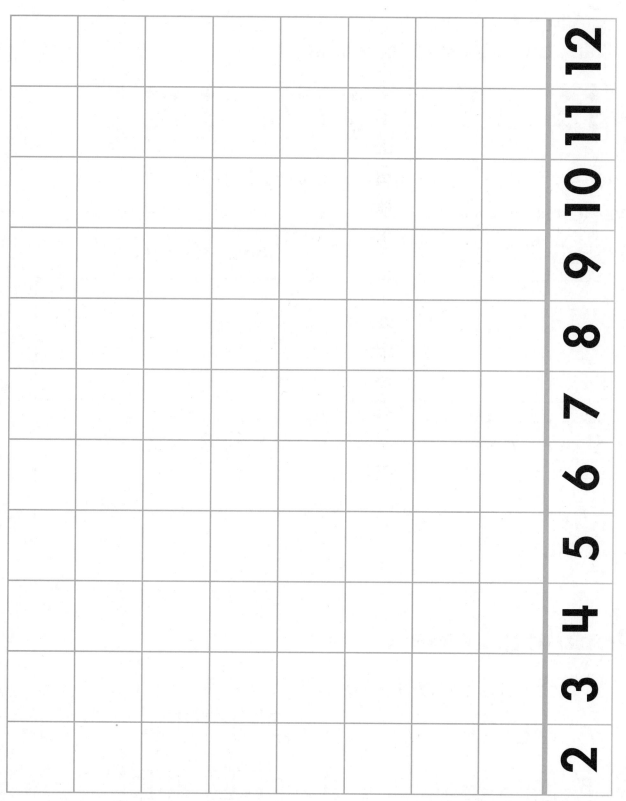

Make a Dot Picture

NOTE Students find ways to organize sets of dots so that they are easy to count.

SMH 21–23

1. Circle the dot pictures that you think are easiest to remember.

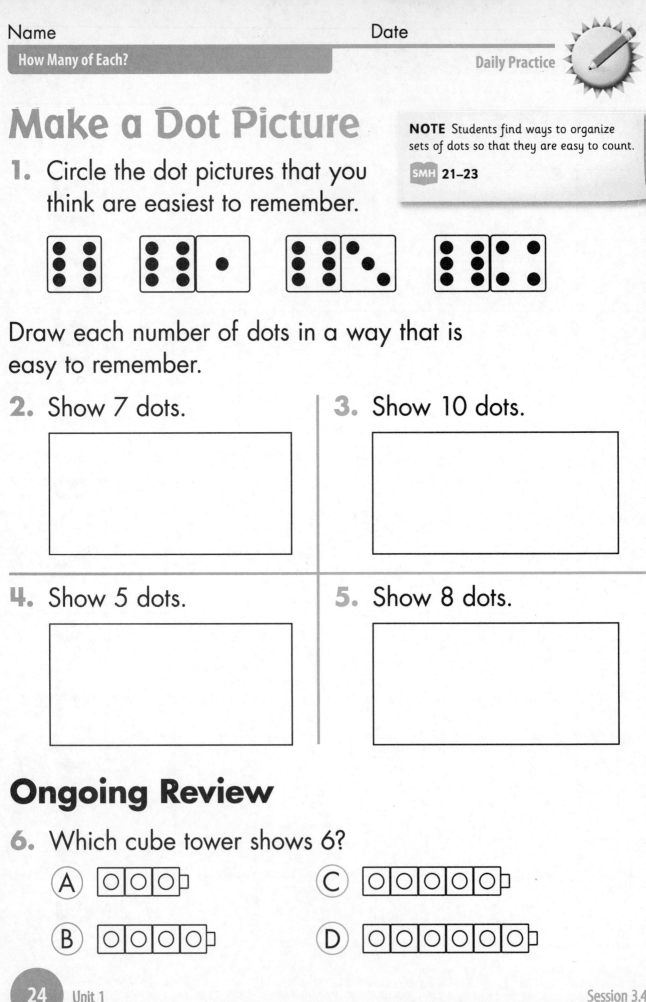

Draw each number of dots in a way that is easy to remember.

2. Show 7 dots.

3. Show 10 dots.

4. Show 5 dots.

5. Show 8 dots.

Ongoing Review

6. Which cube tower shows 6?

Ⓐ

Ⓑ

Ⓒ

Ⓓ

Play *Double Compare* at Home 2 (page 1 of 2)

Play *Double Compare* with someone at home.

You and your partner each turn over two cards. Write the numbers. Circle the pair of cards that shows more.

NOTE For homework, your child will play several rounds of a game with someone at home. The materials should be at home from a previous homework assignment. Encourage your child to explain how he or she compared numbers by asking questions such as these: How do you know that 8 is more than 3? How would you compare 8 + 3 with 8 + 5? Please help your child complete and return this sheet.

SMH G6

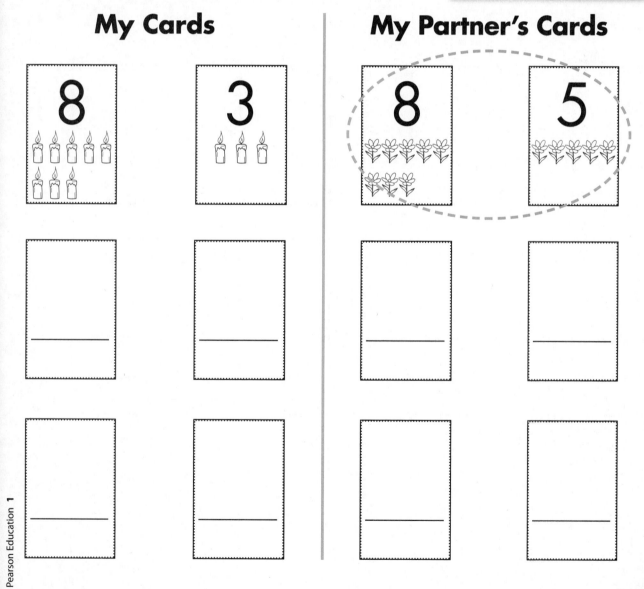

My Cards

My Partner's Cards

Play *Double Compare* at Home 2 (page 2 of 2)

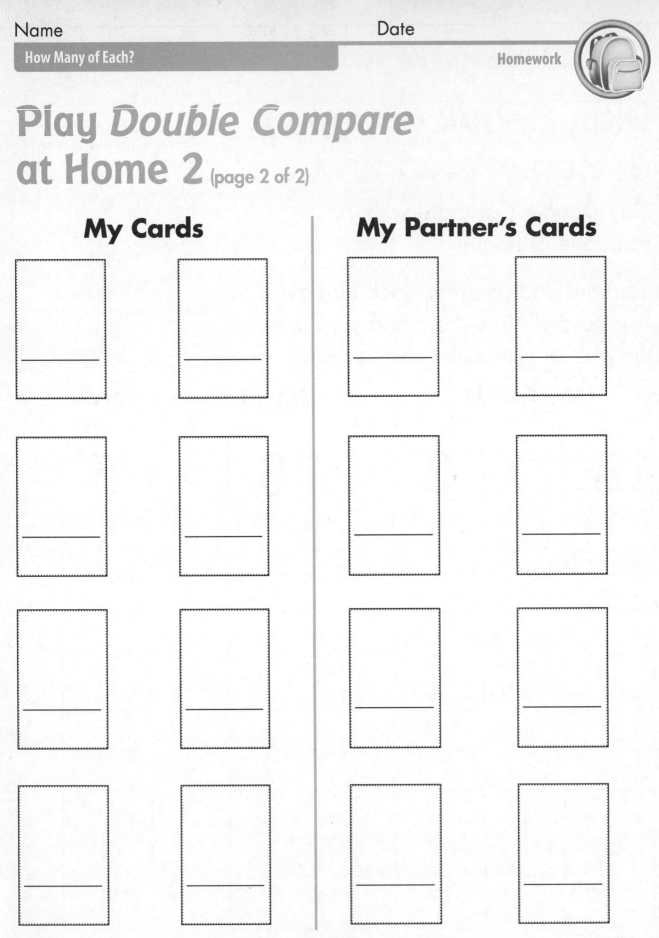

My Cards

My Partner's Cards

How Many Cupcakes?

Solve the problem. Show your work.

Rosa and Max went to the bake sale.
Rosa bought 7 cupcakes.
Max bought 6 cupcakes.
How many cupcakes did they buy?

How Many Dots?

Write the number that tells how many dots.

NOTE Students practice counting and writing numbers.

SMH 6–8, 21–23

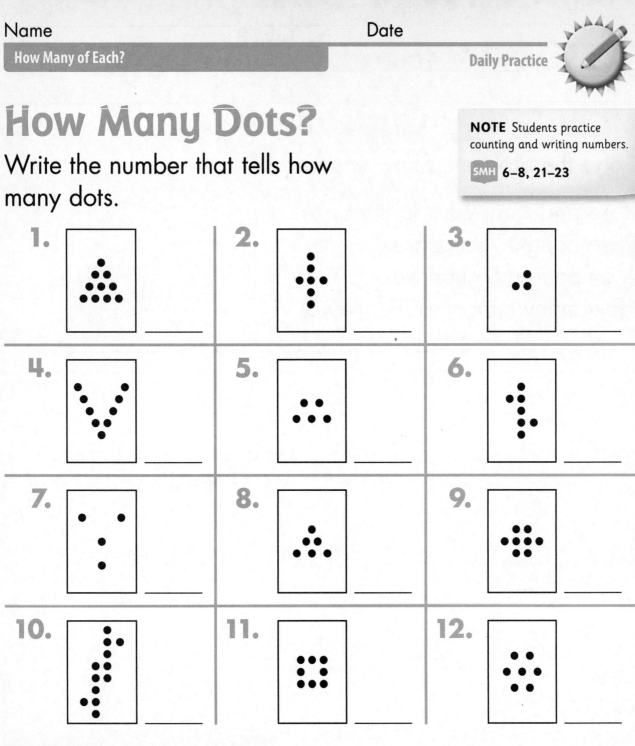

1. ____

2. ____

3. ____

4. ____

5. ____

6. ____

7. ____

8. ____

9. ____

10. ____

11. ____

12. ____

Ongoing Review

Which cube tower shows 5?

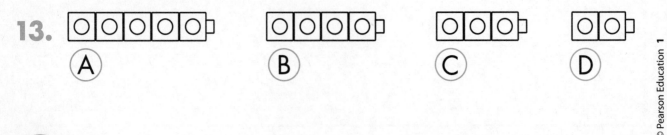

13. Ⓐ Ⓑ Ⓒ Ⓓ

Apples and Oranges

Solve the problem. Show your work.

I went to the store to buy some fruit.
I bought 5 apples and 4 oranges.
How many pieces of fruit did I buy?

NOTE This problem is about combining two numbers. Encourage your child to find his or her own way to solve the problem and record the work.

SMH **33–37**

Double Compare 1

Kim and Sam are playing
Double Compare.

Who has more?
Circle the pair of cards that shows more.

NOTE Students combine two amounts and then figure out which total is larger.

SMH **G6**

Kim's Cards

9

3

Sam's Cards

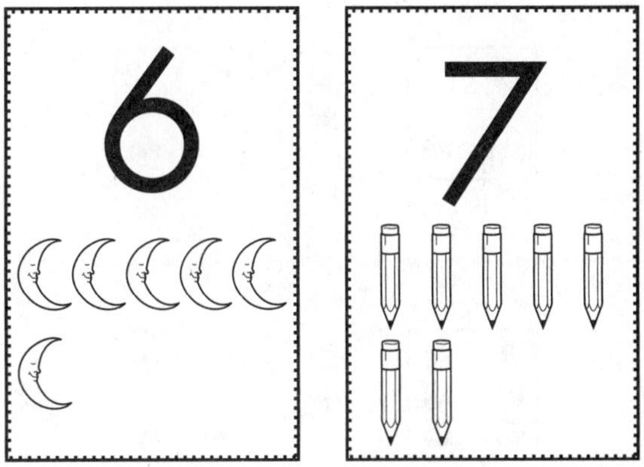

6

7

Show how you know.

Combining Dots
Write the total number.

NOTE Students combine two amounts to find the total.

SMH **G19**

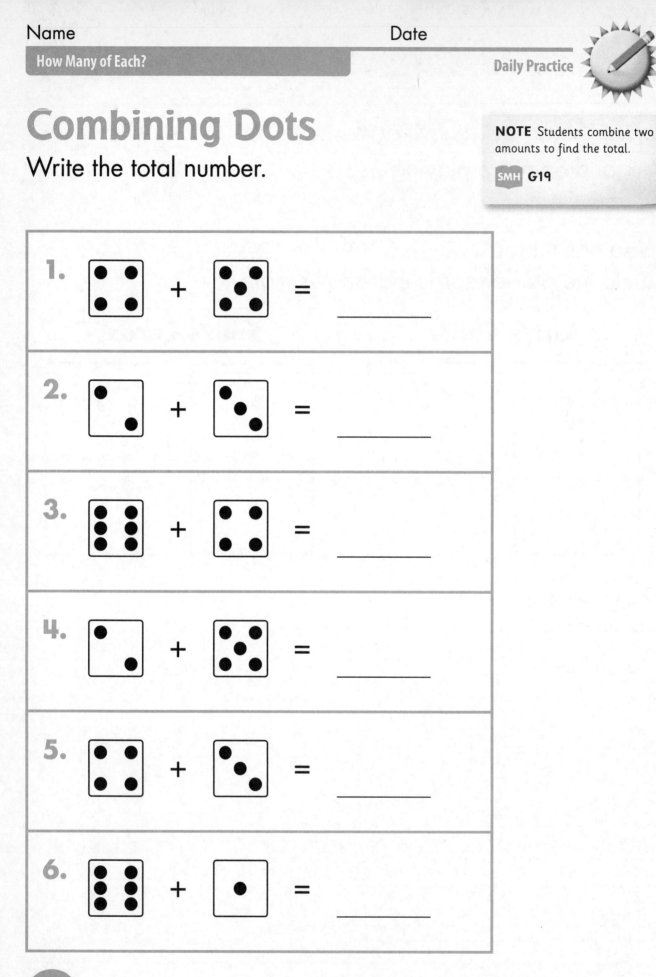

1. ▦ + ▦ = _____

2. ▦ + ▦ = _____

3. ▦ + ▦ = _____

4. ▦ + ▦ = _____

5. ▦ + ▦ = _____

6. ▦ + ▦ = _____

Seven Peas and Carrots

Solve the problem. Show your work.

I have 7 things on my plate.
Some are peas. Some are carrots.
How many of each could I have?
How many peas? How many carrots?

Story Problem 2

Solve the problem. Show your work.

NOTE Students combine two quantities to solve a story problem.

SMH **33–37**

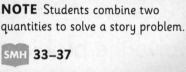

Rosa picked 9 flowers.
Max gave her 4 more.
How many flowers does she have now?

Three Towers Recording Sheet

I used 2 colors of cubes to build 3 towers.

Each tower had _____ cubes in it.

Here is what my towers showed.

Double Compare 2

Kim and Sam are playing
Double Compare.

Who has more?
Circle the pair of cards that shows more.

NOTE Students combine two amounts and then figure out which total is larger.

SMH G6

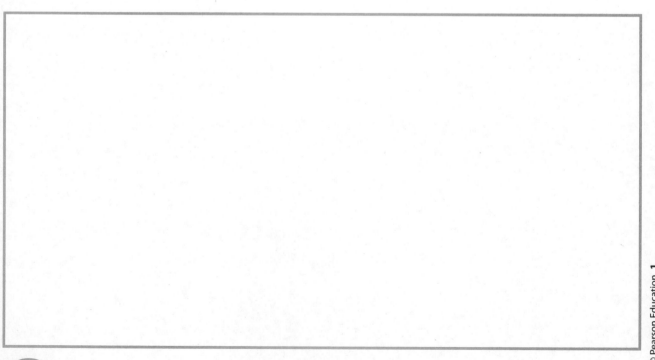

Kim's Cards

Sam's Cards

Show how you know.

Heads and Tails Recording Sheet

Game 1 Total Number _____	
Heads	Tails

Game 2 Total Number _____	
Heads	Tails

Looking at Towers 1

Look at each tower of 10.
Write how many white cubes.
Write how many gray cubes.

NOTE Students practice counting and finding combinations of 10.

SMH 21–23, 48–49

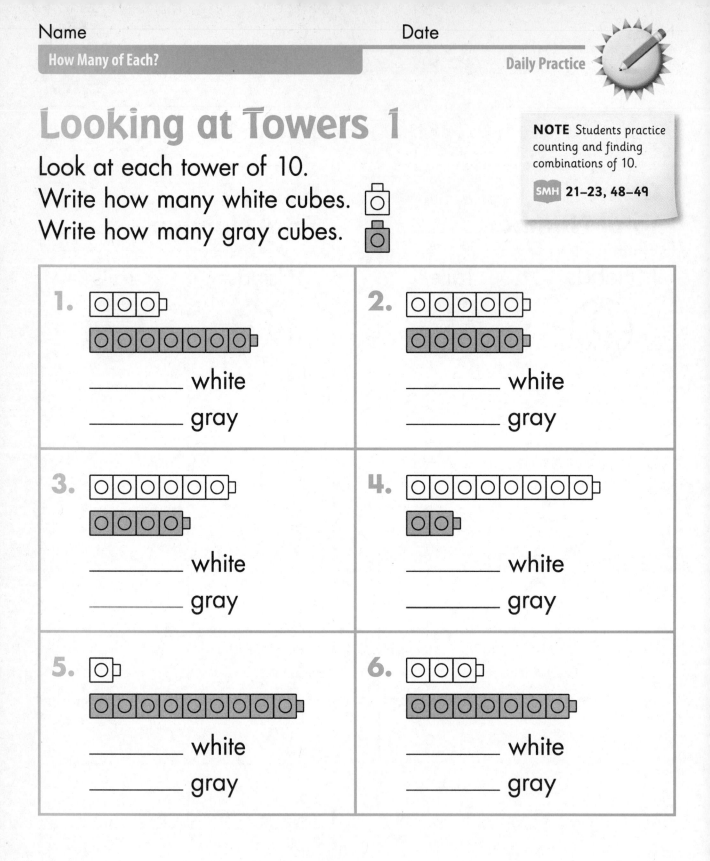

1. _____ white
   _____ gray

2. _____ white
   _____ gray

3. _____ white
   _____ gray

4. _____ white
   _____ gray

5. _____ white
   _____ gray

6. _____ white
   _____ gray

How Many Am I Hiding? Recording Sheet

Total Number _____

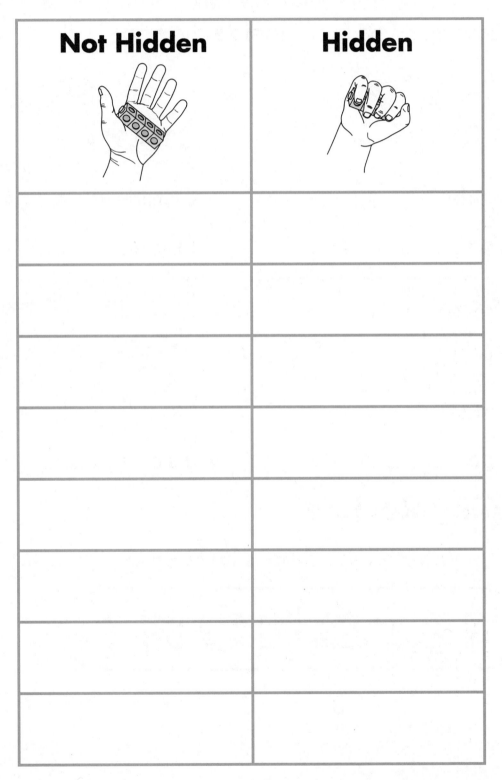

What's in the Bag?

There are 5 balls in all.
Write how many balls are **outside** the bag.
Write how many balls are **inside** the bag.

NOTE Students practice counting and finding combinations of 5.

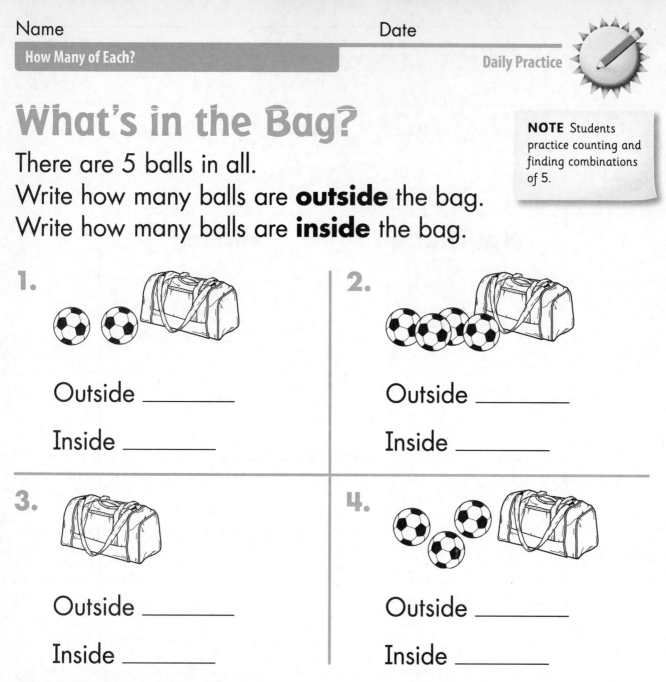

1.

Outside _____

Inside _____

2.

Outside _____

Inside _____

3.

Outside _____

Inside _____

4.

Outside _____

Inside _____

Ongoing Review

5. How many of these shapes have 4 sides?

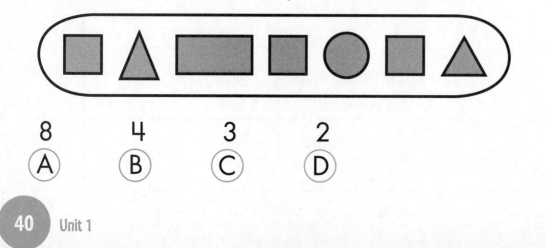

8   4   3   2
Ⓐ   Ⓑ   Ⓒ   Ⓓ

40 Unit 1

Session 4.4

© Pearson Education 1

How Many of Each?   Homework

Play *Heads and Tails* at Home

(page 1 of 2)

> **NOTE** Your child brought home materials to play a game with someone at home. He or she will also need some pennies. Encourage your child to explain how to play the game. Remind your child to return this recording sheet.
>
> **SMH** **G13**

Game 1
Total Number _____

Heads	Tails

Game 2
Total Number _____

Heads	Tails

Play *Heads and Tails* at Home (page 2 of 2)

Game 3 Total Number _____	
Heads	Tails

Game 4 Total Number _____	
Heads	Tails

Nine Peas and Carrots

Solve the problem. Show your work.

I have 9 things on my plate.
Some are peas. Some are carrots.
How many of each could I have?
How many peas? How many carrots?

Looking at Towers 2
Record the combinations for each tower.

NOTE Students practice counting and recording combinations of 10.

SMH 21–23, 48–49

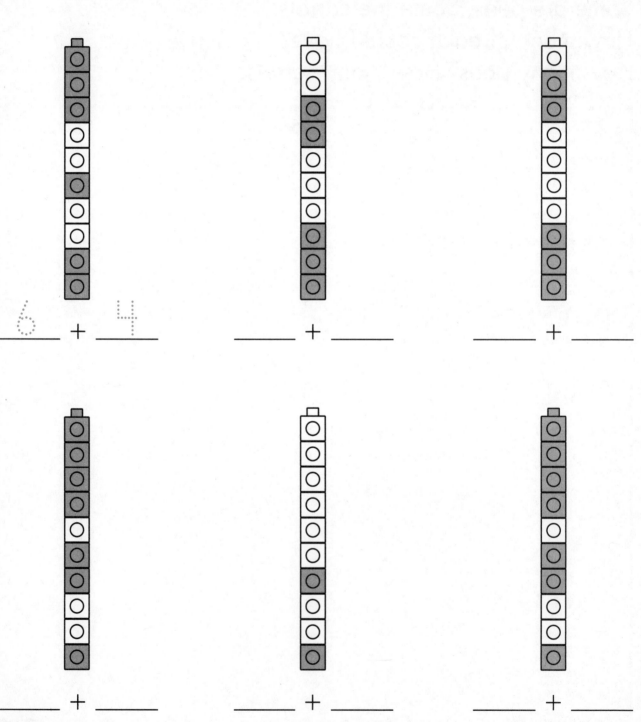

___6___ + ___4___

_____ + _____

_____ + _____

_____ + _____

_____ + _____

_____ + _____

How Many Baseballs?

Solve the problem. Show your work.

Rosa had 4 baseballs.
Sam gave her 5 more.
How many baseballs did they
have altogether?

NOTE This problem is about combining two numbers. Encourage your child to find his or her own way to solve the problem and record the work.

SMH 33–37

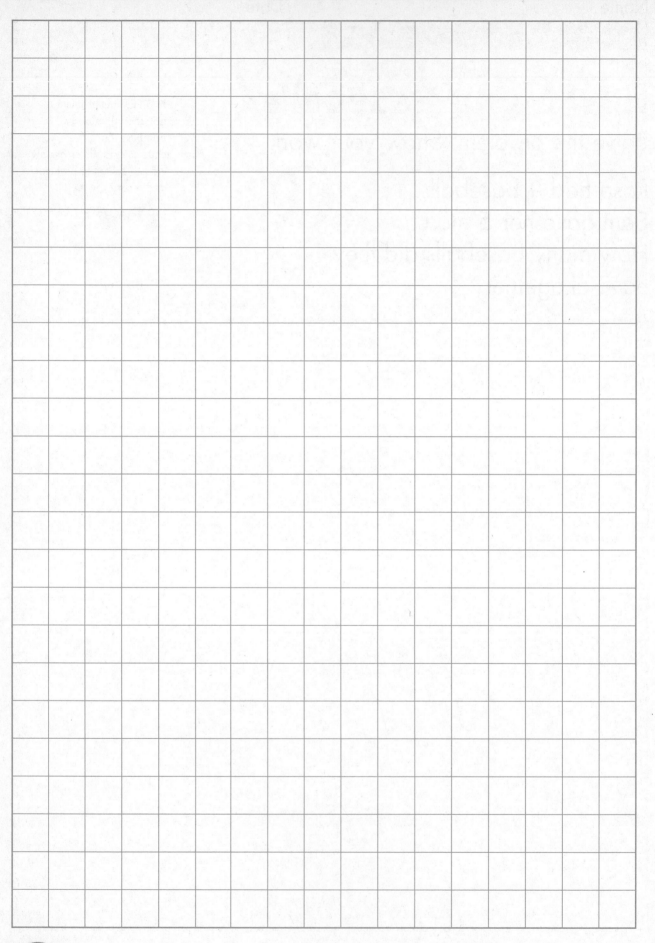

46 Unit 1

Heads and Tails (page 1 of 2)

Pretend that you are playing
Heads and Tails.

Fill in the chart for each game.

Game 1

Total Number _____

Heads 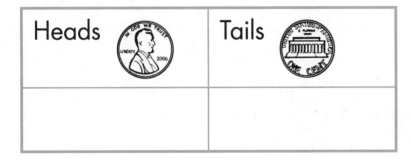	Tails

Game 2

Total Number _____

Heads	Tails

Heads and Tails (page 2 of 2)

Game 3

Total Number _____

Heads 	Tails

Game 4

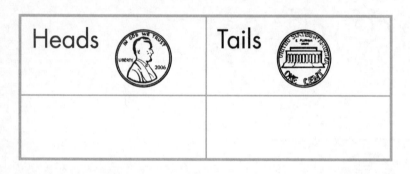

Total Number _____

Heads	Tails

Some Fish!

There are 6 fish in a fish tank.
Some fish are big.
Some fish are small.

Max says that there could be
2 big fish and 4 small fish.

Rosa says that there could be
1 big fish and 4 small fish.

Who is right? _____
Show how you know.

NOTE Students practice combining quantities to solve a story problem.

SMH 33–37

Spiral to Infinity Steve Allen

"Fractal images are often made up of small images-within-images, constantly repeating and going smaller and smaller." – **Steve Allen**

Investigations
IN NUMBER, DATA, AND SPACE®

Student Activity Book

Making Shapes and Designing Quilts   UNIT 2

Making Shapes and Designing Quilts

Investigation 1

Investigation 2

Investigation 3

Pattern-Block Fill-In, Shape A

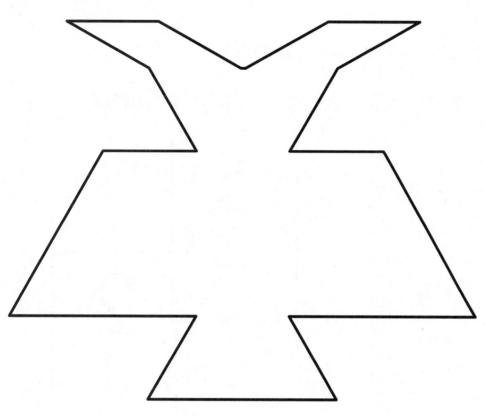

How many blocks did you use?

Shape	⬡	▰	▰	▰	▱	▲	Total
How Many?							

Double Compare

Kim and Sam are playing
Double Compare.

NOTE Students combine two
amounts and then figure out
which total is greater.

SMH **G6**

Circle the pair of cards that has more.

Kim's Cards

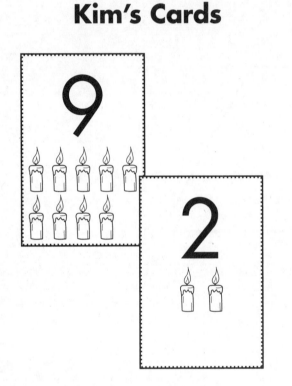

Sam's Cards

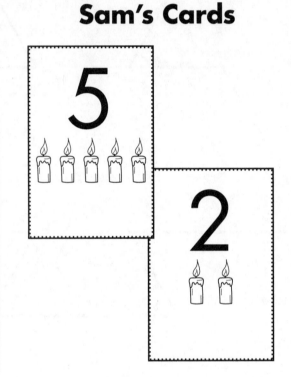

Show how you know.

Pattern-Block Fill-In, Shape B

How many blocks did you use?

Shape	⬡	◢	▱	■	▱	▲	Total
How Many?							

Pattern-Block Fill-In, Shape C

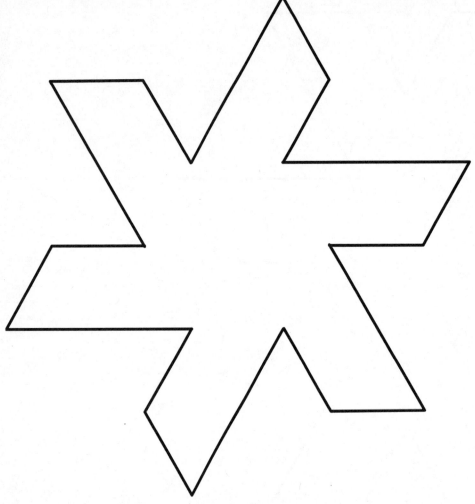

How many blocks did you use?

Shape	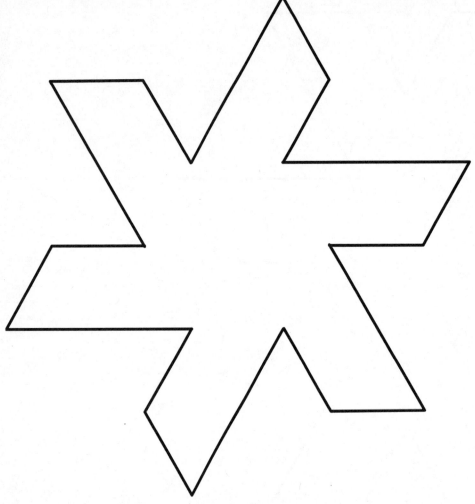						Total
How Many?							

Pattern-Block Fill-In, Shape D

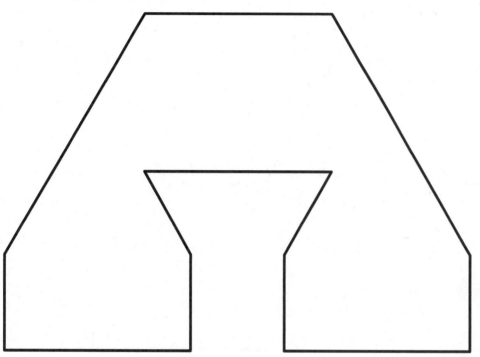

How many blocks did you use?

Shape	⬡	▰	▱	▪	▱	▲	Total
How Many?							

Pattern-Block Fill-In, Shape E

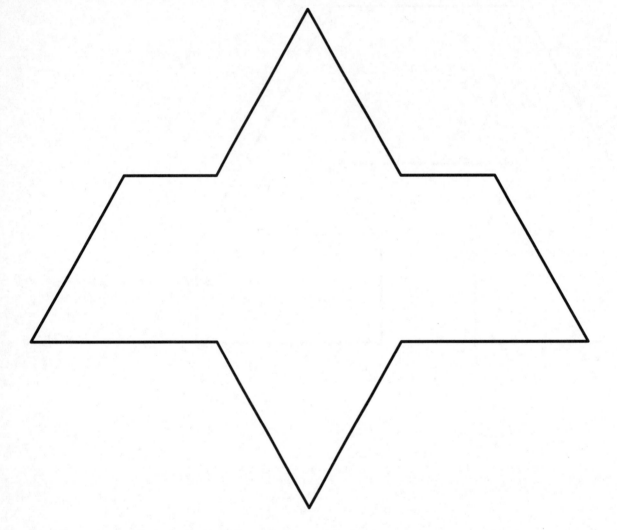

How many blocks did you use?

Shape	⬡	◸	▱	◼	▱	▲	Total
How Many?							

Pattern-Block Counts A

Make a design with 12 pattern blocks.

How many blocks did you use?

Shape	⬡	⬠	▰	■	▱	▲	Total
How Many?							

Pattern-Block Counts B

Make a design with 18 pattern blocks.

How many blocks did you use?

Shape	⬡	⬭	▰	■	▱	▲	Total
How Many?							

Pattern-Block Counts C

Make a design with 25 pattern blocks.

How many blocks did you use?

Shape	⬡	⬠	▱	◼	▰	▲	Total
How Many?							

Pattern-Block Counts D

Make a design with 28 pattern blocks.

How many blocks did you use?

Shape	⬡	⬟	▱	◼	▱	▲	Total
How Many?							

Making Shapes and Designing Quilts

Using a Calendar

Here is a calendar for you. Fill in the month and the dates. Then, find a place to hang it at home.

NOTE Students practice recording dates and creating, reading, and using a calendar as a tool for keeping track of time.

SMH 17–19

Name of Month

Sunday	Monday	Tuesday	Wednesday	Thursday	Friday	Saturday

Special Days _____

_____

Story Problem

Rosa had 8 books.
Max gave her 3 more.
How many books does she have now?

NOTE Students combine two quantities to solve a story problem.

SMH 33–37

Solve the problem. Show your work.

Looking for Rectangles

NOTE Students identify and draw rectangles that they find around their home.

SMH **69**

Look for rectangles around your home.

Draw what you find and write the name of each object.

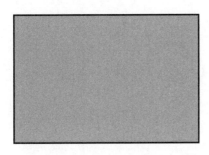

14 Unit 2

Ways to Make Pattern-Block Shapes

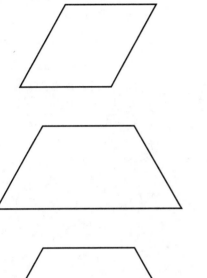
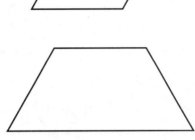
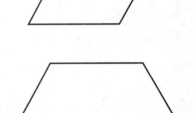

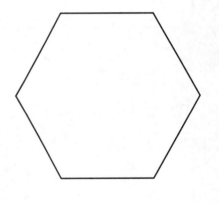

Heads and Tails 1 (page 1 of 2)

Imagine that you are playing
Heads and Tails. Fill in the chart
for each game.

NOTE Students practice
counting and breaking a
number into two parts.

SMH **G13**

Game 1

Total Number: _____

Heads	Tails

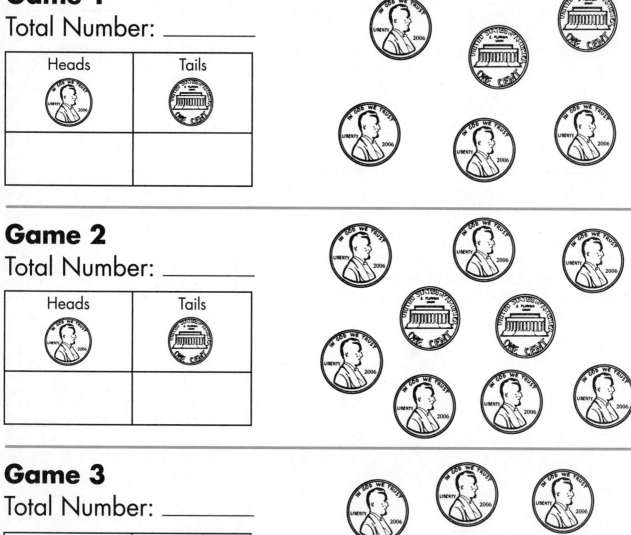

Game 2

Total Number: _____

Heads	Tails

Game 3

Total Number: _____

Heads	Tails

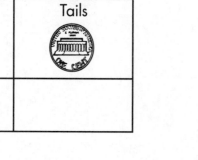

Heads and Tails 1 (page 2 of 2)

Game 4
Total Number: _____

Heads 	Tails

Game 5
Total Number: _____

Heads	Tails

Game 6
Total Number: _____

Heads	Tails

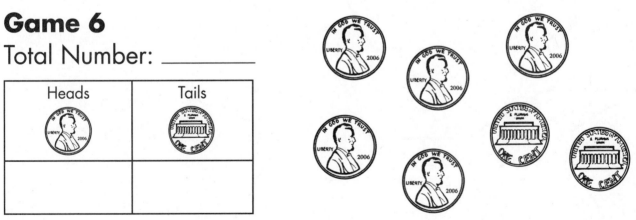

Different Ways to Fill, Shape A

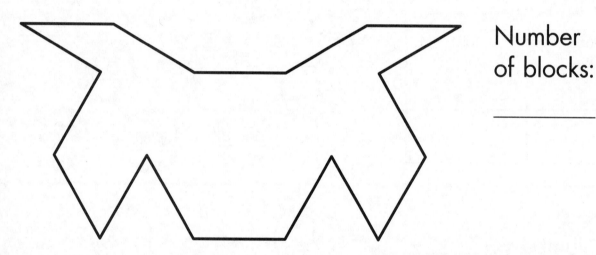

Number
of blocks:

_____

Number
of blocks:

_____

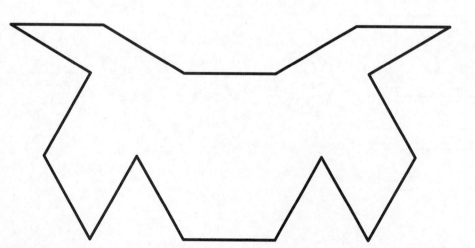

Number
of blocks:

_____

Different Ways to Fill, Shape B

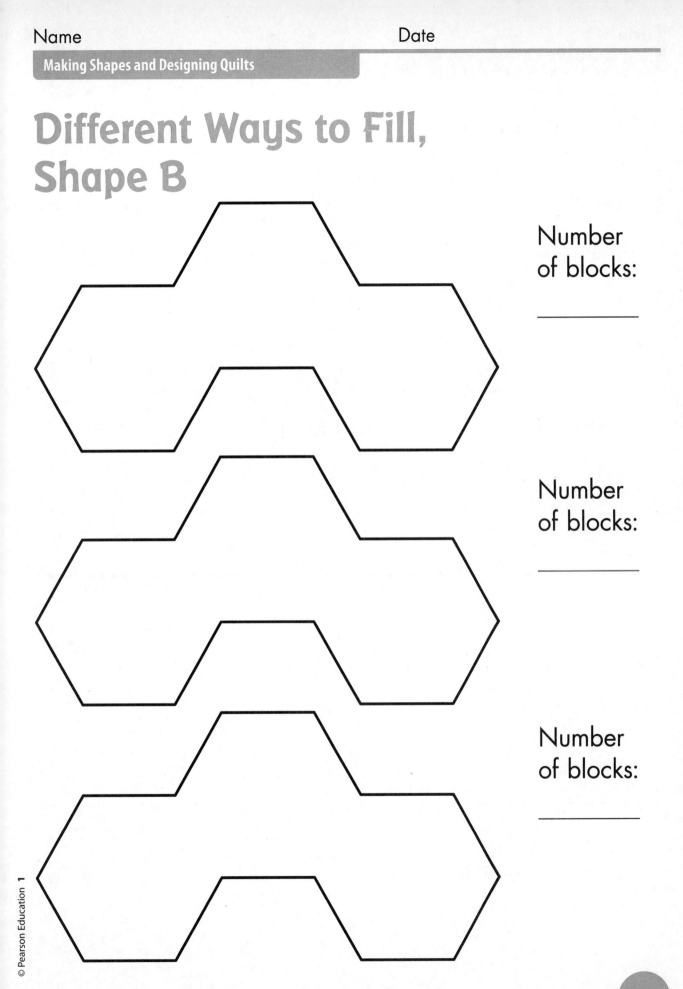

Number of blocks:

_____

Number of blocks:

_____

Number of blocks:

_____

Start With/Get To

Write the missing numbers on the number line.

NOTE Students practice writing numbers and counting.

SMH 26

Here is an example.

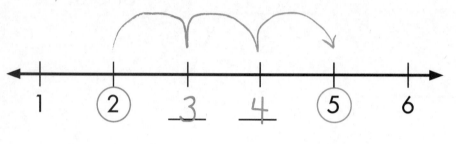

1   2   3   4   5   6

Start with   Get to

Try it.

1.

4   5   ___ ___ ___ ___   10

Start with   Get to

2.

1   2   ___ ___ ___ ___   7

Start with   Get to

Filling with More and Fewer—Shape A

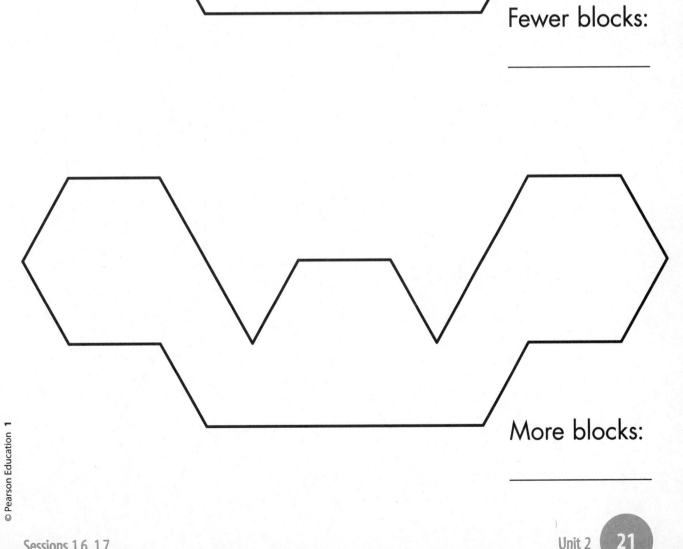

Fewer blocks:

_____

More blocks:

_____

Making Shapes and Designing Quilts

Filling with More and Fewer—Shape B

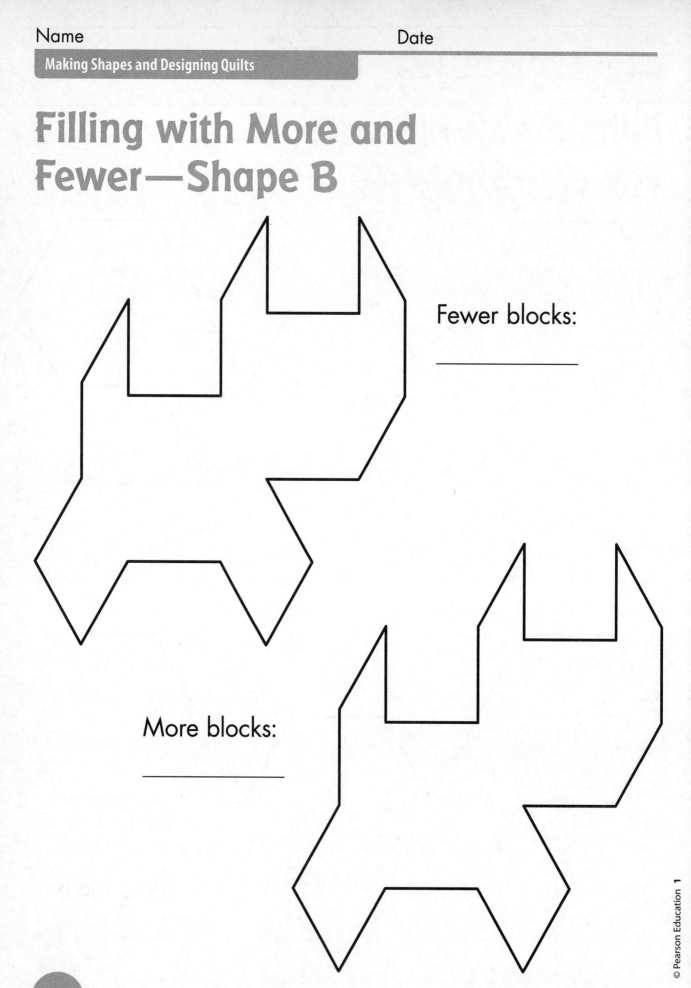

Fewer blocks:

_____

More blocks:

_____

© Pearson Education 1

Filling with More and Fewer—Shape C

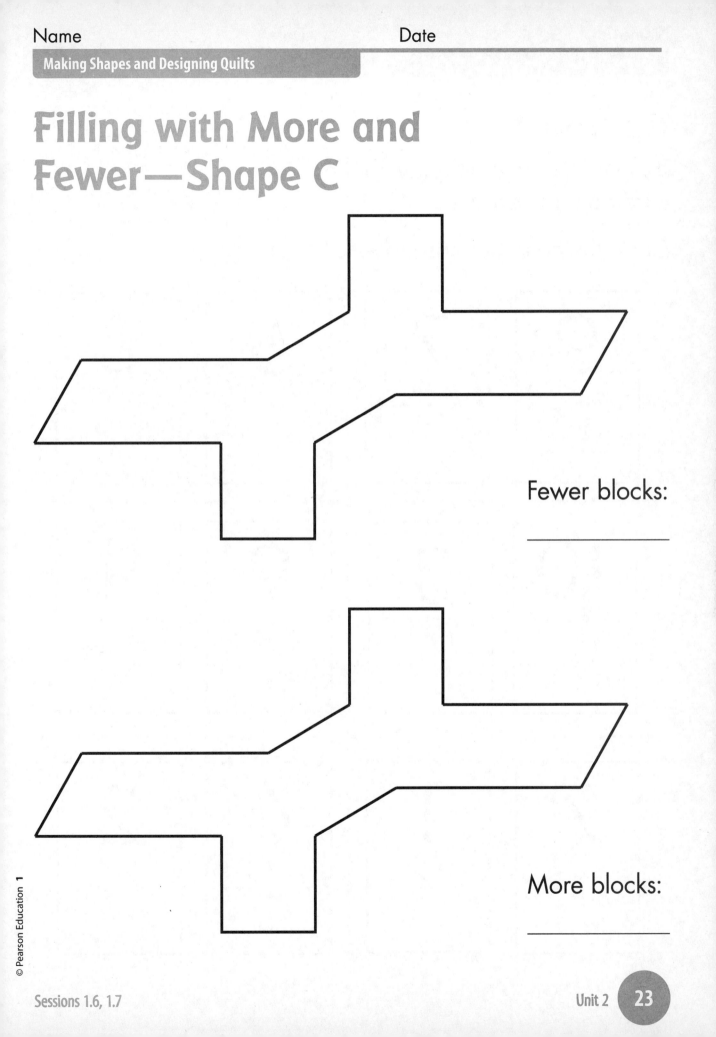

Fewer blocks:

_____

More blocks:

_____

Compare

Imagine that you are playing the card game *Compare*.

Circle the card that has more.

NOTE Students compare two numbers and figure out which is greater.

SMH **G2**

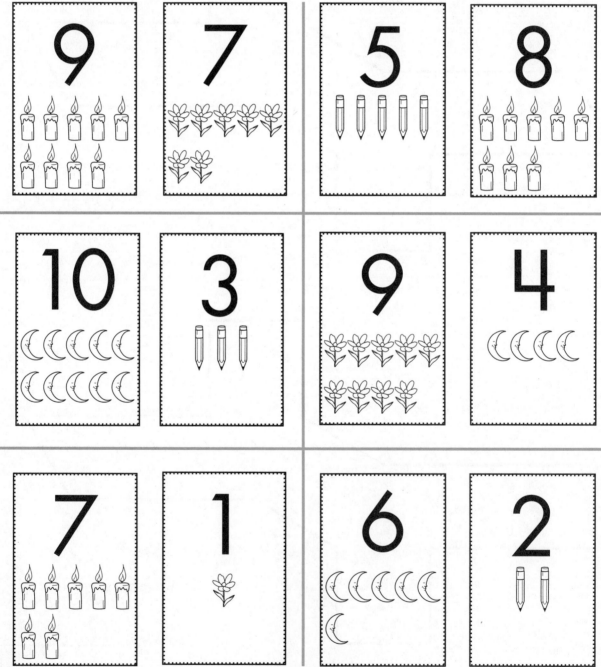

What Do You See?

Draw a line to match each sentence with a shape or shapes.

NOTE Students identify shapes.

SMH 71

1. I see a square.

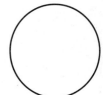

2. I see a circle.

3. I see a triangle in a circle.

4. I see a circle in a square.

25B Unit 2

More Story Problems

NOTE Student practice adding 2 numbers.

SMH 33–37

Sam had 5 balloons.
Kim gave him 6 more.
How many balloons does he have now?

Solve the problem. Show your work.

Heads and Tails 2 (page 1 of 2)

Imagine that you are playing *Heads and Tails*. Fill in the chart for each game.

NOTE Students practice counting and breaking a number into two parts (7 = 3 + 4).

SMH G13

Game 1
Total Number: _____

Heads 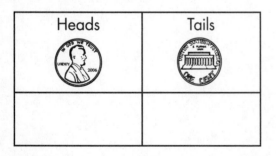	Tails

Game 2
Total Number: _____

Heads	Tails

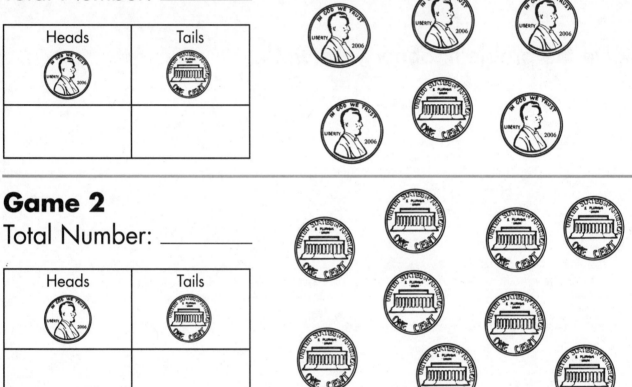

Game 3
Total Number: _____

Heads	Tails

Heads and Tails 2 (page 2 of 2)

Game 4
Total Number: _____

Heads	Tails

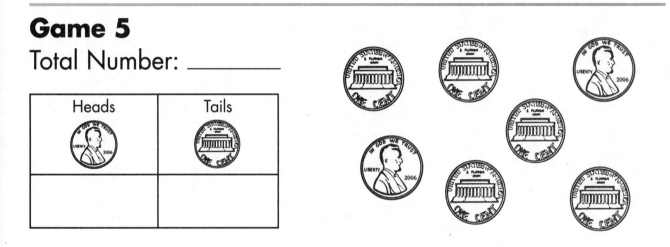

Game 5
Total Number: _____

Heads	Tails

Game 6
Total Number: _____

Heads	Tails

Circling Triangles ✏️

NOTE Students identify triangles and list two attributes that all triangles have in common.

SMH **72, 74–75**

1. Circle all of the triangles in this group of shapes.

2. Write two things that are the same for all of the triangles you circled.

_____

_____

Dot Paper

Circle 3 dots. Draw a triangle by connecting the dots. How many triangles can you draw?

How many triangles did you draw? _____

Finding the Total

Write the total number.

NOTE Students combine two amounts to find the total.

SMH G19

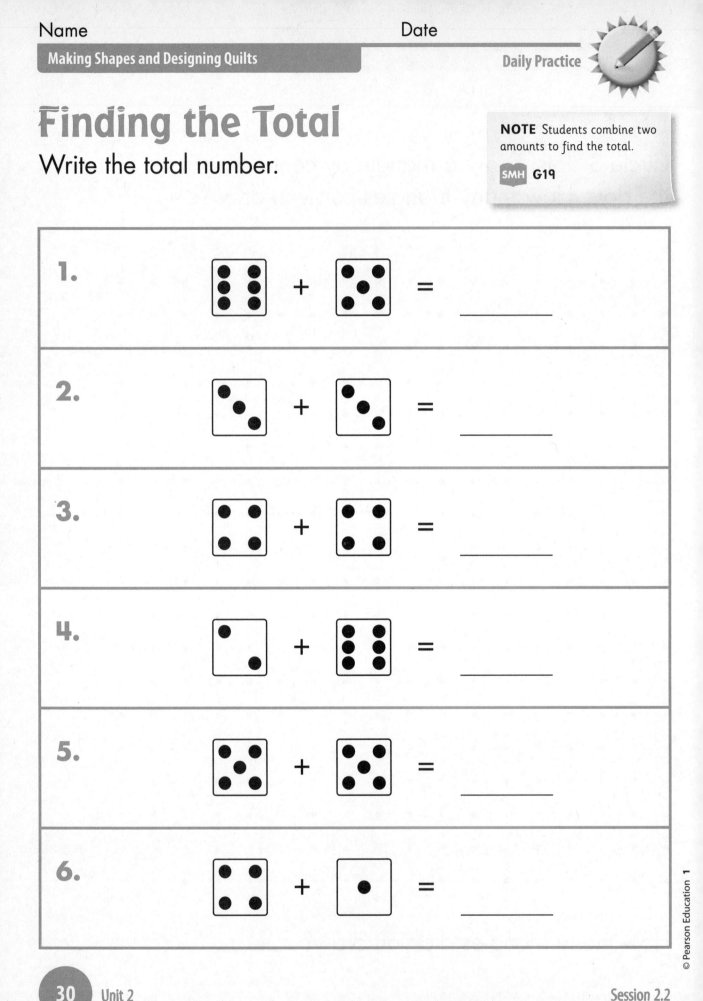

1. ▦ + ▥ = _____

2. ⚂ + ⚂ = _____

3. ⚃ + ⚃ = _____

4. ⚁ + ▦ = _____

5. ⚄ + ⚄ = _____

6. ⚃ + ⚀ = _____

Draw These Shapes

Draw a closed shape that matches the description.

NOTE Students draw shapes with particular attributes.

SMH 71

1. It has 3 sides.

2. It has 4 sides.

3. It has 5 sides.

4. Draw your own.

How many sides does it have? ____

Draw More Shapes

Draw a closed shape that matches the description.

NOTE Students draw shapes with particular attributes.

SMH 71

1. It has 4 sides.

2. It has 4 sides that have the same length.

3. It has 4 sides that have different lengths.

4. It has 4 sides. 2 sides have the same length.

Double Compare

Kim and Sam and Max and Rosa
are playing *Double Compare*.

Circle the pair of cards that has more.

NOTE Students combine
two amounts and then figure
out which total is greater.

SMH G6

1.   **Kim's Cards**   **Sam's Cards**

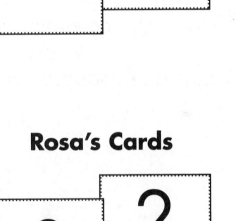

Show how you know.

2.   **Max's Cards**   **Rosa's Cards**

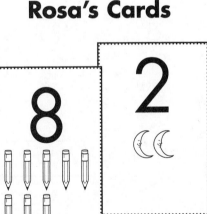

Show how you know.

Take a Closer Look

NOTE Students practice identifying triangles and squares.

SMH **71–73, 75**

1. Color each triangle blue.

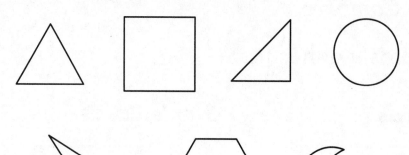

2. How many sides do triangles have? _____

3. How many corners? _____

4. Color each square red.

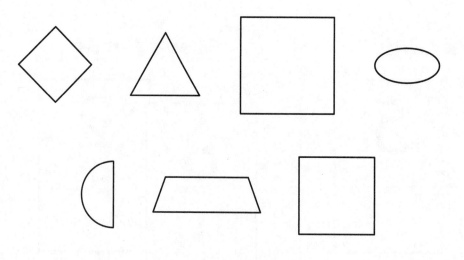

5. How many sides do squares have? _____

6. How many corners? _____

Guess My Rule

Circle the shapes that fit the rule.

NOTE Students practice comparing and sorting shapes according to a given attribute.

SMH 75–79

1. **Rule 1:** Has 4 corners

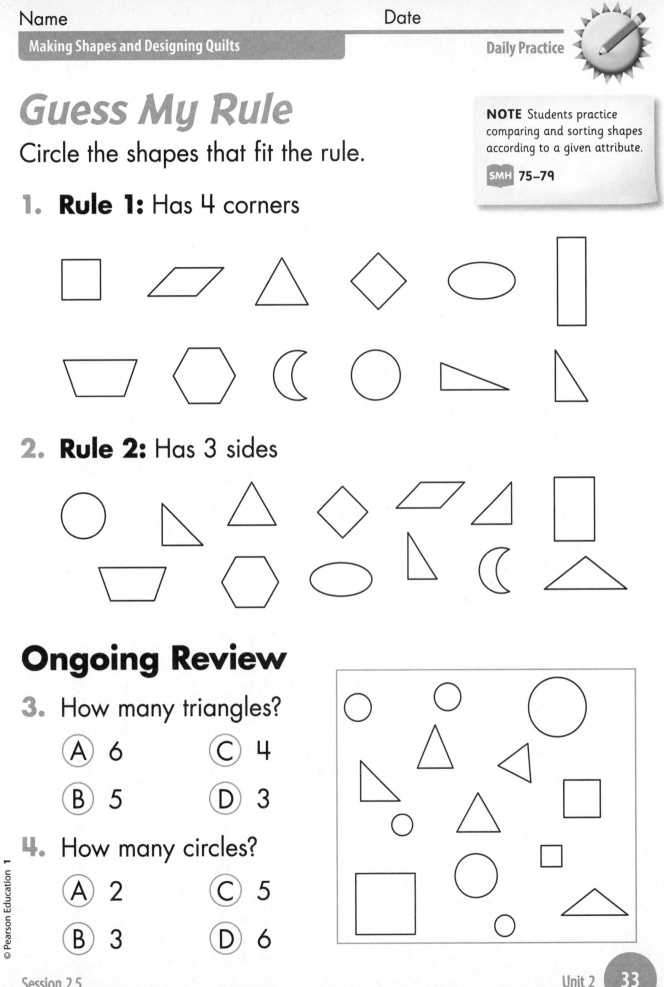

2. **Rule 2:** Has 3 sides

Ongoing Review

3. How many triangles?

(A) 6   (C) 4

(B) 5   (D) 3

4. How many circles?

(A) 2   (C) 5

(B) 3   (D) 6

Quilt Squares

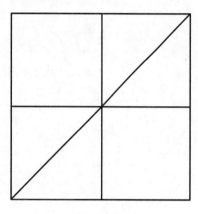

Quilt Pattern A

Quilt Pattern B

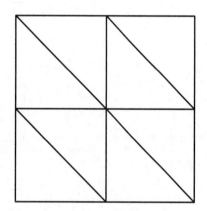

Quilt Pattern C

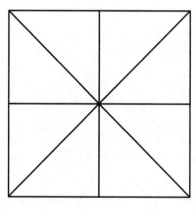

Quilt Pattern D

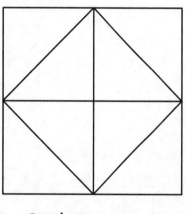

Quilt Pattern E

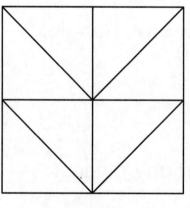

Quilt Pattern F

What Do You See?

Draw a line to match each sentence
with a shape or shapes.

NOTE Students practice comparing
and identifying shapes.

SMH 71

1. I see a triangle.

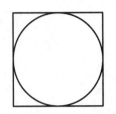

2. I see a square
inside a circle.

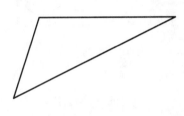

3. I see a circle inside
a square.

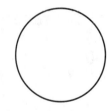

4. I see a shape with
no straight lines.

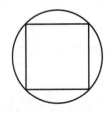

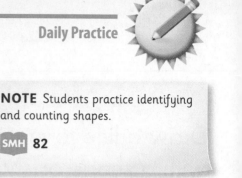

Quilt Patterns

Look at Patterns A and B.
Answer the questions.

NOTE Students practice identifying and counting shapes.

SMH 82

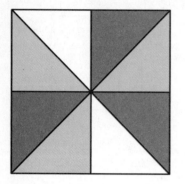

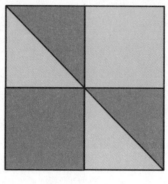

Pattern A   Pattern B

1. How many blue triangles ▲ are in Pattern A? _____

2. How many gray triangles ▲ are in Pattern A? _____

3. How many white triangles △ are in Pattern A? _____

4. How many blue triangles ▲ are in Pattern B? _____

5. How many gray triangles ▲ are in Pattern B? _____

6. How many blue squares ■ are in Pattern B? _____

7. How many gray squares ■ are in Pattern B? _____

Ongoing Review

8. How many balls are in the jar?

Ⓐ 3   Ⓑ 4   Ⓒ 5   Ⓓ 6

Guess My Rule

What do all of the shapes in the circle have in common? Guess the rule and write it below.

NOTE Students guess and list the "rule," or attribute, that the shapes in the circle have in common. They draw one more shape that fits the rule and one more shape that does NOT fit the rule. The shapes outside the circle do NOT fit the rule.

SMH 78–79

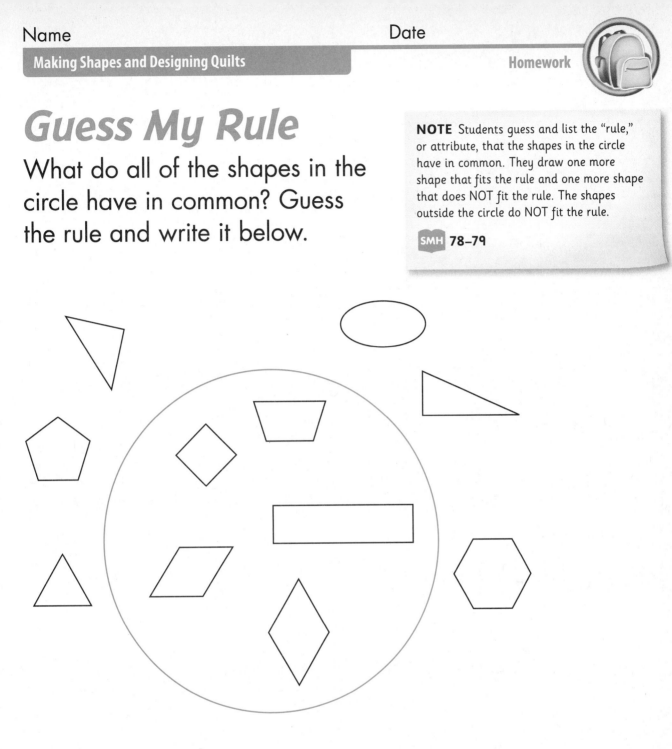

1. Guess my rule: _____

2. Draw 1 shape that fits the rule.

3. Draw 1 shape that does **not** fit the rule.

38 Unit 2

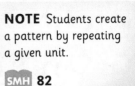

Quilt Patterns

Use this quilt square to make a quilt pattern.

NOTE Students create a pattern by repeating a given unit.

SMH 82

Choose one color to be the dark color. Choose another color to be the light color.

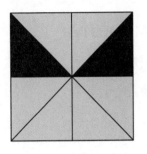

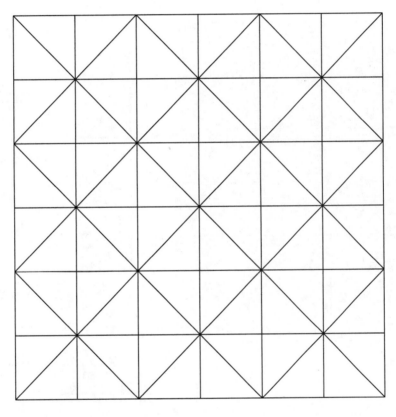

Ongoing Review

Which picture shows the **most** butterflies?

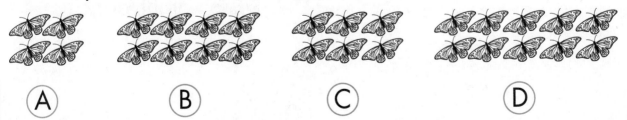

(A)   (B)   (C)   (D)

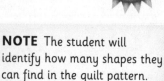

Shapes Inside of Shapes

Look for the shapes below in the quilt square. Count how many of each you find.

NOTE The student will identify how many shapes they can find in the quilt pattern.

SMH **71, 82**

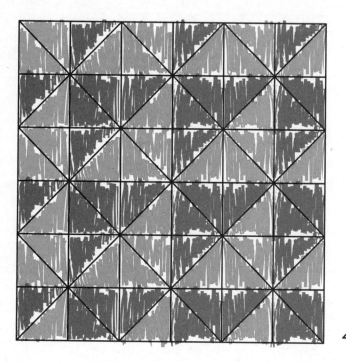

How many triangles?
light/dark

How many squares?
light/dark

How many trapezoids?
light/dark

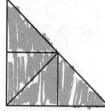

How many large triangles?
light/dark

"Fractal images are often made up of small images-within-images, constantly repeating and going smaller and smaller." – **Steve Allen**

Investigations

IN NUMBER, DATA, AND SPACE®

Solving Story Problems

Investigation 3

Investigation 4

Nine Toys:
How Many of Each?

Solve the problem. Show your work.

I have 9 toys.
Some are blocks. Some are marbles.
How many of each could I have?
How many blocks? How many marbles?

Find as many combinations as you can.

Using a Calendar

Here is a calendar for you.
Fill in the month and dates.
Then find a place to hang it at home.

NOTE Students practice recording dates, and creating, reading, and using a calendar as a tool for keeping track of time.

SMH **17, 18, 19**

Name of Month

Sunday	Monday	Tuesday	Wednesday	Thursday	Friday	Saturday

Special Days

_____   _____

How Many Am I Hiding? Recording Sheet

Total Number _____

Not Hidden	Hidden

Counters in a Cup Recording Sheet

Total Number _____

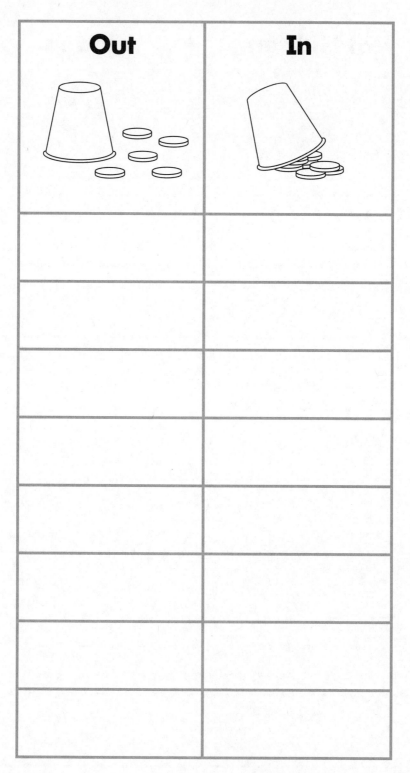

Out	In

What's Inside the Cup?

There are **7** counters in all.
Write how many are outside the cup.
Write how many are inside the cup.

NOTE Students find combinations of 7 when one part is hidden.

SMH **G4**

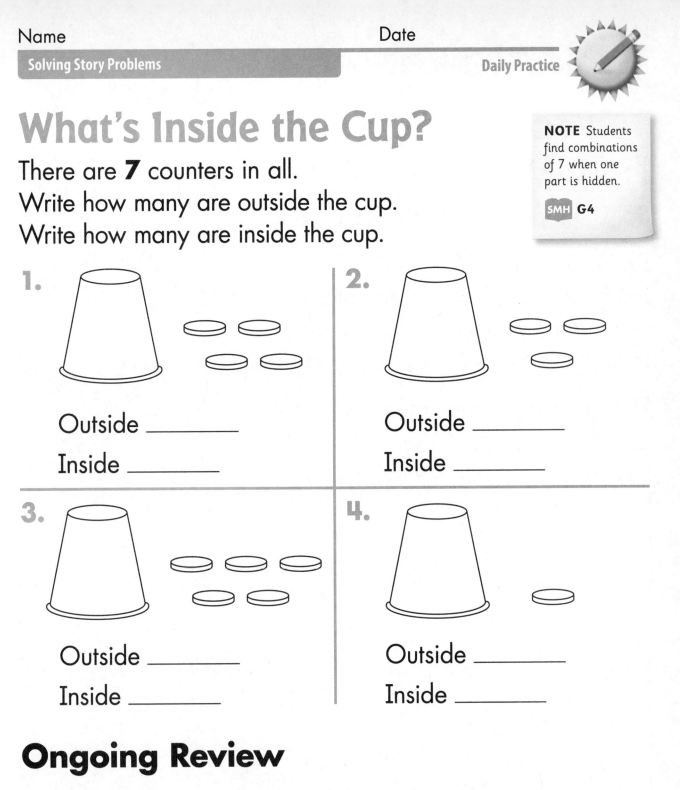

1.

Outside _____
Inside _____

2.

Outside _____
Inside _____

3.

Outside _____
Inside _____

4.

Outside _____
Inside _____

Ongoing Review

5. Which pair of cards has a total of 7?

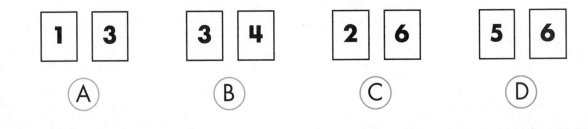

1 3	3 4	2 6	5 6
A	B	C	D

Ten Toys:
How Many of Each?

Solve the problem. Show your work.

I have 10 toys.
Some are blocks. Some are marbles.
How many of each could I have?
How many blocks? How many marbles?

Find as many combinations as you can.

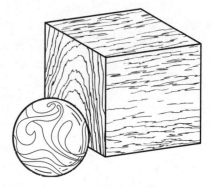

Start With/Get To

Write the missing numbers on the number line. Use the first number line to help you.

NOTE Students practice counting and writing numbers.

SMH **26, 31, 32**

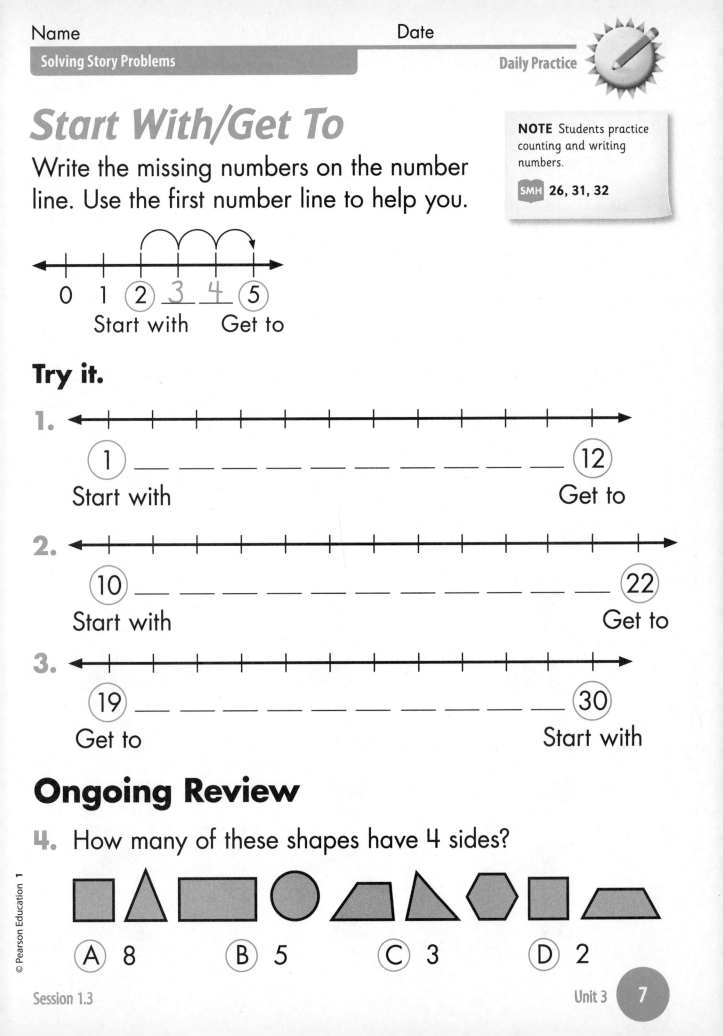

0 1 ② 3 4 ⑤
   Start with   Get to

Try it.

1.

① — — — — — — — — — — ⑫
Start with   Get to

2.

⑩ — — — — — — — — — — ㉒
Start with   Get to

3.

⑲ — — — — — — — — — — ㉚
Get to   Start with

Ongoing Review

4. How many of these shapes have 4 sides?

Ⓐ 8   Ⓑ 5   Ⓒ 3   Ⓓ 2

The Match Game

> **NOTE** Students determine the total number of blocks used in each design and then match the design to the correct list of blocks.

1. Write how many blocks were used in each design.

2. Then match each design with the chart that tells how many of each kind were used.

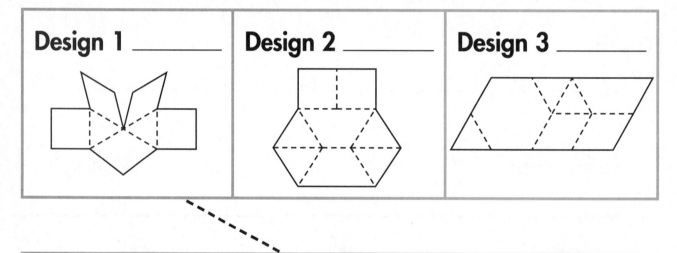

| Design 1 _____ | Design 2 _____ | Design 3 _____ |

1	⬣	0	⬣	0	⬣
1	⬯	0	⬯	2	⬯
2	▰	1	▰	0	▰
0	◼	2	◼	2	◼
0	▱	2	▱	0	▱
3	▲	2	▲	4	▲

Eight Toys: How Many of Each?

Solve the problem. Show your work.

NOTE This problem is about finding combinations of numbers that equal 8. There are a number of possible solutions.

SMH 46

I have 8 toys.
Some are blocks. Some are marbles.
How many of each could I have?
How many blocks? How many marbles?

Find as many combinations as you can.

Dot Addition: What's Missing?

> **NOTE** Students use what they know about combinations to make each total.
>
> **SMH** G5

Fill in the missing cards.
You can use these cards.

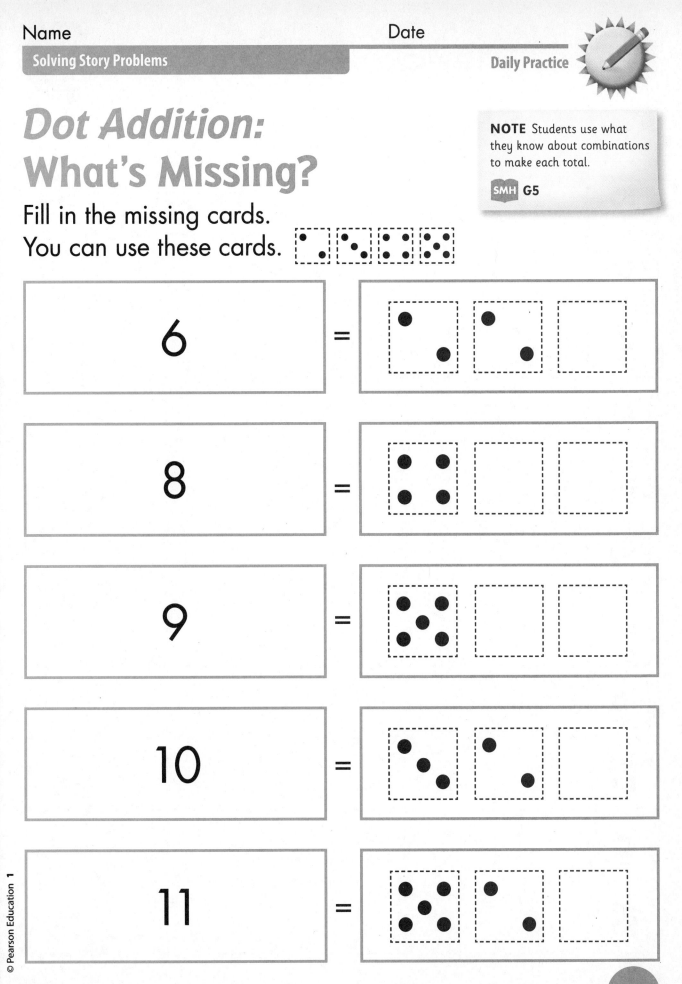

6 =

8 =

9 =

10 =

11 =

Solving Story Problems

Roll and Record Recording Sheet

	2							
	3							
	4							
	5							
	6							
	7							
	8							
	9							
	10							
	11							
	12							

More What's Inside the Cup?

There are **10** counters in all.
Write how many are outside the cup.
Write how many are inside the cup.

NOTE Students find combinations of 10, when one part is hidden.

SMH **G4**

1.

Outside _____
Inside _____

2.

Outside _____
Inside _____

3.

Outside _____
Inside _____

4.

Outside _____
Inside _____

Ongoing Review

5. Which pair of cards has a total of 12?

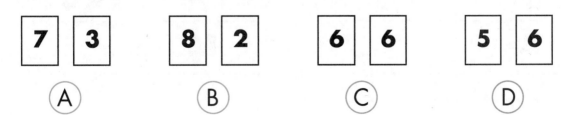

| 7 | 3 | | 8 | 2 | | 6 | 6 | | 5 | 6 |
| A | | | B | | | C | | | D | |

Pennies: Heads and Tails

Pretend that you are playing *Heads and Tails*. Fill in the chart for each game.

NOTE Students continue to find combinations of numbers.

SMH G13

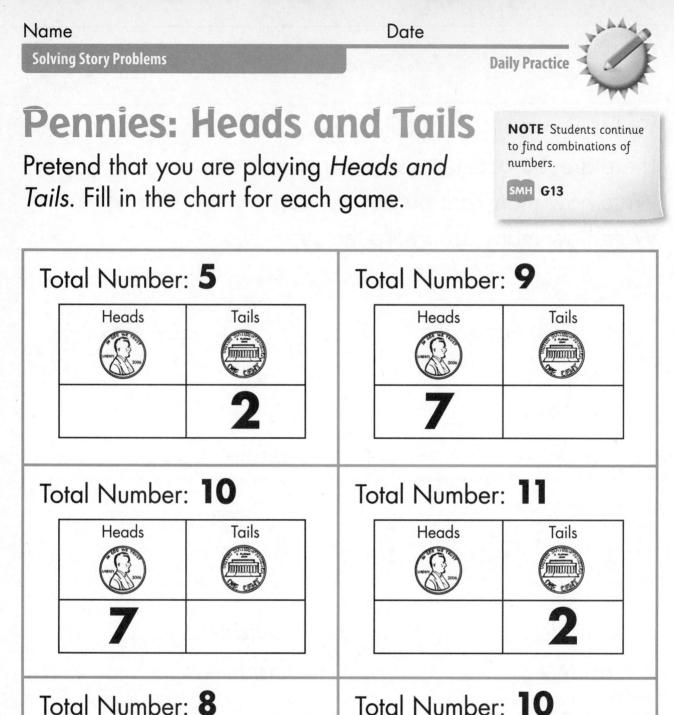

Total Number: **5**

Heads	Tails
	2

Total Number: **9**

Heads	Tails
7	

Total Number: **10**

Heads	Tails
7	

Total Number: **11**

Heads	Tails
	2

Total Number: **8**

Heads	Tails
4	

Total Number: **10**

Heads	Tails
4	

How Many Toy Cars? (page 1 of 2)

Solve the problem. Show your work.

Kim has 7 toy cars.
Sam has 6 toy cars.

How many toy cars do they have?

How Many Toy Cars? (page 2 of 2)

Solve the problem. Show your work.

Max has 6 toy cars.
Rosa has 5 toy cars.
Kim has 4 toy cars.

How many toy cars do they have?

How Many Marbles?

Solve the problem. Show your work.

NOTE Students combine three quantities to solve an addition story problem.

SMH **33–37**

Sam has 4 marbles.
Rosa has 4 marbles.
Kim has 3 marbles.

How many marbles do they have in all?

Solving a Story Problem

Solve the problem. Show your work.

Kim bought 9 pencils.
Sam gave her 7 more pencils.

How many pencils does Kim have now?

NOTE Students combine two quantities to solve a story problem.

SMH 33–37

True or False?

Circle the word to show whether the equation
is true or false.

1. $6 + 4 = 10$ True   False

2. $10 = 6 + 4$ True   False

3. $10 = 6 + 16$ True   False

4. $5 + 4 = 5 + 2 + 2$ True   False

5. $8 = 8$ True   False

6. $2 + 2 + 2 = 3 + 3$ True   False

7. $2 + 2 + 2 = 6 + 3$ True   False

8. $9 - 6 = 3$ True   False

9. $9 - 3 = 6$ True   False

10. $9 = 6 - 3$ True   False

More True or False?

Circle the word to show whether the equation is true or false.

NOTE Students determine whether equations are true or false.

SMH **44**

1. $8 + 2 = 11$ True   False

2. $10 = 8 + 2$ True   False

3. $10 - 2 = 12$ True   False

4. $8 = 10 - 2$ True   False

5. $4 + 4 = 8 + 2$ True   False

6. $8 - 2 = 6 + 2$ True   False

7. $6 + 2 = 6 - 2$ True   False

8. $4 + 2 = 5 + 1$ True   False

9. $7 - 5 = 2 + 5$ True   False

10. $10 - 2 = 6 + 2$ True   False

Roll and Record: Subtraction
Recording Sheet

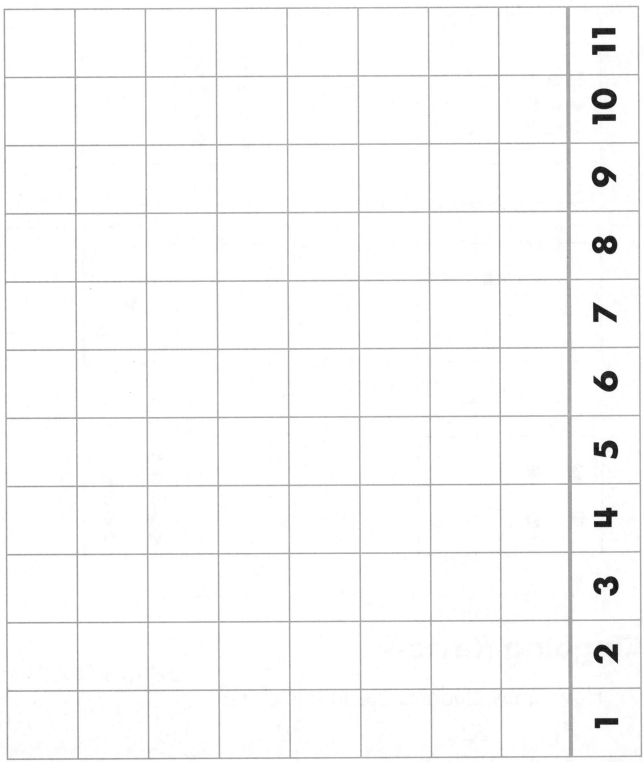

15 Is the Number

Draw dots so that there are 15 in all.
Write how many dots are in each part.

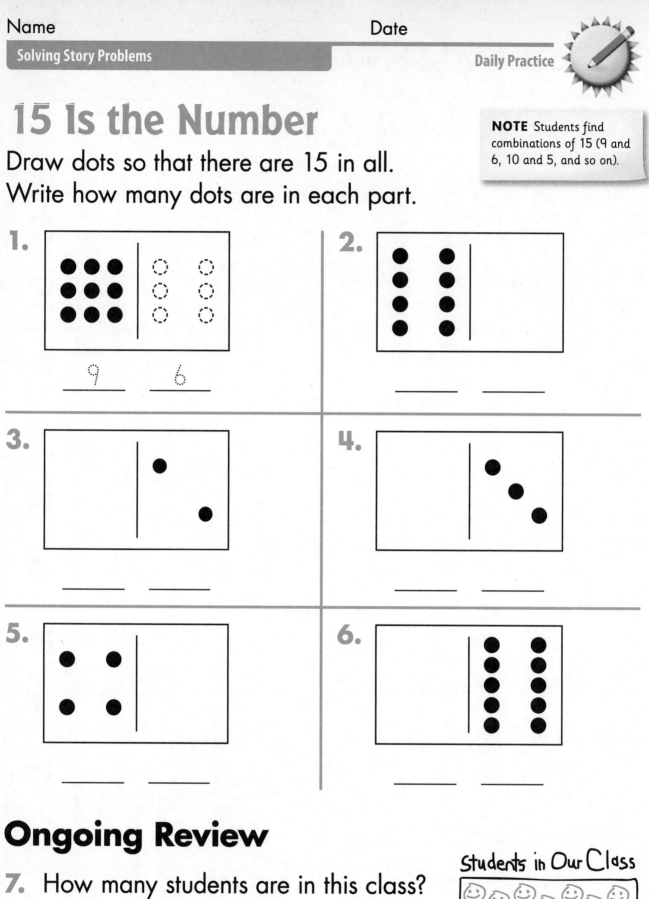

1.

___9___ ___6___

2.

___ ___

3.

___ ___

4.

___ ___

5.

___ ___

6.

___ ___

Ongoing Review

7. How many students are in this class?

24	22	21	19
Ⓐ	Ⓑ	Ⓒ	Ⓓ

Students in Our Class

How Many Squirrels? (page 1 of 2)

Solve the problem. Show your work.

There were 12 squirrels on the ground.
Then 4 of them ran up a tree.
How many stayed on the ground?

How Many Squirrels? (page 2 of 2)

Solve the problem. Show your work.

I saw 15 squirrels in the park.
Then 8 ran away.
How many squirrels were left?

Finding the Total
Write the total number.

NOTE Students combine two given amounts to find the total.

SMH G19

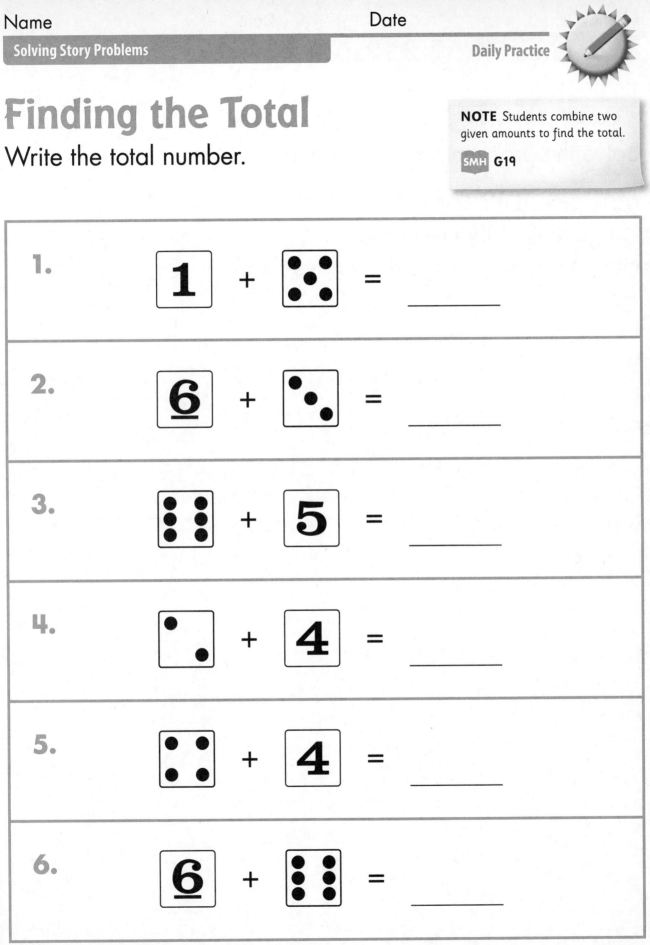

1. **1** + [⚄ five dots] = _____

2. **6** + [three dots] = _____

3. [six dots] + **5** = _____

4. [two dots] + **4** = _____

5. [four dots] + **4** = _____

6. **6** + [six dots] = _____

How Many Apples? (page 1 of 2)

Solve the problem. Show your work.

Max picked 12 apples.
He gave 6 of them to Rosa.
How many apples did Max have then?

How Many Apples? (page 2 of 2)

Solve the problem. Show your work.

Max had 12 apples.
He gave 7 of them to Rosa.
How many apples does Max have left?

Fill in the Dots

Draw dots on the cards to make each number. Use only the dot cards shown.

NOTE Students determine combinations of dot cards that make the given numbers.

SMH G5

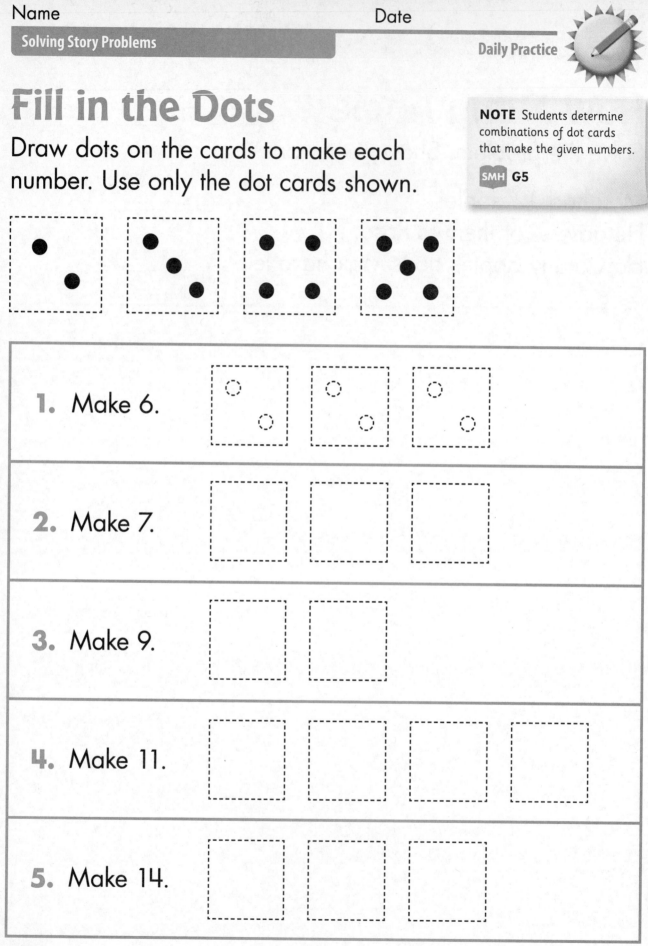

1. Make 6.

2. Make 7.

3. Make 9.

4. Make 11.

5. Make 14.

Story Problems (page 1 of 2)

Solve the problems. Show your work.

1. Rosa had 11 library books.
   She took 4 of them back.
   How many books does Rosa have now?

2. There were 10 children playing at the park.
   Then 8 more came to play.
   How many children were at the park?

Story Problems (page 2 of 2)

Solve the problems. Show your work.

3. A squirrel found 8 nuts.
Then it found 7 more nuts.
How many nuts did it find?

---

4. Max has 5 cookies.
Sam has 7 cookies.
How many do they have in all?

More Story Problems (page 1 of 2)

Solve the problems. Show your work.

1. Rosa had 15 pennies.
   She spent 5 pennies.
   How many pennies did she have left?

---

2. Kim saw 20 ducks on the pond.
   Then 9 ducks flew away.
   How many ducks were still in the pond?

More Story Problems (page 2 of 2)

Solve the problems. Show your work.

3. Rosa was collecting rocks.
She found 6 rocks.
Then she found 1 rock.
Then she found 4 more rocks.
How many rocks did she find?

4. Rosa was picking flowers.
She picked 8 flowers.
Then she picked 2 flowers.
Then she picked 1 flower.
How many flowers did she pick?

Counting on a Number Line

NOTE Students practice writing numbers and counting on from a number other than one.

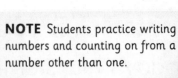

SMH **26, 31, 32**

Write the missing numbers on the number line. Use the first number line to help you.

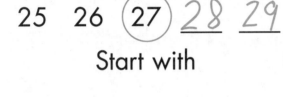

25   26   (27)   28   29   (30)
      Start with   Get to

Try it.

1.

15   16   17   (18) ___ ___ ___ ___ ___ (24)
            Start with   Get to

2.

20   (21) ___ ___ ___ ___ ___ ___ (28)
      Start with   Get to

3.

35   (36) ___ ___ ___ ___ ___ ___ (43)
      Start with   Get to

Solving Story Problems

Today's Number: 9

Today's Number is 9.

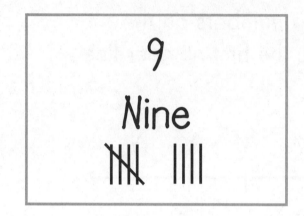

How many ways can you make Today's Number?
Show the ways.

How Did They Do That?

NOTE Students determine which pairs of numbers have sums of 7, 9, 11, 6, and 2.

SMH G9

1. Look at Rosa and Max's Five-in-a-Row gameboard. Circle the pairs of numbers they used to win.

6 and 6   6 and 5

5 and 4   1 and 5

2 and 2   2 and 3

6 and 4   3 and 4

1 and 1   2 and 1

2	12	7	6	12
9	5	4	10	8
7̶	9̶	11̶	6̶	2̶
9	5	11	3	10
11	3	8	4	2

Ongoing Review

2. Which cube train has more cubes than the tower on the right?

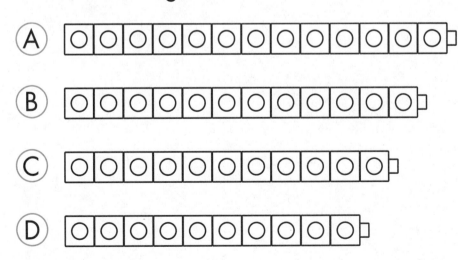

A

B

C

D

Today's Number: 10

Today's Number is 10.

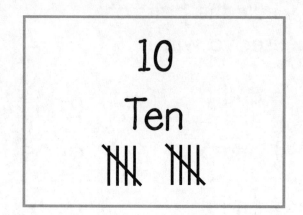

How many ways can you make Today's Number?
Show the ways.

Solving Story Problems

Subtraction Problems

Subtract. Write the answers.

NOTE Students subtract one amount from another.

SMH **G20**

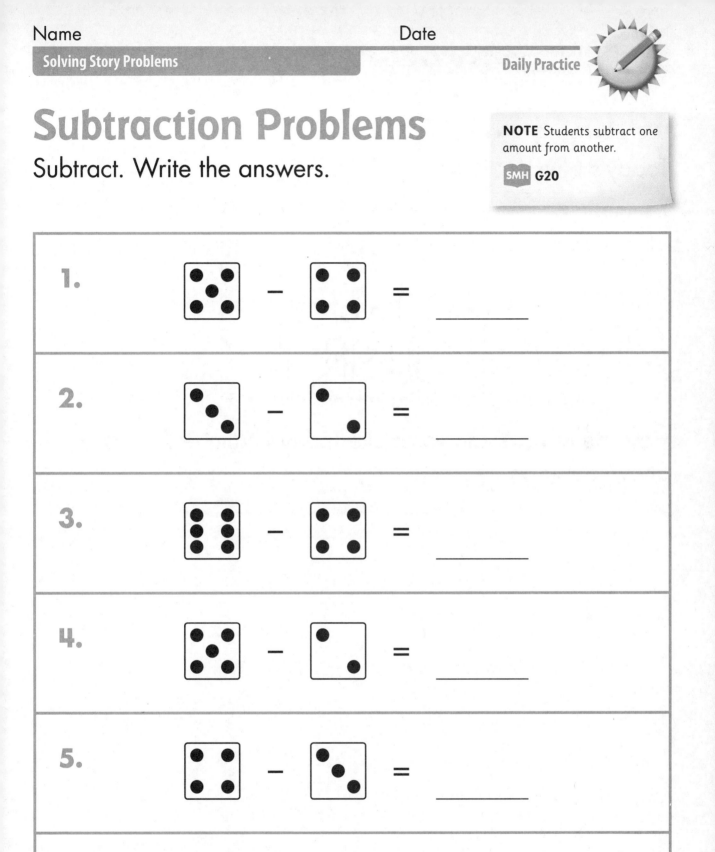

1. ⬚ − ⬚ = _____

2. ⬚ − ⬚ = _____

3. ⬚ − ⬚ = _____

4. ⬚ − ⬚ = _____

5. ⬚ − ⬚ = _____

6. ⬚ − ⬚ = _____

Today's Number: 12

Today's Number is 12.

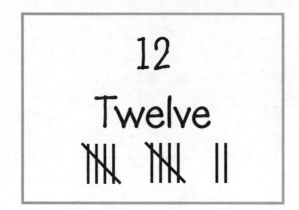

How many ways can you make Today's Number?
Show the ways.

Follow the Rules

Choose a rule and circle it.
Then circle the shapes that fit the rule.

1. Rule 1: Has 4 sides **OR**
   Rule 2: Has curves

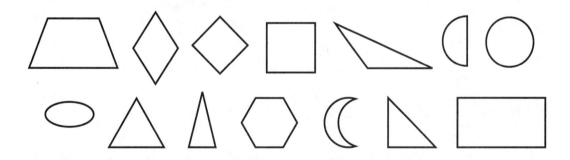

2. Rule 1: Has straight sides **OR**
   Rule 2: Has 3 corners

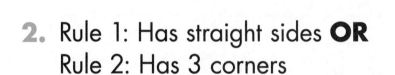

Ongoing Review

3. Max had 8 baseball cards. He gave 3 to his friend Sam. How many baseball cards does Max have now?

   1   5   7   8
   (A)   (B)   (C)   (D)

Solving Story Problems   **Daily Practice**

Roll and Record: What's Missing?

NOTE Students solve addition problems by combining two amounts to find the total or by finding the part that is missing.

SMH G19

1. $\boxed{\underline{9}}$ + $\boxed{}$ = 10

2. (dots: 5) + $\boxed{5}$ = _____

3. $\boxed{}$ + (dots: 6) = 10

4. (dots: 3) + $\boxed{3}$ = _____

5. $\boxed{}$ + $\boxed{2}$ = 10

6. $\boxed{7}$ + (dots: 3) = _____

Missing Numbers

Circle 5, 8, 14, and 19.

NOTE Students practice identifying, counting and writing numbers.

SMH 6–10

1.

1	2	3	4	5	6	7	8	9	10
11	12	13	14	15	16	17	18	19	20

Fill in the missing numbers.

2.

1		3		5		7		9	
11		13		15		17		19	

3.

	2		4		6		8		10
	12		14		16		18		20

4.

21		23	24			27	28		30
	32	33	34	35			38	39	

5.

	22	23		25	26			29	30
31		33			36	37			40

Daily Practice

NOTE Students practice solving addition and subtraction story problems.

SMH **33–37, 38–42**

How Many?

Solve the problems. Show your work.

1. Rosa had 10 shells.
She gave 6 of them to Max.
How many shells does Rosa have left?

2. Kim has 5 marbles.
Sam gives her 7 more.
How many marbles does Kim have now?

What Went Wrong?

Here are parts of 5 counting strips.
Fix the mistakes.

NOTE Students use their knowledge of the counting sequence to identify and fix counting errors.

SMH **6–10, 21–23**

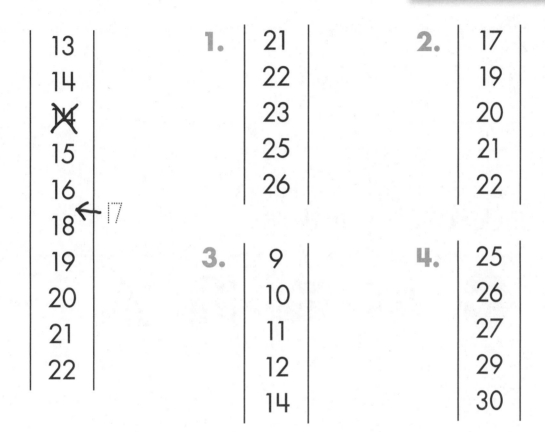

	13
	14
	~~14~~
	15
	16
	18 ← 17
	19
	20
	21
	22

1.

	21
	22
	23
	25
	26

2.

	17
	19
	20
	21
	22

3.

	9
	10
	11
	12
	14

4.

	25
	26
	27
	29
	30

Ongoing Review

5. How many children answered this question?

7	12	16	22
Ⓐ	Ⓑ	Ⓒ	Ⓓ

Do you wear glasses?

Yes	No

And the Total Is . . .

NOTE Students create a pattern-block design and then determine the number of each type of block used and the total number of blocks in their design.

1. Color the pattern blocks to make a design.

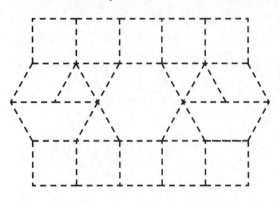

Fill in the chart to tell how many of each kind of block are in your design.

Shape	⬡	⬢	▱	◼	▲	Total
How Many?						

Ongoing Review

2. This train should have 12 cubes.
   How many more cubes are needed?

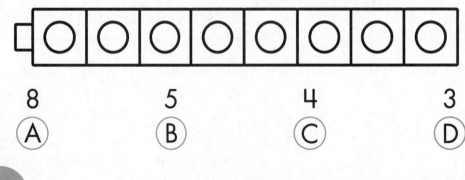

8	5	4	3
Ⓐ	Ⓑ	Ⓒ	Ⓓ

Counting Strips at Home

Write the missing numbers on these counting strips.

NOTE Students practice writing numbers and counting on from a number other than one.

SMH **6–16, 21–23**

12	23	45
13	24	46
14	25	47

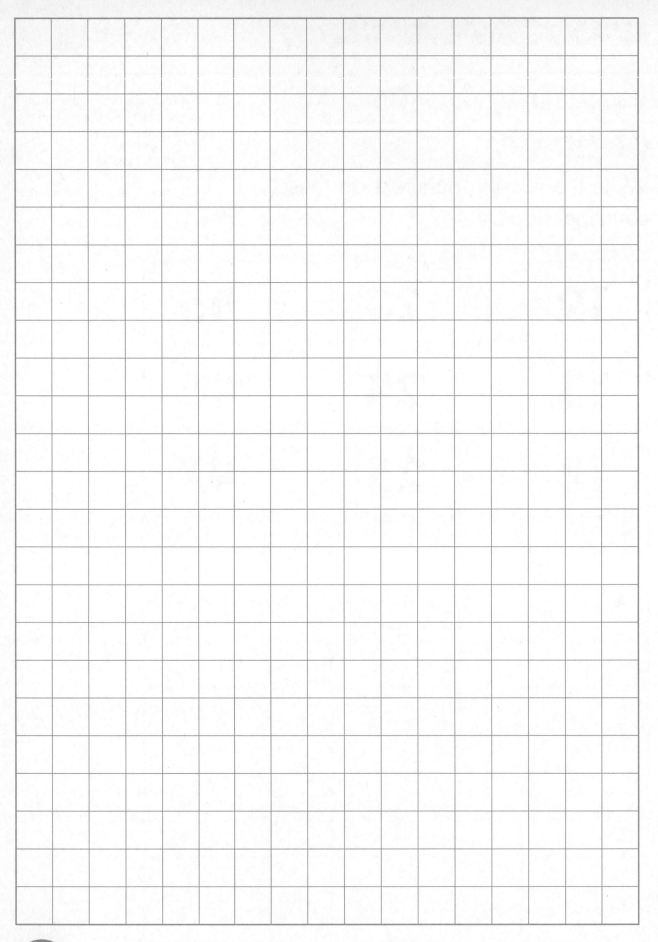

44 Unit 3

How Many Crayons?

Solve the problem. Show
your work.

NOTE Students subtract
one quantity from another
to solve a story problem.

SMH **38–42**

Kim has 11 crayons.
She lets Sam borrow 8 crayons.
How many crayons does Kim have now?

Missing Numbers Recording Sheet

Round 1: I think these numbers are missing.

_____   _____   _____   _____   _____

_____   _____   _____   _____   _____

Round 2: I think these numbers are missing.

_____   _____   _____   _____   _____

_____   _____   _____   _____   _____

Round 3: I think these numbers are missing.

_____   _____   _____   _____   _____

_____   _____   _____   _____   _____

Round 4: I think these numbers are missing.

_____   _____   _____   _____   _____

_____   _____   _____   _____   _____

Fill in the 100 Chart

Fill in the 100 chart. Write the missing numbers.

NOTE Students practice solving addition combinations and sequencing numbers 1–100.

SMH 27–29

1	2	3	4		6	7	8	9	
11	12		14	15	16	17	18	19	20
21	22	23		25	26	27	28	29	30
31		33	34	35	36	37	38	39	40
41	42	43	44	45	46	47	48	49	50
	52	53	54	55	56		58	59	60
61	62	63		65	66	67	68	69	70
71	72	73	74		76	77	78	79	80
81	82	83	84	85		87		89	90
91	92	93	94	95	96	97	98	99	

More Counting Strips at Home

NOTE Students continue to practice writing numbers and counting on from a number other than one.

SMH 6–16, 21–23

Write the missing numbers on these counting strips.

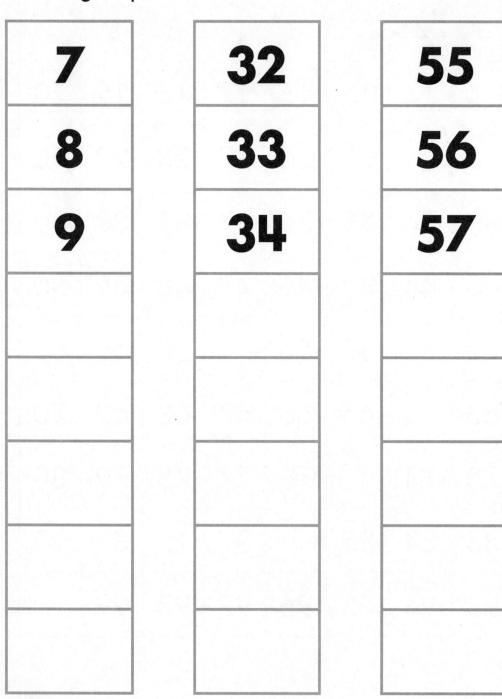

7	32	55
8	33	56
9	34	57

What Numbers Are Missing?

Fill in the 100 chart. Write the missing numbers.

NOTE Students use what they know about the counting sequence and patterns on the 100 chart to fill in the missing numbers.

SMH 27–29

	2	3	4	5	6	7	8	9	10
11	12	13	14	15	16	17		19	20
21	22	23	24		26	27	28	29	30
	32	33	34	35	36	37	38	39	40
41	42		44	45	46	47	48	49	50
51	52	53	54	55	56	57	58	59	
61	62	63		65	66		68	69	70
71	72	73	74	75	76	77	78		80
81	82	83	84	85	86	87	88	89	90
91	92	93	94	95		97	98	99	100

What Can I Buy?

Pretend you have 12 pennies.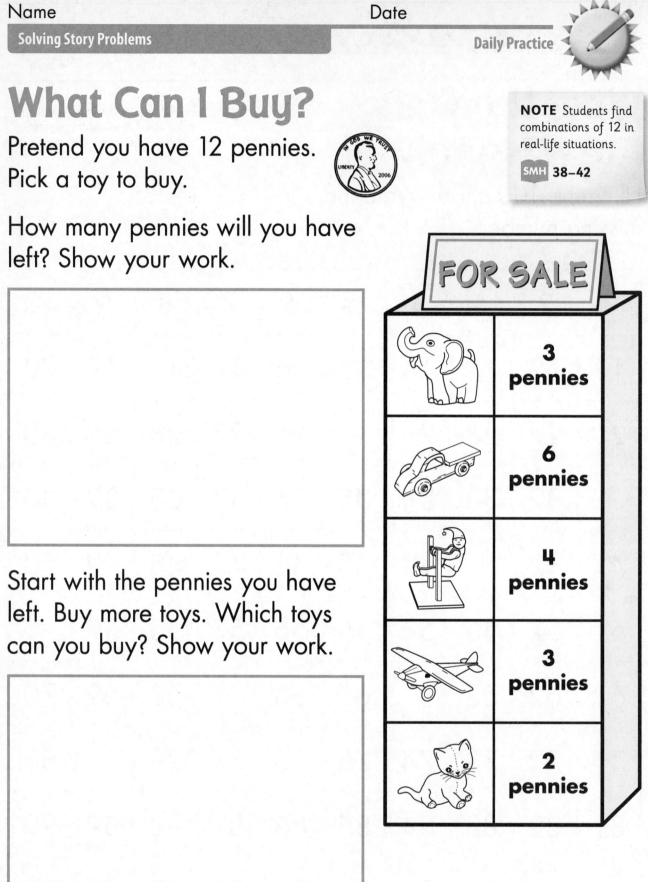
Pick a toy to buy.

NOTE Students find combinations of 12 in real-life situations.

SMH 38–42

How many pennies will you have left? Show your work.

Start with the pennies you have left. Buy more toys. Which toys can you buy? Show your work.

FOR SALE

	3 pennies
	6 pennies
	4 pennies
	3 pennies
	2 pennies

Spiral to Infinity Steve Allen

"Fractal images are often made up of small images-within-images, constantly repeating and going smaller and smaller." – **Steve Allen**

Investigations
IN NUMBER, DATA, AND SPACE®

What Would You Rather Be?

Investigation 3

Describe a Shape

Trace your shape in this box
Look carefully at your shape.

What are some words that
describe your shape?
List as many as you can.

Words that describe my shape:

What Is Missing?

Fill in the missing numbers.

NOTE Students practice writing numbers and work with the order of numbers from 1 to 100.

SMH 27–29

1	2	3	4		6	7		9	10
	12	13		15		17		19	
21		23	24	25				29	30
31	32				36				40
		44			46	47	48	49	
	52	53		55					60
		64				67		69	
71	72	73					78		
	82			85	86		88	89	
91	92		94			97			

Ongoing Review

How many flowers in all?

12	10	5	2
Ⓐ	Ⓑ	Ⓒ	Ⓓ

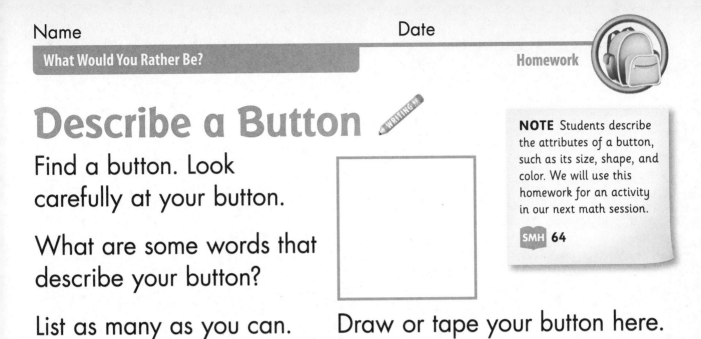

Describe a Button

Find a button. Look carefully at your button.

What are some words that describe your button?

List as many as you can.

Draw or tape your button here.

NOTE Students describe the attributes of a button, such as its size, shape, and color. We will use this homework for an activity in our next math session.

SMH 64

Words that describe my button:

Finding Socks

Jacob was cleaning his room.
He found 3 socks under his bed.
He found 6 socks in his closet.
He found 4 socks on the floor.
How many socks did he find in all?

Solve the problem. Show your work.

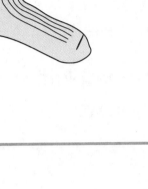

NOTE Students combine three quantities to solve a story problem.

SMH 33–37

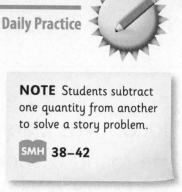

Apple Picking

Talisa picked 17 apples.
She ate 9 of them.
How many apples does
Talisa have left?

Solve the problem.
Show your work.

NOTE Students subtract one quantity from another to solve a story problem.

SMH 38–42

Ongoing Review

How many pattern blocks are in this design?

8   9   10   12
(A)   (B)   (C)   (D)

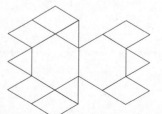

Two Groups

Look at the two groups pictured below. What rule did the teacher use to sort the students?

NOTE Students determine how a set of data has been sorted and then continue sorting according to this rule.

SMH 64

We do not fit the rule.	We fit the rule.

1. Does [image] fit the rule? _____

2. Does [image] fit the rule? _____

3. Does [image] fit the rule? _____

4. Does [image] fit the rule? _____

5. The rule is _____.

Heads and Tails

Imagine that you are playing *Heads and Tails.*

NOTE Students practice counting and breaking a number into two parts ($7 = 3 + 4$).

SMH G13

Fill in the chart for each game.

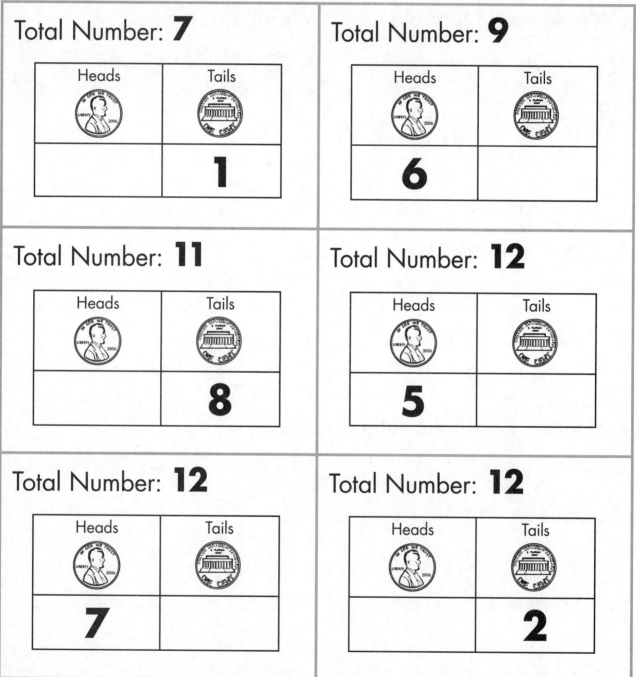

Total Number: **7**

Heads	Tails
	1

Total Number: **9**

Heads	Tails
6	

Total Number: **11**

Heads	Tails
	8

Total Number: **12**

Heads	Tails
	5

Total Number: **12**

Heads	Tails
7	

Total Number: **12**

Heads	Tails
	2

Eleven Shapes: How Many of Each?

I have 11 shapes.

Some are circles. ◯

Some are triangles. △

How many of each could I have?

Solve the problem. Show your work.

NOTE Students find combinations of two numbers that equal 11. There are a number of possible solutions. Encourage students to find more than one.

SMH 46–47

Ongoing Review

There should be 8 crayons in the box.
How many more are needed?

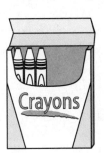

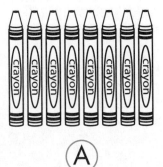 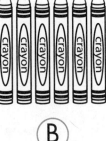  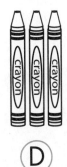

Ⓐ   Ⓑ   Ⓒ   Ⓓ

Our Plan for Collecting Data ✏

1. What is your question?

_____

_____

_____

2. Who will ask the question?

_____

_____

3. Who will record students' responses?

_____

_____

4. How will you record students' responses?

_____

_____

_____

5. How will you make sure that you asked everyone?

_____

_____

_____

Monthly Calendar

Here is a calendar for you. Fill in the month and dates. Then, find a place to hang it at home.

> **NOTE** Students practice recording dates and making, reading, and using a calendar as a tool for keeping track of time.
>
> **SMH** 17–19

Name of Month

Sunday	Monday	Tuesday	Wednesday	Thursday	Friday	Saturday

Special Days

_____   _____

_____   _____

What We Found Out ✏️

1. What was your question?

_____

_____

_____

2. What did you find out?

_____

_____

_____

3. What surprised or interested you?

_____

_____

_____

4. Write an equation that shows what you found out.

_____

_____

_____

Counting Strips

Write the missing numbers on these counting strips.

NOTE Students practice counting and writing numbers.

SMH 6–12, 21–23

17	35	67
18	36	68
19	37	69

Would You Rather ...?

Would you rather drink white milk or chocolate milk?

Students answered this question by putting a cube next to the white milk carton or the chocolate milk carton.

NOTE Students describe the resulting data to a survey question.

SMH **65–66, 68**

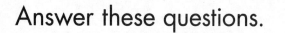

Answer these questions.

1. How many students responded? _____

2. How many students responded white milk? _____

3. How many students responded chocolate milk? _____

4. Draw two towers to show how students responded.

NOTE Students describe resulting attendance data.

SMH **65–66, 68**

Attendance Data

The chart shows how many students are in class today and how many are not.

Room 110's Attendance	
HERE	NOT HERE
★ ★ ★ ★ ★ ★ ★ ★ ★ ★ ★ ★ ★ ★ ★	★ ★ ★ ★ ★ ★

1. How many students are here today? _____

2. How many students are absent today? _____

3. How many students are in the class? _____

Ongoing Review

4. How many hands and feet in all?

10	20	22	40
Ⓐ	Ⓑ	Ⓒ	Ⓓ

Roll and Record: Addition

Write the total number.

> **NOTE** Students combine two amounts to find the total.
>
> **SMH** **G19**

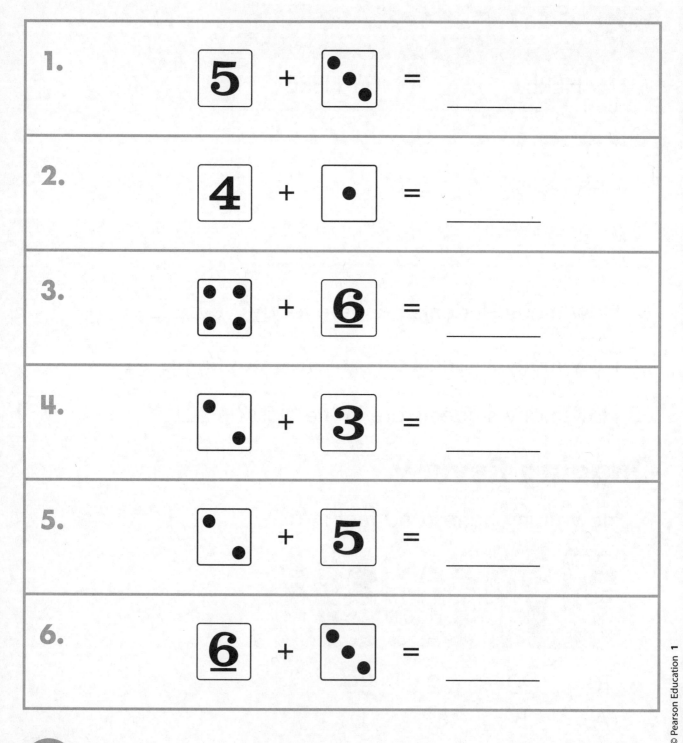

1. **5** + ⚂ = _____

2. **4** + ⚀ = _____

3. ⚃ + **6** = _____

4. ⚁ + **3** = _____

5. ⚁ + **5** = _____

6. **6** + ⚂ = _____

Start With/Get To

Write the missing numbers on the number line.

NOTE Students practice writing numbers and counting on a number line.

SMH **26, 31, 32**

Example:

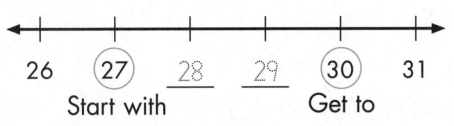

26   (27)   28   29   (30)   31

Start with   Get to

Now it is your turn.

1.

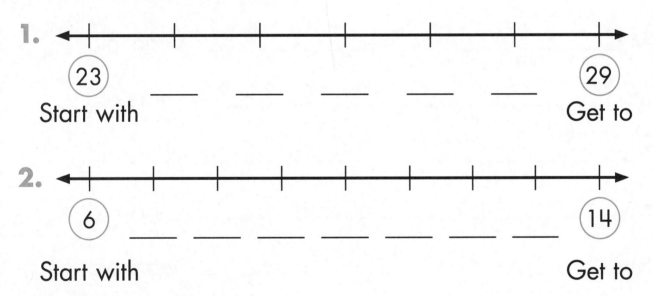

(23) __ __ __ __ __ (29)

Start with   Get to

2.

(6) __ __ __ __ __ __ __ (14)

Start with   Get to

Ongoing Review

3. There are 5 birds eating. 5 more birds come to eat. How many birds are eating now?

5   7   9   10
(A)   (B)   (C)   (D)

Family Ages

Find out the ages of people in your family. Write each person's name, age, and family role. For example:

NOTE Students collect data on the ages of people in their families. We will use this homework for an activity in the next math session.

SMH 65

My <u>mother</u> is <u>33</u> years old.

My <u>brother, Chris,</u> is <u>9</u> years old.

You do not have to fill in all the blanks.

My _____ is _____ years old.

My _____ is _____ years old.

My _____ is _____ years old.

My _____ is _____ years old.

My _____ is _____ years old.

My _____ is _____ years old.

My _____ is _____ years old.

My _____ is _____ years old.

Comparing Classes

Look at your representation of the ages of students in your class.

Look at your representation of the ages of students in another class.

How are the ages similar in the two classes?

How are the ages different in the two classes?

Roll and Record: Subtraction

NOTE Students subtract one amount from another.

SMH **G20**

Subtract and write the answer.

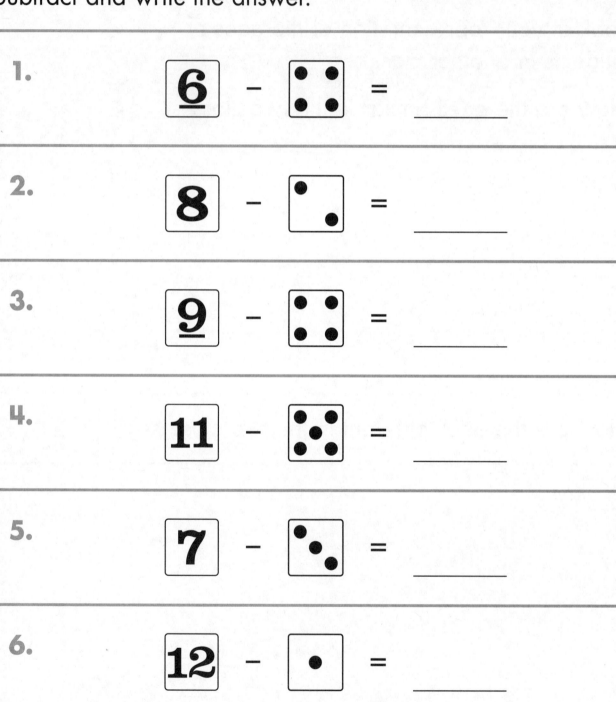

1. $\underline{6}$ – [⊡ 4] = _____

2. 8 – [⋰ 2] = _____

3. $\underline{9}$ – [⊡ 4] = _____

4. 11 – [⚄ 5] = _____

5. 7 – [⋰ 3] = _____

6. 12 – [• 1] = _____

What Does It Show?

This chart shows how old some third-grade students are.

NOTE Students read a chart and describe the data in the chart.

SMH **65–68**

Age	Number of Students
7	|
8	|||| |||| ||
9	|||| ||||
10	

1. How many students are 7 years old? _____

2. How many students are 8 years old? _____

3. How many students are 9 years old? _____

4. How many students are 10 years old? _____

5. How old are most of the students? _____

6. Are there more 8-year-olds or 9-year-olds? _____

7. Are there fewer 7-year-olds or 9-year-olds? _____

More True or False?

Circle the word to show whether the equation is true or false.

NOTE Students determine whether equations are true or false.

SMH **44**

1. $10 + 2 = 12$ True   False

2. $7 + 7 = 10 + 4$ True   False

3. $14 = 7 - 7$ True   False

4. $5 + 5 + 2 = 6 + 6$ True   False

5. $8 - 4 = 4 + 0$ True   False

6. $8 - 4 = 4 + 4$ True   False

Fruit Snack

It's Max's turn to bring in the class snack. He wants to bring in fruit, but he can bring only two kinds of fruit. Max asked his classmates what their favorite fruits are.

NOTE Students organize and interpret data.

SMH 65–66, 68

Favorite Fruits

apple	pear	grapes	watermelon	banana
Sacha Neil	Carol Bruce Toshi Libby Talisa	Keena Jacob Edgar	Allie Diego Paula Lyle Vic Leah	Marta DeShawn

What two fruits should Max bring in for the class snack? How do you know?

_____

_____

_____

Spiral to Infinity Steve Allen

"Fractal images are often made up of small images-within-images, constantly repeating and going smaller and smaller."– **Steve Allen**

Investigations

IN NUMBER, DATA, AND SPACE®

Fish Lengths and Animal Jumps

How Many Cubes Long?

Name of Object	How long?
	_____ cubes
	_____ cubes
	_____ cubes
	_____ cubes
	_____ cubes
	_____ cubes
	_____ cubes
	_____ cubes

Which is your shortest object? _____

Which is your longest object? _____

Make a list of your objects from shortest to longest.

Using a Calendar

Here is a calendar for you. Fill in the month and dates. Then find a place to hang it at home.

NOTE Students practice recording dates and creating, reading, and using a calendar as a tool for keeping track of time.

SMH 17–19

Name of Month

Sunday	Monday	Tuesday	Wednesday	Thursday	Friday	Saturday

Special Days

_____   _____

How Long Is It?

Name of Object	How long?	What did you use?		
		cubes	tiles	clips
		cubes	tiles	clips
		cubes	tiles	clips
		cubes	tiles	clips
		cubes	tiles	clips
		cubes	tiles	clips

It's Longer

Circle the longer object.

NOTE Students have been exploring the lengths of objects. You may wish to have your child compare a spoon with different objects and determine which object is longer. Make sure that he or she is aligning the two objects on one end before comparing their lengths.

SMH **93, 94, 95**

1.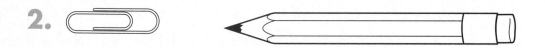

2.

3.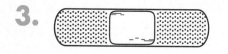

4.

5.

Measuring Keepers (page 1 of 2)

Which kind of fish are you measuring?

Alewife   Perch   Mackerel

How long does a keeper have to be?

_____ inches

	How many inches long?	Is it a keeper?
Fish A	_____ inches	Yes No
Fish B	_____ inches	Yes No
Fish C	_____ inches	Yes No
Fish D	_____ inches	Yes No
Fish E	_____ inches	Yes No
Fish F	_____ inches	Yes No

Measuring Keepers (page 2 of 2)

Which kind of fish are you measuring?

   Alewife   Perch   Mackerel

How long does a keeper have to be?

_____ inches

	How many inches long?	Is it a keeper?
Fish A	_____ inches	Yes No
Fish B	_____ inches	Yes No
Fish C	_____ inches	Yes No
Fish D	_____ inches	Yes No
Fish E	_____ inches	Yes No
Fish F	_____ inches	Yes No

Measuring with Paper Clips

Write how many paper clips were used to measure each picture.

NOTE Students use paper clips as a unit of measurement to determine the length or height of different objects.

SMH 96, 97–98

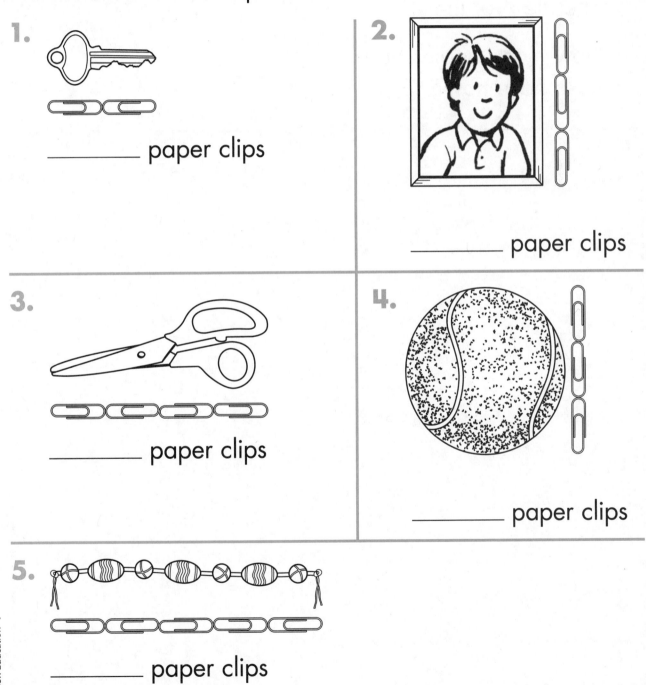

1.

_____ paper clips

2.

_____ paper clips

3.

_____ paper clips

4.

_____ paper clips

5.

_____ paper clips

Rosa's Apples (page 1 of 2)

Solve the problems. Show your work.

NOTE These problems are about subtracting one quantity from another. Encourage your child to find his or her own way to solve the problem and record the work.

SMH 38–42

1. Rosa picked 18 apples.

She ate 7 of them.

How many apples does Rosa have now?

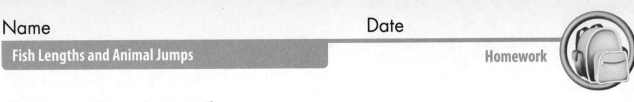

Rosa's Apples (page 2 of 2)

2. Rosa went to the store and bought 19 apples.

She used 8 of them to make applesauce.

How many apples does Rosa have now?

Fish Stories (page 1 of 2) ✏️

Solve the problems about fish.
Show your work.

1. Sam caught a perch that is 8 inches long.
He caught an alewife that is 11 inches long.
How much longer is the alewife than the perch?

2. Kim caught a perch that is 5 inches long.
Sam caught a perch that is 6 inches long.
How much longer is Sam's perch than Kim's perch?

Fish Stories (page 2 of 2)

3. Rosa caught a perch that is 2 inches long.

Keepers must be 6 inches long.

How much longer would Rosa's fish need to be to keep it?

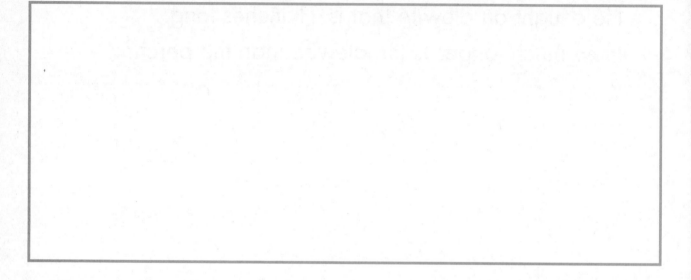

4. Max's perch is 3 inches long.

Rosa's perch is 5 inches long.

How much shorter is Max's perch than Rosa's perch?

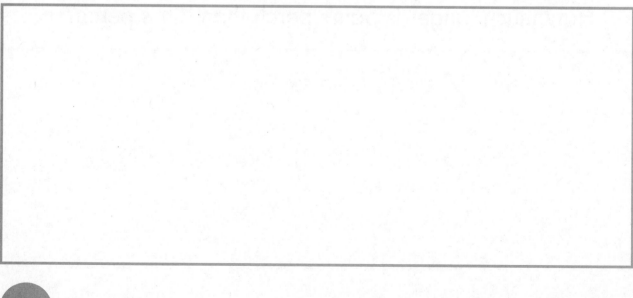

Measuring with Squares

Write the number that tells how many squares were used to measure each picture.

NOTE Students use squares as a unit of measurement to determine the length or height of several items.

SMH 96

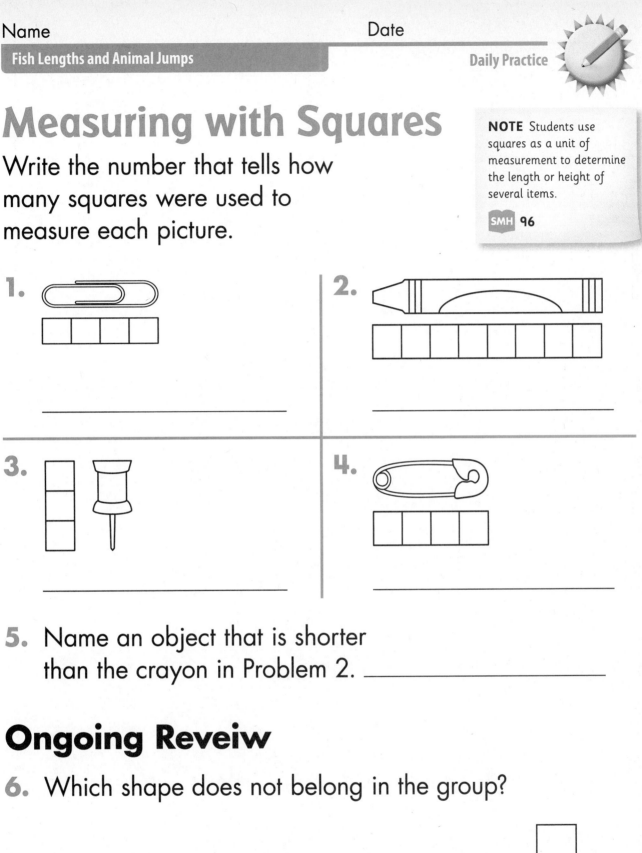

1.

_____

2.

_____

3.

_____

4.

_____

5. Name an object that is shorter than the crayon in Problem 2. _____

Ongoing Reveiw

6. Which shape does not belong in the group?

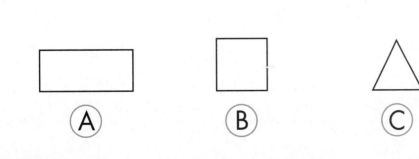 

Ⓐ   Ⓑ   Ⓒ   Ⓓ

True or False?

Circle the word to show whether the equation is true or false.

NOTE Students determine whether equations are true or false.

SMH 44

1. $4 + 5 = 8$ True   False

2. $8 + 4 = 4$ True   False

3. $8 = 4 + 4$ True   False

4. $8 - 5 = 3$ True   False

5. $8 = 3 - 5$ True   False

6. $8 - 3 = 5$ True   False

Start With/Get To

Write the missing numbers on the number line.

NOTE Students practice writing numbers and counting backwards.

SMH **26, 32**

Here is an example. Start with ⑤. Get to ②.

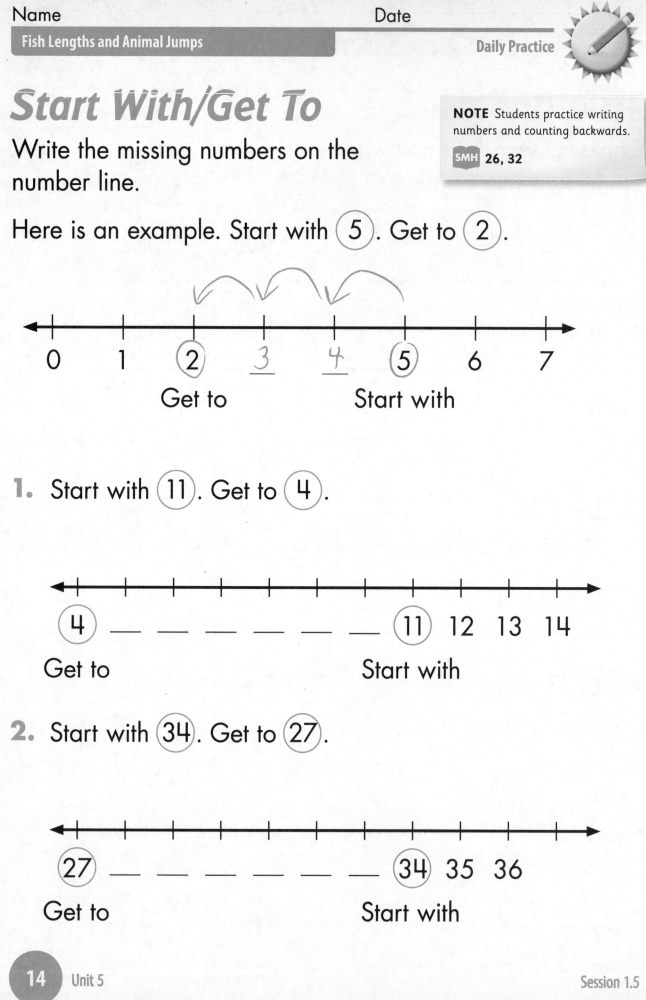

1. Start with ⑪. Get to ④.

2. Start with ㉞. Get to ㉗.

© Pearson Education 1

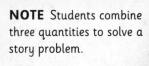

On the Bus

Solve the problem. Show your work.

NOTE Students combine three quantities to solve a story problem.

SMH 33–37

There were 3 children on the school bus.
At the first stop, 7 more children
got on the bus.
At the next stop, 4 more children
got on the bus.

How many children were on the school bus?

Distances in the Classroom (page 1 of 2)

Measure the tapes by using kid steps, and find out which is longer.

1. How long is Tape A? _____ kid steps

   How long is Tape B? _____ kid steps

   Which is longer?   Tape A   Tape B

2. How long is Tape C? _____ kid steps

   How long is Tape D? _____ kid steps

   Which is longer?   Tape C   Tape D

3. How long is Tape E? _____ kid steps

   How long is Tape F? _____ kid steps

   Which is longer?   Tape E   Tape F

4. How long is Tape G? _____ kid steps

   How long is Tape H? _____ kid steps

   Which is longer?   Tape G   Tape H

Distances in the Classroom (page 2 of 2)

Choose two tapes you have not compared yet.
Record which is longer.

5. Tape _____ is _____ kid steps long.

Tape _____ is _____ kid steps long.

Which tape is longer? _____

6. Tape _____ is _____ kid steps long.

Tape _____ is _____ kid steps long.

Which tape is longer? _____

Heads and Tails

Imagine that you are playing *Heads and Tails.* Fill in the chart for each game.

NOTE Students practice counting and breaking a number into two parts (7 = 3 + 4).

SMH **G13**

Total Number: _____

Heads	Tails
2	**6**

Total Number: **10**

Heads	Tails
	7

Total Number: **11**

Heads	Tails
4	

Total Number: **13**

Heads	Tails
6	

Total Number: _____

Heads	Tails
4	**8**

Total Number: **9**

Heads	Tails
	5

Kid Steps at Home

Count the number of kid steps for each distance.

NOTE Your child will measure distances in your home using his or her own steps. Remind your child to place the heel of one shoe in front of the toe of the other shoe while measuring.

SMH 103

Distance	Kid Steps
From the stove to the sink	
From the sink to the table	
From your bed to the bedroom door	
From the bathroom to your bed	

Now measure other distances at your home.

Distance	Kid Steps
From _____ to _____	
From _____ to _____	

20 Unit 5

Measuring with Different Units

Choose a tape.
Choose 2 units.
Measure the tape with each unit.
Record.

1. We measured Tape _____.

     It is _____ baby steps long.

     It is _____ basketball player steps long.

     It is _____ craft sticks long.

2. We measured Tape _____.

     It is _____ baby steps long.

     It is _____ basketball player steps long.

     It is _____ craft sticks long.

3. We measured Tape _____.

     It is _____ baby steps long.

     It is _____ basketball player steps long.

     It is _____ craft sticks long.

Hats

Solve the problem. Show your work.

NOTE Students subtract one quantity from another to solve a story problem.

SMH 38–42

Kim had 13 hats for her party.
She gave 7 of them to her guests.

How many hats does she have left?

What Time Is It?

Read each clock, and write the time.

NOTE Students practice telling time to the hour.

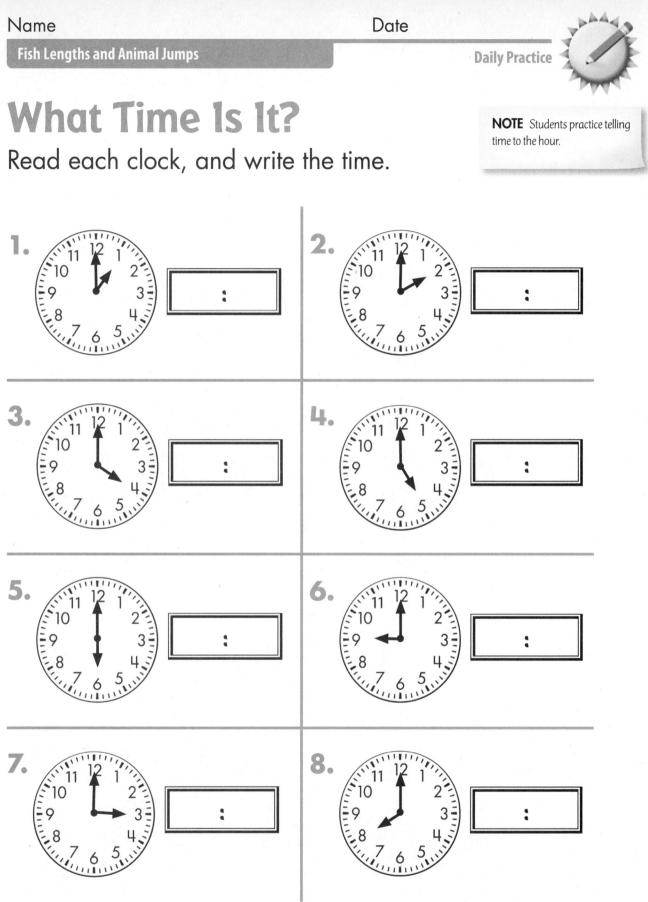

1.

:

2.

:

3.

:

4.

:

5.

:

6.

:

7.

:

8.

:

Reporting What We Found ✎

1. What tape do you have? Tape _____

---

2. Which measurement of the tape used the <u>greatest</u> number of units?

Baby steps   Basketball player steps   Craft sticks

---

3. Which measurement of the tape used the <u>least</u> number of units?

Baby steps   Basketball player steps   Craft sticks

---

4. Why were the numbers different?

How Many Snowballs?

NOTE Students combine two quantities to solve a story problem.

SMH 33–37

Solve the problem. Show your work.

Rosa made 8 snowballs.
Max also made 8 snowballs.

How many snowballs did they make?

Animal Jumps

What unit did you use to measure? (Circle one)

Baby steps   Craft sticks

1. The rabbit's jump was _____ units long.

2. The frog's jump was _____ units long.

3. The mouse's jump was _____ units long.

4. Max's jump was _____ units long.

5. The squirrel's jump was _____ units long.

6. The grasshopper's jump was _____ units long.

List the animal names in order by how long their jumps were.

Longest _____

Next longest _____

Next longest _____

Next longest _____

Next longest _____

Shortest _____

Jumping Word Problems (page 1 of 2) ✏️WRITING

Solve each problem. Show your work.

1. Sam's cat jumped 6 craft sticks. Rosa's cat jumped 3 craft sticks. Which cat jumped farther? How much farther did it jump?

```
┌─────────────────────────────────────────┐
│                                           │
│                                           │
│                                           │
│                                           │
└─────────────────────────────────────────┘
```

2. A rabbit jumped 8 basketball player steps. Then it jumped 5 basketball player steps. How far did it jump in all?

```
┌─────────────────────────────────────────┐
│                                           │
│                                           │
│                                           │
│                                           │
└─────────────────────────────────────────┘
```

3. Kim jumped 8 craft sticks. Max jumped 10 craft sticks. How much farther did Max jump than Kim?

```
┌─────────────────────────────────────────┐
│                                           │
│                                           │
│                                           │
│                                           │
└─────────────────────────────────────────┘
```

Jumping Word Problems (page 2 of 2)

4. Sam jumped 2 basketball player steps.
Then he jumped 3 basketball player steps.
Then he jumped 4 basketball player steps.
How far did he jump in all?

5. A frog jumped to the pond. It jumped
4 kid steps. Then it jumped 6 kid steps.
How many kid steps did the frog jump?

6. A squirrel jumped 6 craft sticks. A rabbit
jumped 9 craft sticks. How much farther
did the rabbit jump than the squirrel?

How Many in All?
Write the total number.

NOTE Students combine two amounts to find the total.

SMH **G19**

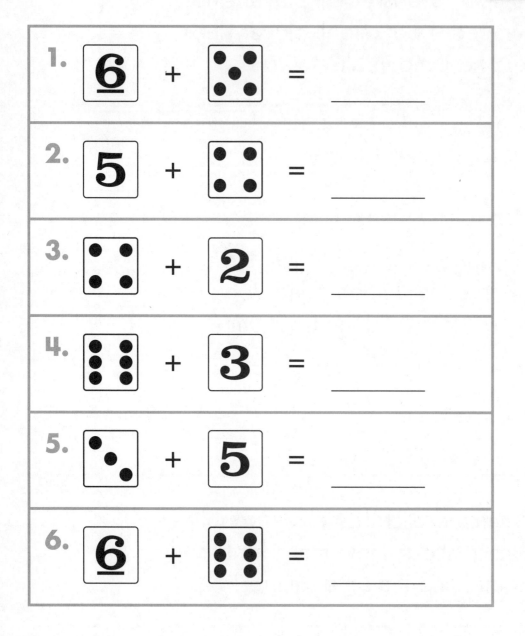

1. **6** + [::] = _____

2. **5** + [::] = _____

3. [::] + **2** = _____

4. [:::] + **3** = _____

5. [:] + **5** = _____

6. **6** + [:::] = _____

Comparing Lengths

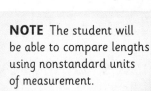

NOTE The student will be able to compare lengths using nonstandard units of measurement.

SMH 96

Rosa is going to measure her book.
First she will measure using crayons.
Then she will measure using paper clips.

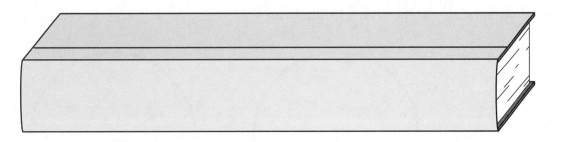

Will it take more crayons or paper clips to

measure her book? _____

Why do you think so? _____

The length of Rosa's book is 2 crayons.

How many paper clips long is Rosa's book? _____

How do you know? _____

Half-and-Half Pizzas

Max's family loves pizza.
They order half cheese and half pepperoni.

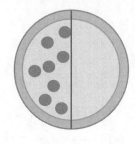

Make your own half-and-half pizzas.

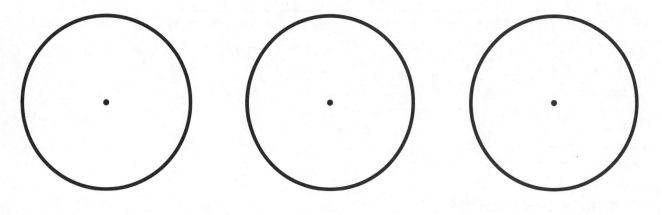

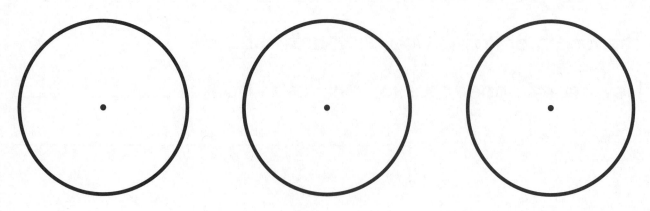

Half-and-Half

NOTE Students solve problems about halves of circles.

1. Draw a line that cuts the circle in half. Then, color half of the circle.

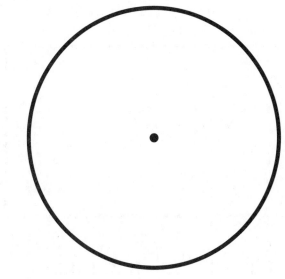

2. Circle the pizzas that are half-and-half.

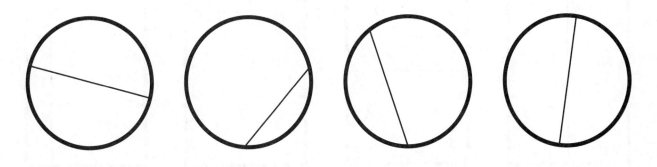

More Half-and-Half

NOTE Students solve problems about halves of rectangles.

1. Draw a line that cuts the rectangle in half. Then, color half of the rectangle.

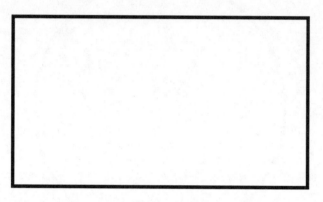

2. Circle the rugs that are half-and-half.

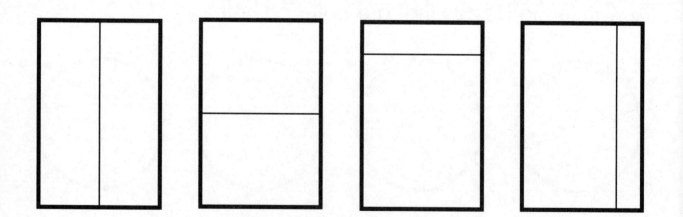

Area Rugs: Circles

Draw lines that cut the circles into fourths.
Choose 4 different colors to make a rug.

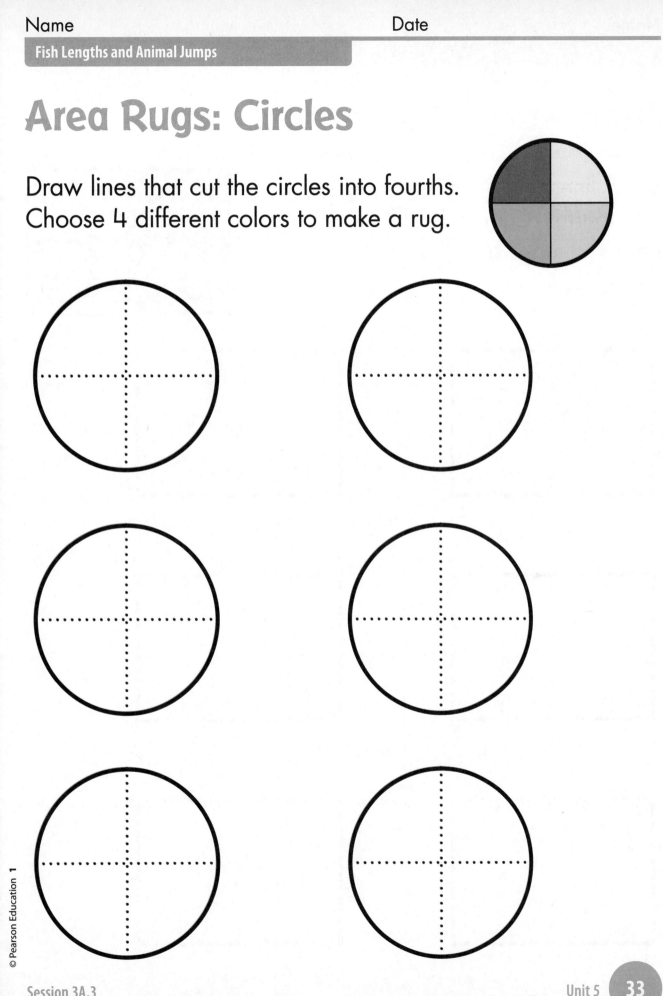

Area Rugs: Rectangles

Draw lines that cut the rectangles into fourths. Choose 4 different colors to make a rug.

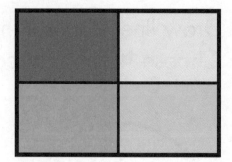

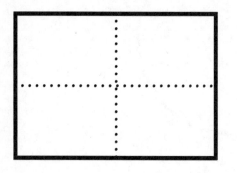

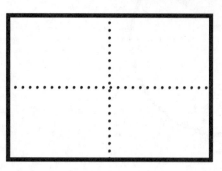

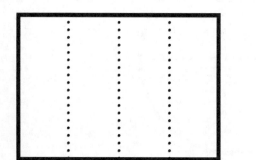

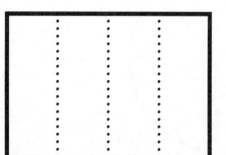

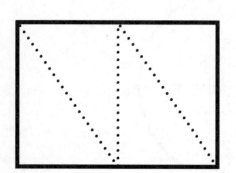

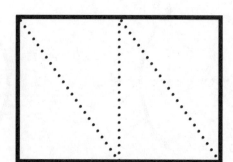

Area Rugs: Squares

Choose a rug to make.

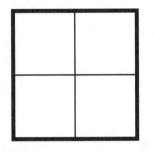 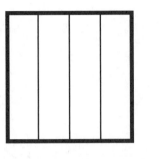 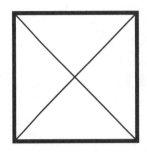

Draw lines to make fourths. Choose 4 different colors for your shape. Glue the shapes to make a rug.

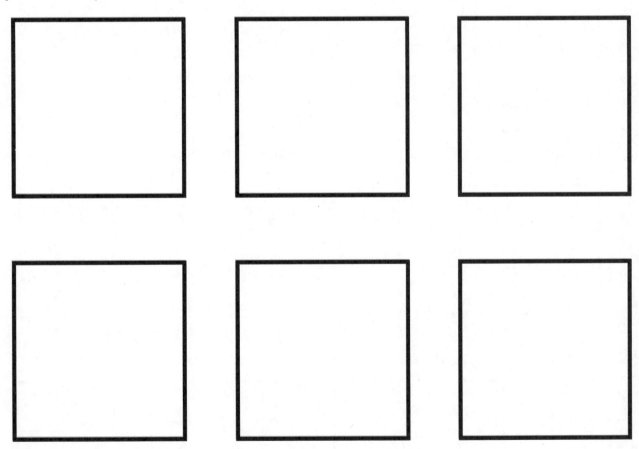

Fourths

NOTE Students solve problems about fourths.

1. Draw lines to cut the circle into fourths.

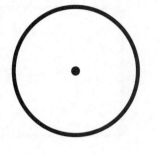

2. Color one fourth of the square.

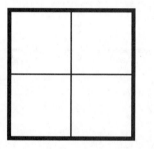

3. Color one fourth of the rectangle.

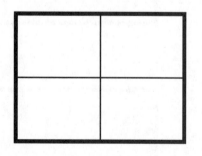

4. Circle the rugs that show fourths.

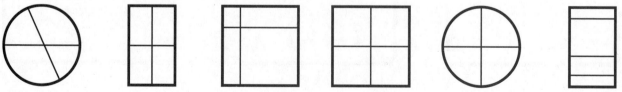

Daily Practice

Identifying Halves and Fourths

NOTE Students identify halves and fourths.

1. Circle the figures that show **halves**.

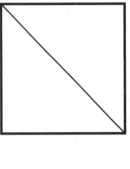 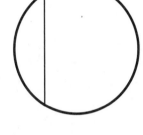 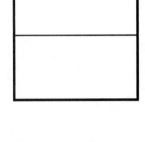

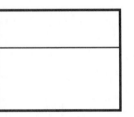 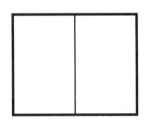 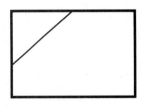

2. Circle the figures that show **fourths**.

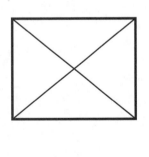 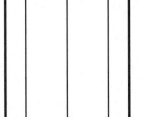 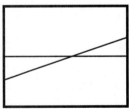

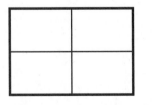 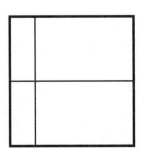

Spiral to Infinity Steve Allen

"Fractal images are often made up of small images-within-images, constantly repeating and going smaller and smaller." – **Steve Allen**

Investigations
IN NUMBER, DATA, AND SPACE®

Number Games and Crayon Puzzles

Today's Number: 10

Today's Number is 10.

How many ways can you make Today's Number?
Show the ways.

Using a Calendar

Here is a calendar for you.
Fill in the month and dates.
Then find a place to hang it at home.

NOTE Students practice recording dates and creating, reading, and using a calendar as a tool for keeping track of time.

SMH 17–19

Name of Month

Sunday	Monday	Tuesday	Wednesday	Thursday	Friday	Saturday

Special Days

Halves

Draw a line that cuts each shape in half.
Color one half of each shape.

1.

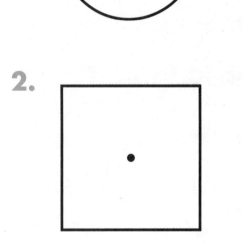

2.

3. Circle the shapes that are cut in half.

3B Unit 6

Three Towers Recording Sheet

Equations

_____   _____   _____

Tower 1   Tower 2   Tower 3

Number Games and Crayon Puzzles

Which Is Larger?

Circle the pair of numbers that makes the larger total.

NOTE Students find which of two totals is greater by using pairs of Primary Number Cards.

SMH G6

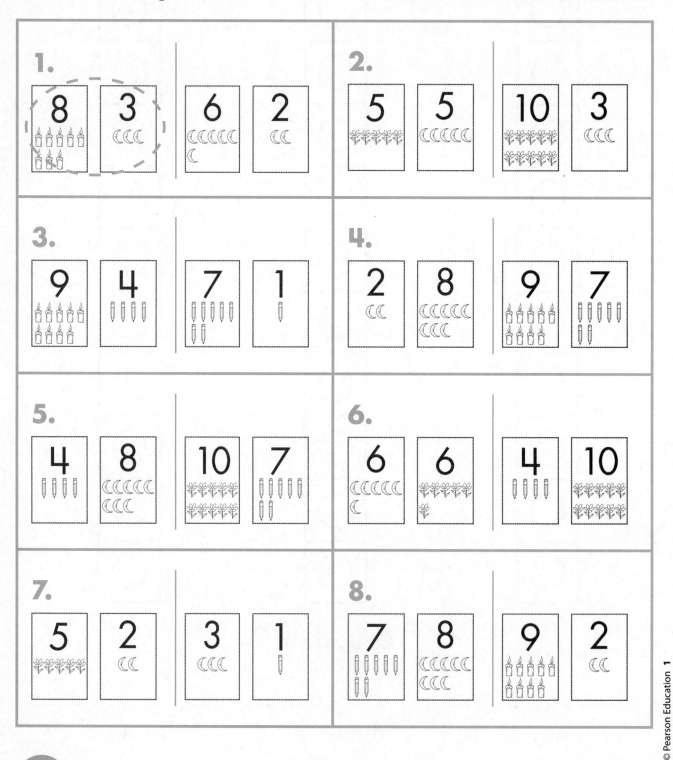

How Many Ducks?

Solve the problem. Show your work.

NOTE Students combine three quantities to solve a story problem.

SMH **33–37**

Sam saw 2 ducks flying in the air.
He saw 8 ducks in the grass and
5 more ducks in the pond.
How many ducks did Sam see?

Number Games and Crayon Puzzles

Daily Practice

Give Me 10!

Write a number on the card to make 10 in all.

NOTE Students make combinations of 10 using number cards.

SMH 48–49

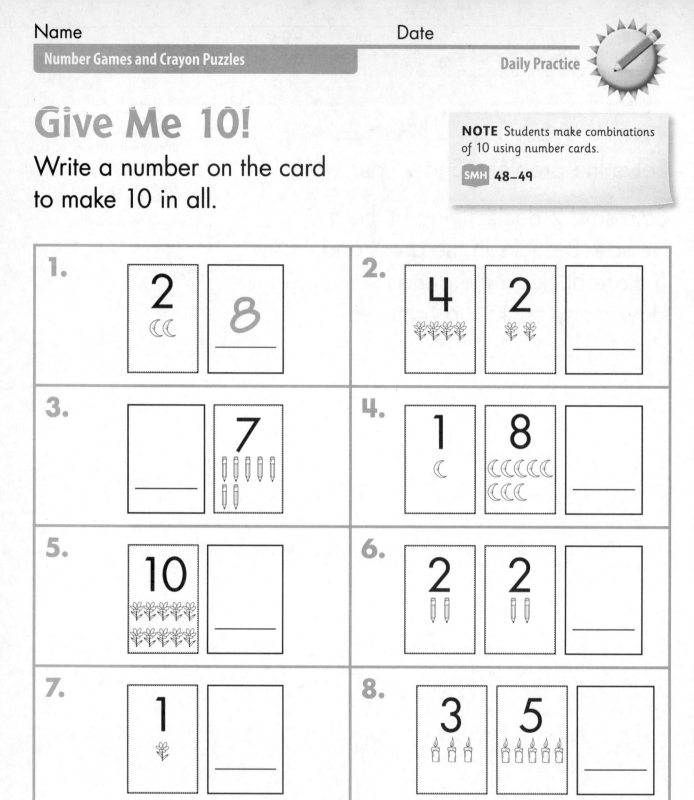

Make 10 Recording Sheet

Play this game at home.
Use the game rules and game
materials you took home.

After you play, write about
the game.

NOTE Please play this game with your
child, and then help your child fill out
and return this sheet. The more times
children play a mathematical game, the
more practice they get with important
skills and with reasoning mathematically.

SMH 48–49, G15

1. Who played the game?

_____

_____

2. What happened when you played?

_____

_____

_____

_____

_____

_____

_____

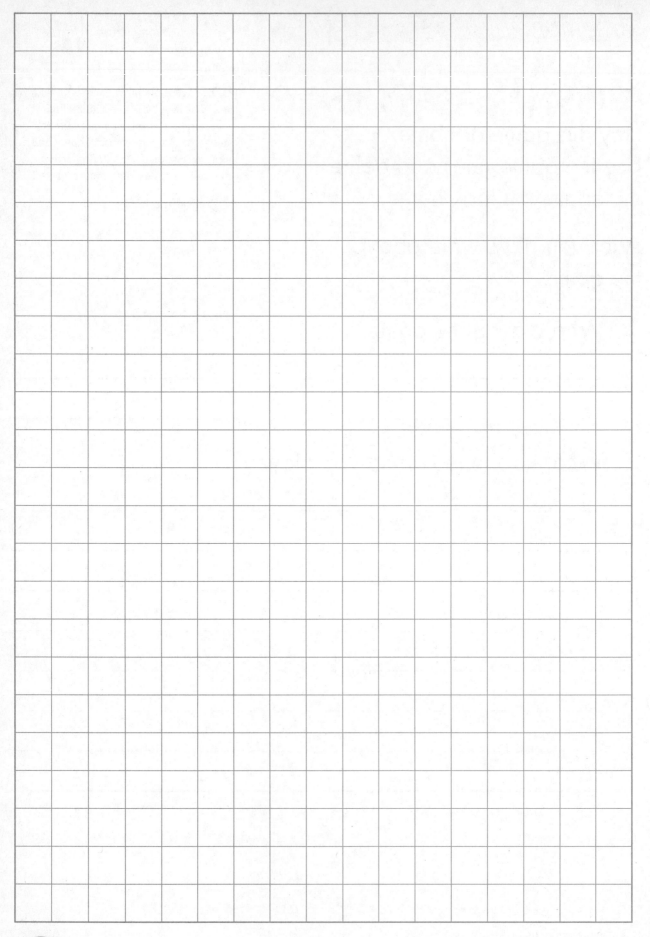

8   Unit 6

Counters in a Cup Recording Sheet

Total Number _____

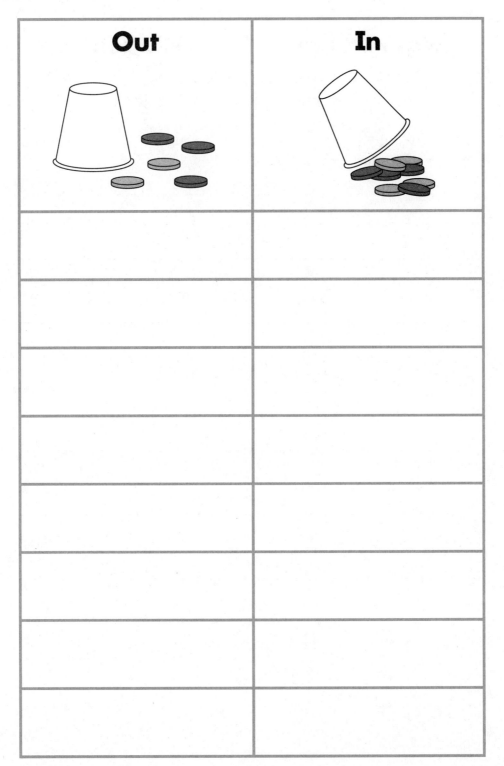

Number Games and Crayon Puzzles

How Many Am I Hiding? Recording Sheet

Total Number _____

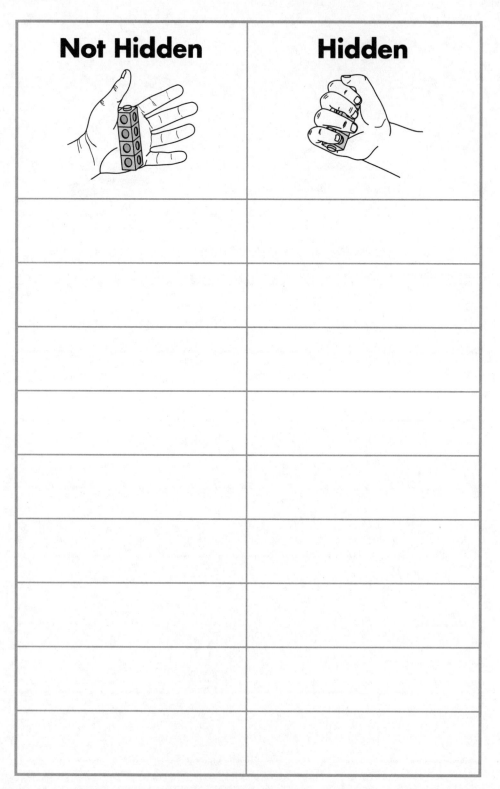

Not Hidden	Hidden

Addition Problems

Write the total number or the missing part.

NOTE Students solve addition problems by combining two amounts to find the total or by finding the missing part.

SMH G6

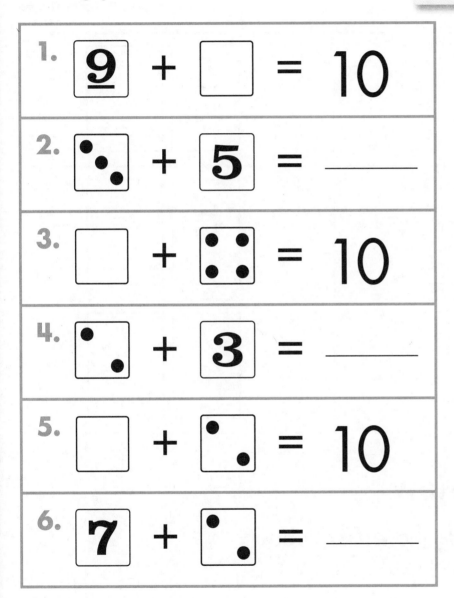

1. $\underline{9}$ + ☐ = 10

2. ⚃ + **5** = _____

3. ☐ + ⚃ = 10

4. ⚁ + **3** = _____

5. ☐ + ⚁ = 10

6. **7** + ⚁ = _____

What Is Missing?

Each pair of cards should make 10.
Write the missing number.

NOTE Students continue to practice combinations of 10.

SMH **48–49**

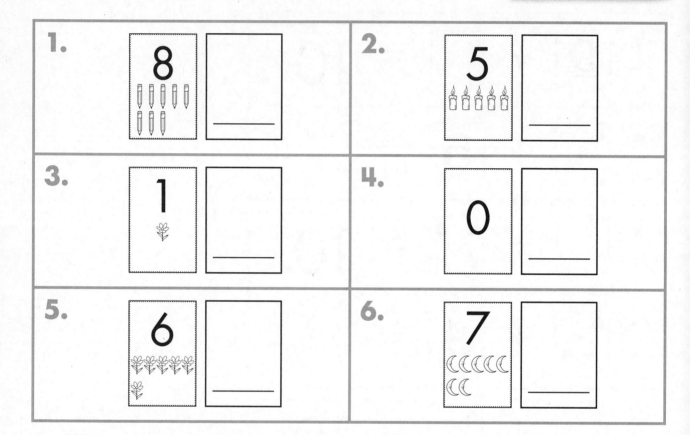

1. 8

2. 5

3. 1

4. 0

5. 6

6. 7

Ongoing Review

7. Which tower has the **most** cubes?

    (A)   (B)   (C)   (D)

8. Which tower has the **fewest** cubes?

    (A)   (B)   (C)   (D)

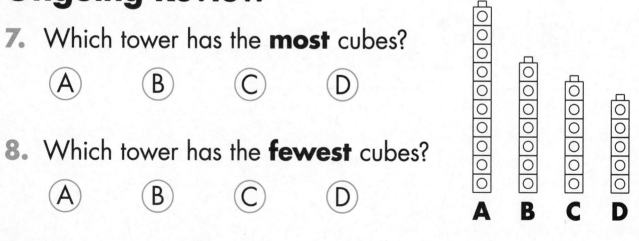

A   **B**   **C**   **D**

What's the Sum?

Write the sum of the two numbers.

NOTE Students practice adding two numbers.

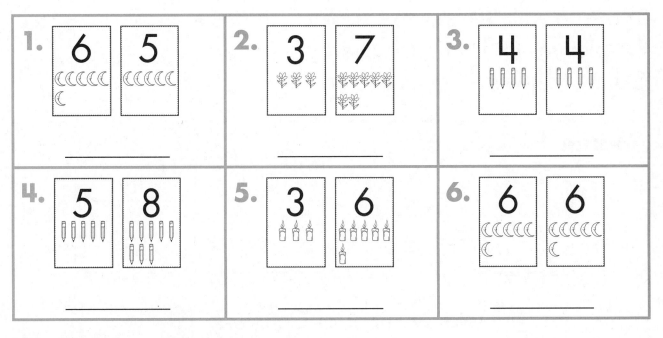

1. 6   5 _____

2. 3   7 _____

3. 4   4 _____

4. 5   8 _____

5. 3   6 _____

6. 6   6 _____

Ongoing Review

7. Which block has the **most** sides?

   (A)   (B)   (C)   (D)

8. Which block has the **fewest** sides?

   (A)   (B)   (C)   (D)

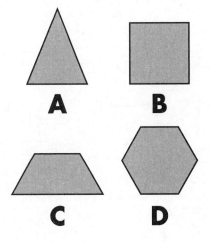

A   B

C   D

Counters in a Cup at Home

Pretend you are playing *Counters in a Cup* with 10 counters. Use the pictures to fill in each chart. Game 1 shows you what to do.

> **NOTE** Students work with a total of 10 counters. They use the number of visible counters to determine the number of hidden counters. This work encourages students to practice counting and breaking a number into two parts (10 = 6 + 4).
>
> **SMH** 48–49, G4

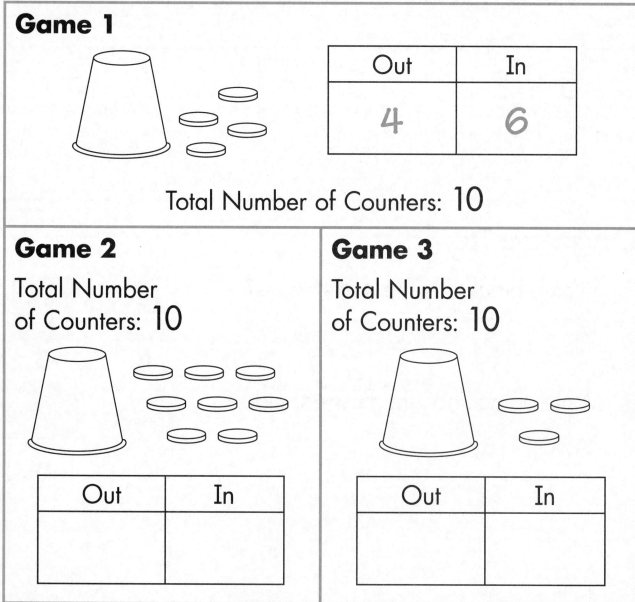

Game 1

Out	In
4	6

Total Number of Counters: **10**

Game 2

Total Number of Counters: **10**

Out	In

Game 3

Total Number of Counters: **10**

Out	In

Story Problems with Missing Parts (page 1 of 2)

Solve each problem. Show your work.

1. Kim used 3 round beads to make a bracelet.
   She also used some square beads.
   The bracelet has 7 beads in all.
   How many square beads did Kim use?

2. Some beads on Kim's bracelet are blue.
   There are 4 purple beads.
   There are 7 beads altogether.
   How many of the beads are blue?

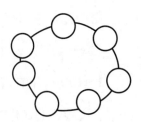

Story Problems with Missing Parts (page 2 of 2)

Solve each problem. Show your work.

3. Sam bought 5 books about animals.
He also bought some books about trains.
He bought 7 books altogether.
How many books about trains did
Sam buy?

4. Sam put some books on the top shelf.
He put 2 books on the bottom shelf.
Now there are 7 books on both shelves.
How many books did Sam put on the
top shelf?

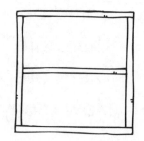

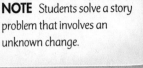

A Story Problem with an Unknown Change

NOTE Students solve a story problem that involves an unknown change.

Solve the problem. Show your work.

1. Rosa has 4 shells in her pail.
   She finds more shells in the sand.
   Now she has 6 shells.
   How many shells did Rosa find in the sand?

More Story Problems with Missing Parts (page 1 of 2)

Solve each problem. Show your work.

1. There were 6 birds in a tree.
   Some of the birds flew away.
   4 birds were left in the tree.
   How many birds flew away?

2. Rosa had some stickers.
   She gave 2 stickers to her friend.
   Then she had 4 stickers left.
   How many stickers did Rosa start with?

More Story Problems with Missing Parts (page 2 of 2)

Solve each problem. Show your work.

3. Max had 7 pencils in his desk.
He gave some of the pencils away.
He had 4 pencils left in his desk.
How many pencils did Max give away?

4. There were some frogs in a pond.
3 frogs hopped away.
There were 4 frogs left in the pond.
How many frogs were in the pond
at first?

Another Story Problem with an Unknown Change

NOTE Students solve a story problem that involves an unknown change.

Solve the problem. Show your work.

1. There were 8 balls in the gym.
   Some balls were put away.
   There were 5 balls still in the gym.
   How many balls were put away?

Twelve Crayons in All: How Many of Each?

Solve the problem. Show your work.

I have 12 crayons.
Some are red. Some are blue.
How many of each could I have?
How many red? How many blue?

Find as many combinations as you can.

Nine Shapes:
How Many of Each?

NOTE Students find combinations of two numbers that equal 9. There are a number of possible solutions.

SMH **46–47**

Solve the problem. Show your work.

I have 9 shapes.
Some are circles. Some are triangles.
How many of each could I have?
How many circles? How many triangles?

Find as many combinations as you can.

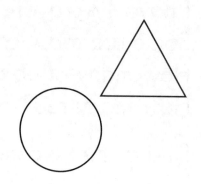

Crayon Puzzles
About More (page 1 of 2)

Solve the problems. Show your work.

1. I have 7 crayons.
   Some are blue and some are red.
   I have more blue crayons.
   How many of each could I have?

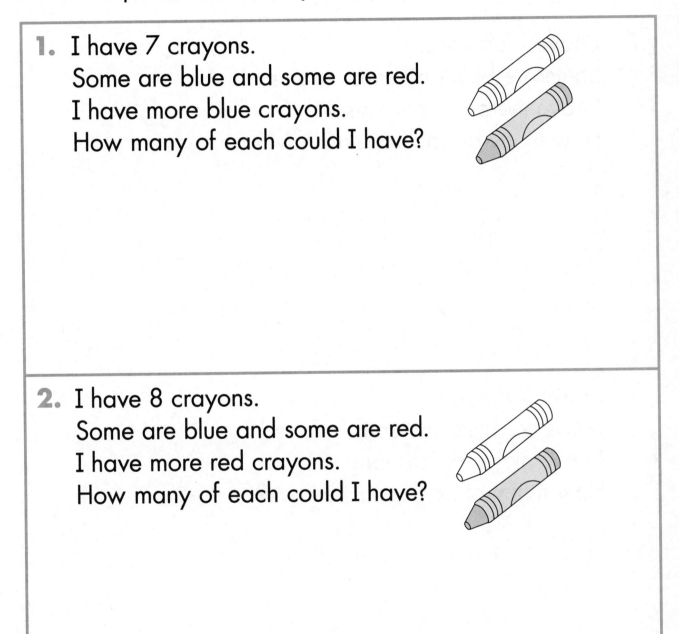

2. I have 8 crayons.
   Some are blue and some are red.
   I have more red crayons.
   How many of each could I have?

Crayon Puzzles
About More (page 2 of 2)

Solve the problems. Show your work.

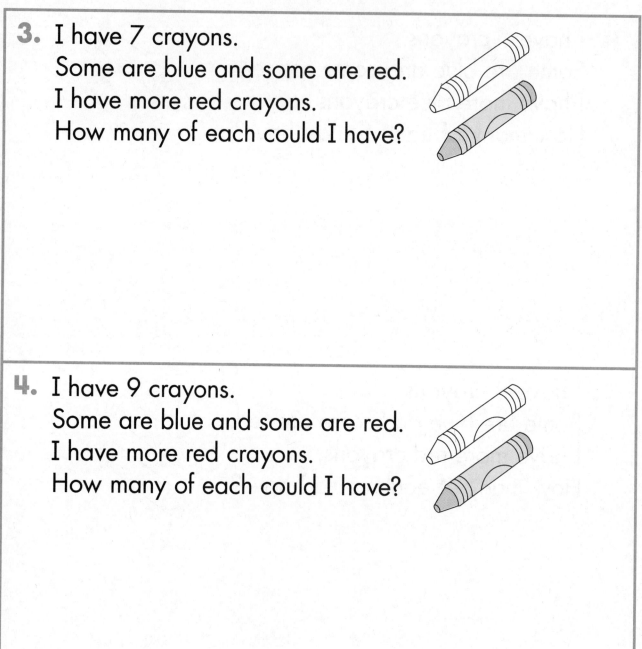

3. I have 7 crayons.
Some are blue and some are red.
I have more red crayons.
How many of each could I have?

4. I have 9 crayons.
Some are blue and some are red.
I have more red crayons.
How many of each could I have?

Inside and Outside

There are 9 soccer balls in all.
Write how many are outside the bag.
Write how many are inside the bag.

NOTE Students practice counting and breaking a number into two parts $(9 = 6 + 3)$.

1.

Outside _____

Inside _____

2.

Outside _____

Inside _____

3.

Outside _____

Inside _____

4.

Outside _____

Inside _____

Ongoing Review

5. Which group of marbles matches the number of cubes?

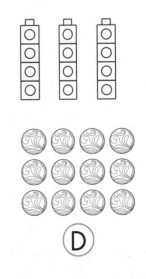

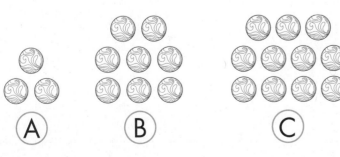

(A)   (B)   (C)   (D)

Eleven Crayons: How Many of Each?

NOTE Students find combinations of numbers that equal 11. There are a number of possible solutions. Encourage your child to find as many as she or he can.

SMH 46–47

Solve the problem. Show your work.

I have 11 crayons.
Some are red. Some are blue.
How many of each could I have?
How many red? How many blue?

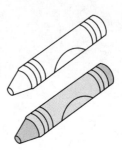

Find as many combinations as you can.

Totals and Missing Parts

Pretend you are playing *Heads and Tails*.
Fill in the chart for each game.

NOTE Students practice counting and breaking a number into two parts (7 = 3 + 4).

SMH **G13**

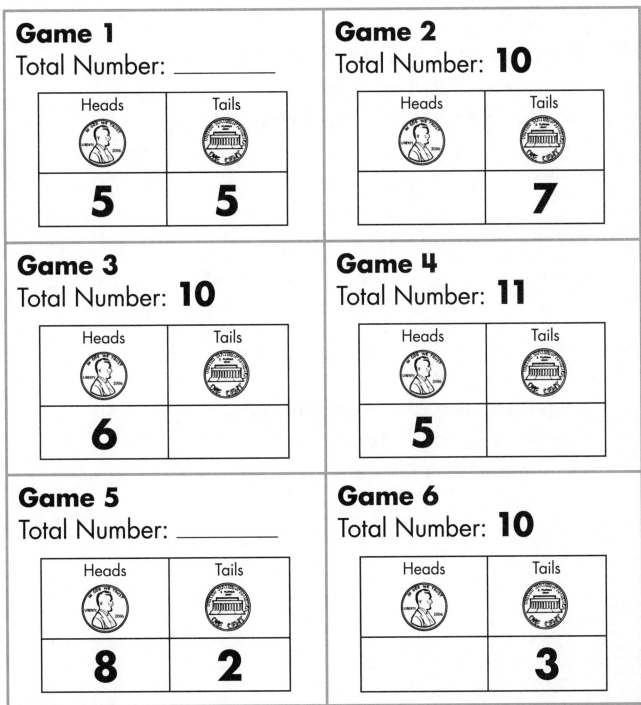

Game 1
Total Number: _____

Heads	Tails
5	5

Game 2
Total Number: **10**

Heads	Tails
	7

Game 3
Total Number: **10**

Heads	Tails
6	

Game 4
Total Number: **11**

Heads	Tails
5	

Game 5
Total Number: _____

Heads	Tails
8	2

Game 6
Total Number: **10**

Heads	Tails
	3

More Crayon Puzzles
About More (page 1 of 2)

Solve the problems. Show your work.

1. I have 9 crayons.
   Some are blue and some are red.
   I have more blue crayons.
   How many of each could I have?

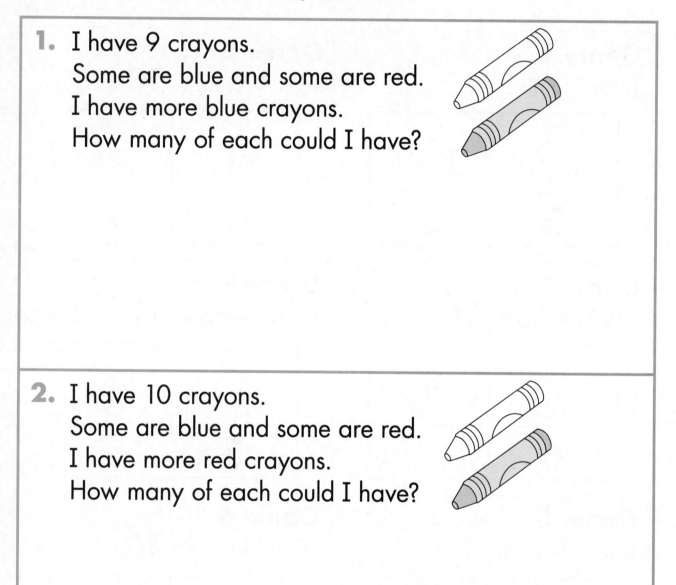

2. I have 10 crayons.
   Some are blue and some are red.
   I have more red crayons.
   How many of each could I have?

More Crayon Puzzles
About More (page 2 of 2)

Solve the problems. Show your work.

3. I have 12 crayons.
Some are blue and some are red.
I have more blue crayons.
How many of each could I have?

4. I have 13 crayons.
Some are blue and some are red.
I have more red crayons.
How many of each could I have?

Jack and Jill

Where are Jack and Jill going?

NOTE Students continue to find combinations of 10. It may be helpful to students to cross out combinations that do not equal 10.

SMH 48–49

1. Circle the combinations of 10. Draw a line connecting the combinations of 10 to find out.

2. Circle the place where Jack and Jill are going.

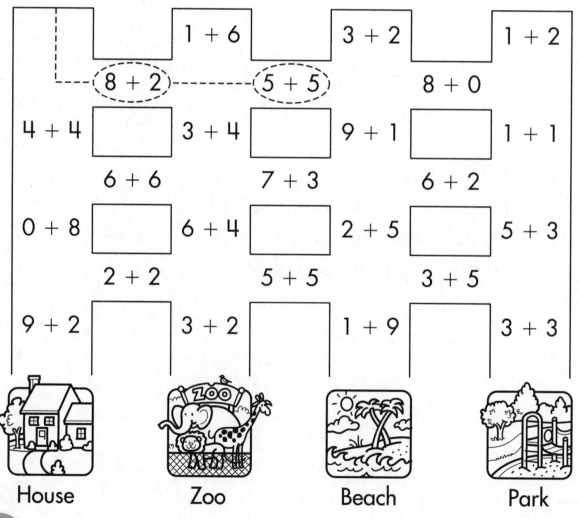

	$1 + 6$	$3 + 2$	$1 + 2$
	$8 + 2$	$5 + 5$	$8 + 0$
$4 + 4$	$3 + 4$	$9 + 1$	$1 + 1$
	$6 + 6$	$7 + 3$	$6 + 2$
$0 + 8$	$6 + 4$	$2 + 5$	$5 + 3$
	$2 + 2$	$5 + 5$	$3 + 5$
$9 + 2$	$3 + 2$	$1 + 9$	$3 + 3$

House   Zoo   Beach   Park

Make 10 at Home

Play *Make 10* with someone at home.

Write numbers to show some cards that you put together to make 10. The picture shows what to do.

NOTE Students play a game with someone at home. The Primary Number Cards should be at home from a previous homework assignment. Encourage your child to explain how to play the game. Please help your child fill out and return this sheet.

SMH 48–49, G15

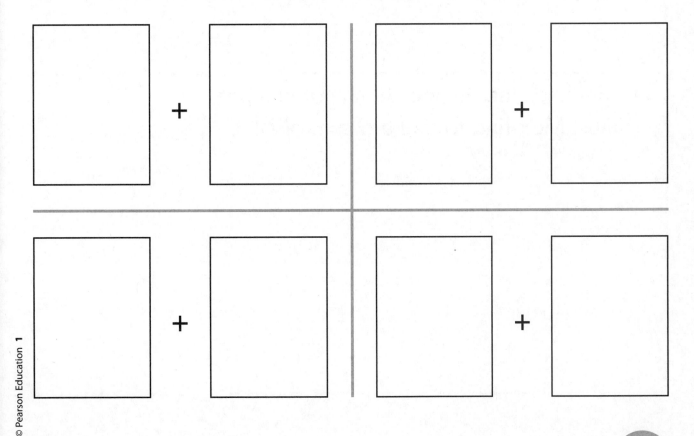

We put these cards together to make 10.

Unknown Numbers

Solve each problem. Show your work.

NOTE Students solve story problems that involve an unknown change.

Max and Kim are going on a Number Hunt.
They are hunting for numbers that have a sum of 6.

1. Max finds the number 2. What number must Kim find to make a sum of 6?

2. Kim finds the number 4. What number must Max find to make a sum of 6?

Number Games and Crayon Puzzles

How Many Nuts?

Solve the problem.
Show your work.

NOTE Students combine two
quantities to solve a story problem.

SMH **33–37**

A squirrel found 12 nuts under the elm tree.

Then it found 5 nuts under the oak tree.

How many nuts did the squirrel find?

True or False?

Part 1

Circle the word to show whether the equation
is true or false.

1. $9 = 3 + 5$ True   False

2. $3 + 4 = 7$ True   False

3. $8 = 3 + 6$ True   False

4. $9 - 7 = 2$ True   False

5. $9 - 2 = 6$ True   False

Part 2

Write a number that makes the equation true.

1. $5 + 5 = 2 + \boxed{}$

2. $5 + 5 = \underline{} + 2$

3. $3 + 4 = \boxed{} + 1$

4. $5 + 2 = 1 + \underline{}$

5. $8 - 4 = \underline{} + 4$

More True or False?

Circle the word to show whether the equation is true or false.

NOTE Students determine whether equations are true or false and they complete equations to make them true.

SMH 44

1. $11 = 9 + 3$ True   False

2. $3 + 9 = 12$ True   False

3. $12 - 9 = 3$ True   False

Write a number that makes the equation true.

4. $3 + 3 = \underline{\hspace{1cm}} + 2$

5. $3 + 3 = 2 + \boxed{}$

6. $3 + 2 = 6 - \underline{\hspace{1cm}}$

Counting on a Number Line

NOTE Students practice writing numbers and counting on a number line.

SMH 26

Write the missing numbers on the number line.

Here is an example.

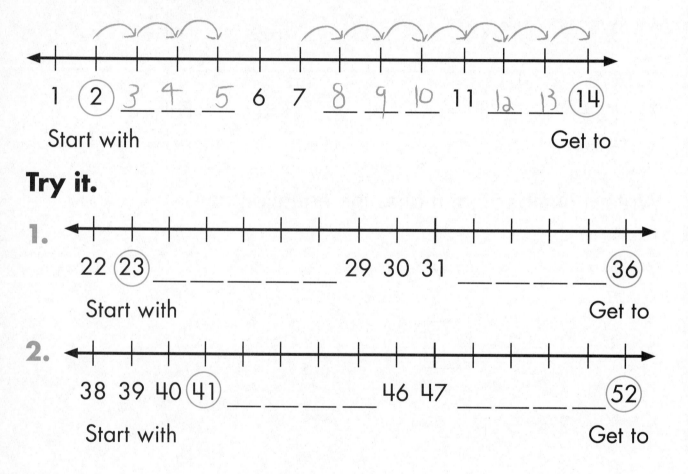

1 (2) _3_ _4_ _5_ 6 7 _8_ _9_ _10_ 11 _12_ _13_ (14)

Start with   Get to

Try it.

1.

22 (23) ___ ___ ___ ___ 29 30 31 ___ ___ ___ (36)

Start with   Get to

2.

38 39 40 (41) ___ ___ ___ ___ 46 47 ___ ___ ___ (52)

Start with   Get to

Half Hours

Read each clock, and write the time.

NOTE Students practice telling time to the half hour.

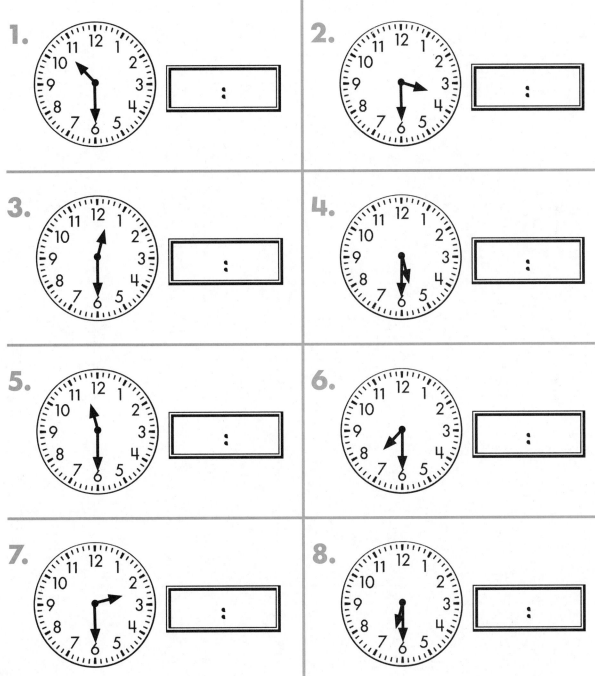

Roll and Record: Subtraction

Recording Sheet

								11
								10
								9
								8
								7
								6
								5
								4
								3
								2
								1

Match to *Make 10*
Match cards that equal a sum of 10.

NOTE Students continue to practice combinations of 10.

SMH 48–49

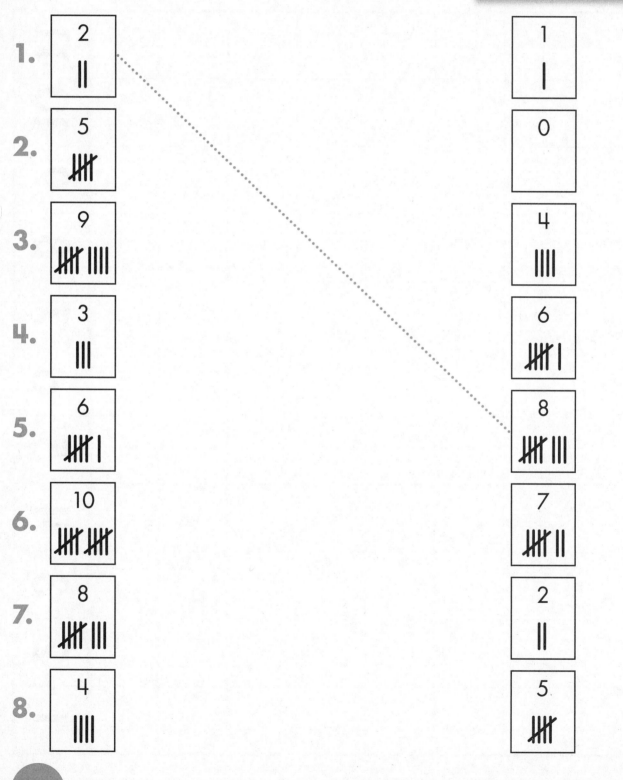

Dot Addition at Home

NOTE Students use what they know about combinations to find another way to make each total.

SMH G5

Use the Dot Addition Cards to find each total, or show each total by drawing Dot Addition Cards.

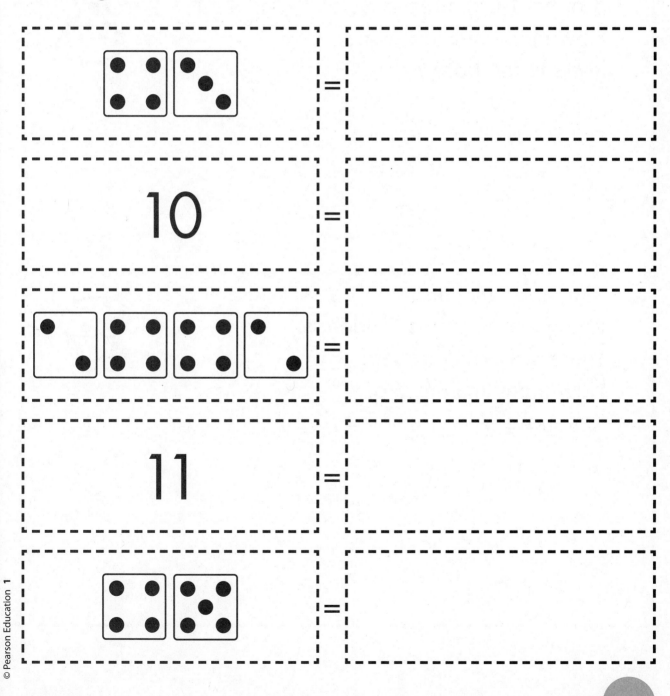

Story Problems

Solve each problem. Show your work.

NOTE Students solve story problems that involve an unknown change.

1. Rosa is having a party.
   She invites 8 friends.
   3 of her friends are boys.
   How many girls does she
   invite to the party?

2. Kim made muffins.
   She gave 5 muffins to friends.
   There are 3 muffins left.
   How many muffins did
   Kim make?

Subtraction Problems

Subtract. Write the answer.

NOTE Students subtract one amount from another.

SMH **G20**

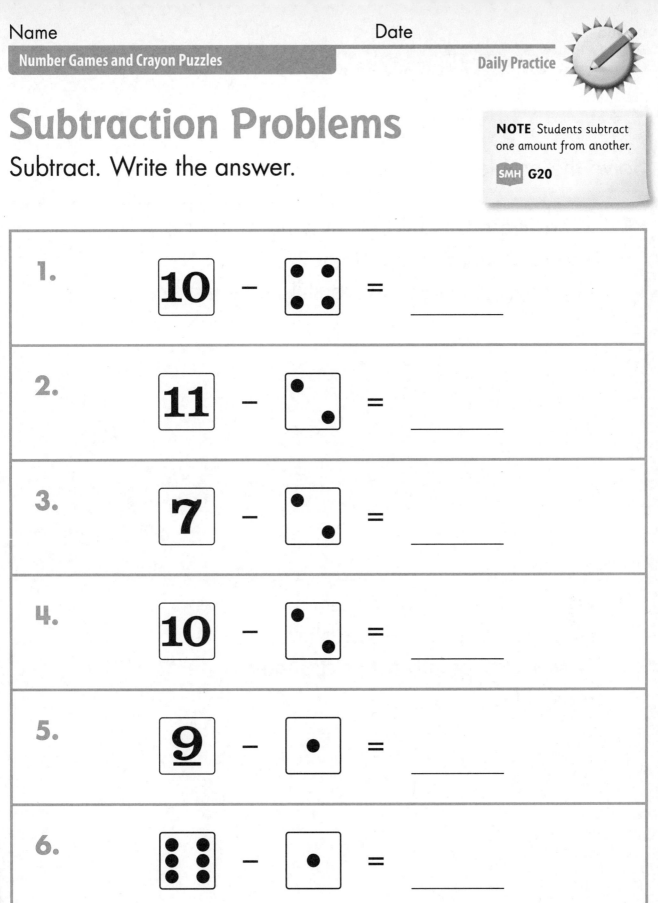

1. $10 - \boxed{\vcenter{\hbox{⁘}}} = $ _____

2. $11 - \boxed{\vcenter{\hbox{⠂}}} = $ _____

3. $7 - \boxed{\vcenter{\hbox{⠂}}} = $ _____

4. $10 - \boxed{\vcenter{\hbox{⠂}}} = $ _____

5. $\underline{9} - \boxed{\vcenter{\hbox{•}}} = $ _____

6. $\boxed{⠿} - \boxed{\vcenter{\hbox{•}}} = $ _____

Story Problems (page 1 of 4)

Solve the problems. Record your work.

1. There were 14 children playing in the park.
Then 5 children went home.
How many children were still in the park?

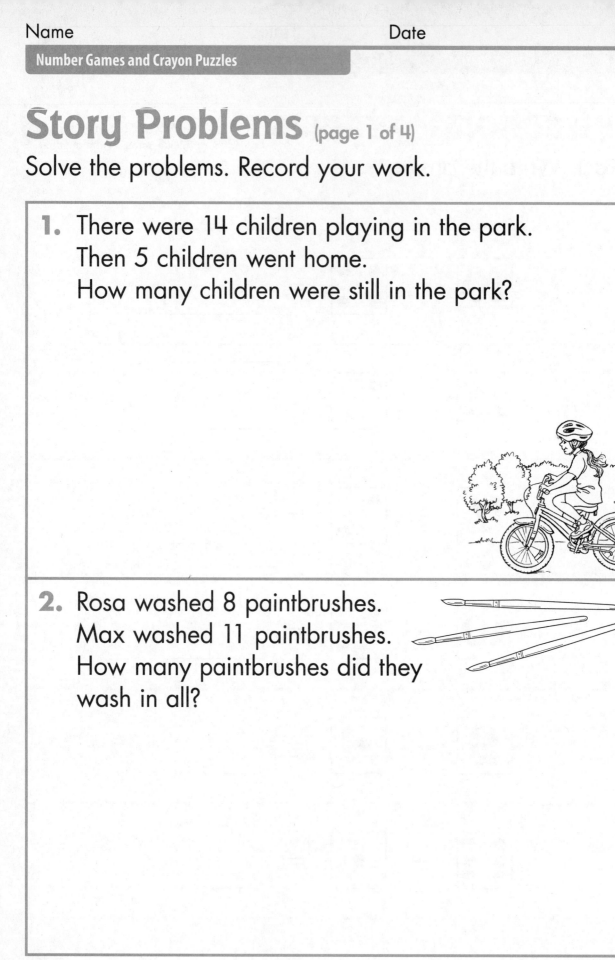

2. Rosa washed 8 paintbrushes.
Max washed 11 paintbrushes.
How many paintbrushes did they
wash in all?

Story Problems (page 2 of 4)

Solve the problems. Record your work.

3. The class needs boxes.
Kim got 7 boxes. Sam got 4 boxes.
Then Kim got 3 more boxes.
How many boxes does the class
have now?

4. Max had 16 flowers.
He gave 5 to his mom.
How many flowers did he have left?

Story Problems (page 3 of 4)

Solve the problems. Record your work.

5. Rosa had 11 cherries.
   She gave 2 cherries to Sam.
   She gave 4 cherries to Kim.
   How many cherries does Rosa
   have now?

6. There were 9 children on the playground.
   8 more children came to the playground.
   Now how many children are at the
   playground?

Story Problems (page 4 of 4)

Solve the problems. Record your work.

7. Max, Rosa, and Kim went to the beach.
Kim found 3 shells.
Rosa found 2 shells.
Max found 7 shells.
How many shells did they find in all?

8. Sam had 14 pumpkins.
He gave away 7 of them.
How many pumpkins were left?

Solving a Story Problem

NOTE Students subtract one quantity from another to solve a story problem.

SMH **38–42**

Solve the problem. Show your work.

Max's soccer team has 15 balls.
His team let Rosa's soccer team
borrow 6 balls.
How many balls does Max's team have left?

More Story Problems

Solve each problem. Show how you solve it.

NOTE Students solve addition and subtraction story problems.

SMH 33–37, 38–42

1. Sam has 4 big boats and 7 little boats.
How many boats does he have in all?

_____

2. Kim had 14 stuffed dogs. She gave 4 to Rosa.
How many stuffed dogs does Kim have now?

_____

3. There are 5 red kites and 8 green kites flying in the sky.
How many kites are flying in the sky?

_____

4. The clown was holding 15 balloons.
9 of them popped.
How many balloons are left?

_____

How Many Pennies?

Solve the problems.
Show your work.

NOTE Students solve two story problems about pennies. One problem involves addition and the other, subtraction. Encourage your child to record his or her work. You may want to give your child some pennies to act out the stories.

SMH **33–37, 38–42**

1. Max had 17 pennies.
   He used 5 pennies to buy a toy.
   How many pennies does he have now?

2. Rosa had 11 pennies.
   Sam gave her 7 more pennies.
   How many pennies does Rosa have now?

Solve and Record

Solve each problem.
Record your work.

> **NOTE** Students solve addition and subtraction story problems involving larger numbers and then they record their strategies.
>
> **SMH** 33–37, 38–42

1. Kim had 11 stamps in her collection.
Then her grandpa gave her 4 more stamps.
How many stamps does Kim have now?

_____

2. There are 7 goldfish, 3 black fish, and 9 striped fish in the tank.
How many fish are in the tank?

_____

3. There are 18 children in the class.
3 children are absent today.
How many children are present?

_____

Can You *Make 10?*

NOTE Students practice identifying number combinations that are equal to 10.

SMH 48–49

1. Color each shape that has a pair of cards that adds up to 10.

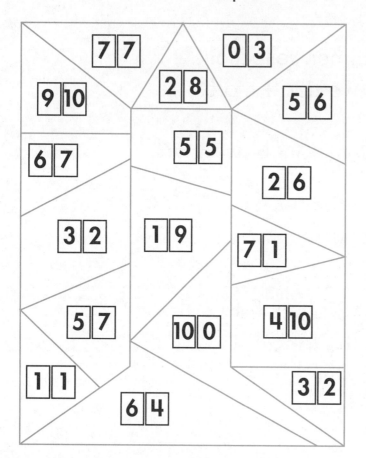

Ongoing Review

2. What comes next?

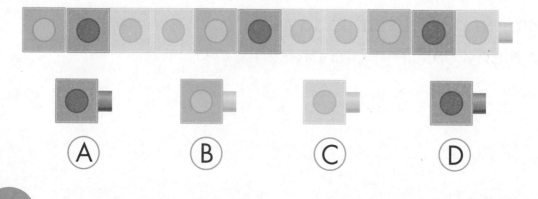

Ⓐ   Ⓑ   Ⓒ   Ⓓ

Play Time!

Solve the problem.
Show your work.

There are 12 cat toys.

How many toys could each cat have?

NOTE Students solve real-world problems involving the math content of this unit.

SMH 46–47

Spiral to Infinity Steve Allen

"Fractal images are often made up of small images-within-images, constantly repeating and going smaller and smaller." – **Steve Allen**

Investigations
IN NUMBER, DATA, AND SPACE®

Color, Shape, and Number Patterns

Investigation 2

Cube Patterns

Make a pattern with the cubes.
Then color it in below.

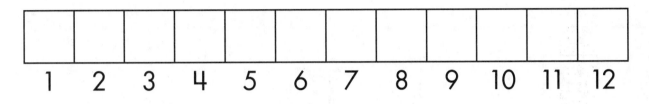

1 2 3 4 5 6 7 8 9 10 11 12

Make another pattern with the cubes.
Then color it in below.

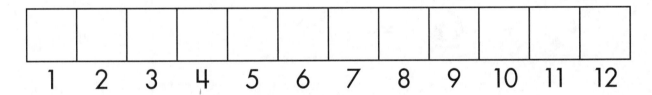

1 2 3 4 5 6 7 8 9 10 11 12

Addition Practice

Write in the missing numbers.

NOTE Students combine two amounts to find the total or determine the missing addend.

SMH G19

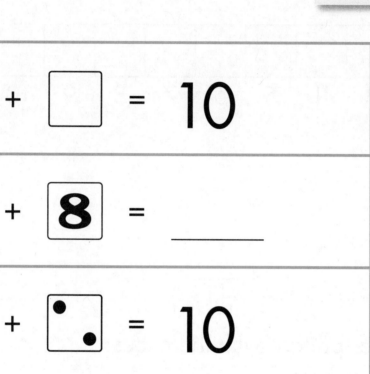

1. [3] + [ ] = 10

2. [·· ··] + [8] = _____

3. [ ] + [· ·] = 10

4. [· · ·] + [6] = _____

5. [ ] + [9] = 10

6. [·· ··] + [6] = _____

Body Movement Patterns

Choose a cube train. Color it in below.

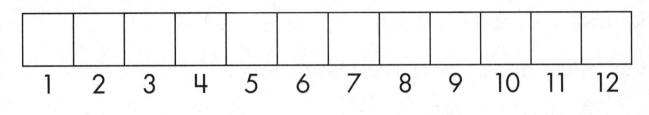

1	2	3	4	5	6	7	8	9	10	11	12

Decide on your body movements.
Write your code for them below.

Max's Apples

Max bought 18 apples.

NOTE Students subtract two numbers to solve a story problem.

SMH **38–42**

He gave 7 of them to Rosa.

How many apples does Max have now?

Solve the problem. Show your work.

Ongoing Review

What is the total of the two number cards?

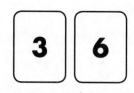

3   6   9   12

(A)   (B)   (C)   (D)

More True or False?

Circle the word to show whether the equation is true or false.

NOTE Students determine whether equations are true or false and complete equations to make them true.

SMH **44**

1. $7 = 3 + 4$ True   False

_____

2. $7 - 3 = 4$ True   False

_____

3. $7 = 3 - 4$ True   False

Write a number that makes the equation true.

4. $5 + 3 = 1 +$ ☐

5. $3 + 2 = 6 -$ ____

6. $8 - 3 =$ ☐ $+ 4$

What Comes Here? Part 1

Choose a cube train. Color it in here.

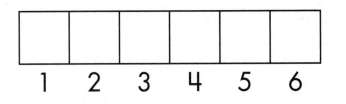

1	2	3	4	5	6

Think about what happens if the color pattern continues in the same way.

1. What color will cube 8 be? _____

2. What color will cube 10 be? _____

3. What color will cube 12 be? _____

4. How do you know what color cube 12 will be?

Daily Practice

Subtraction Practice

Subtract and write the answer.

NOTE Students subtract one amount from another.

SMH **G20**

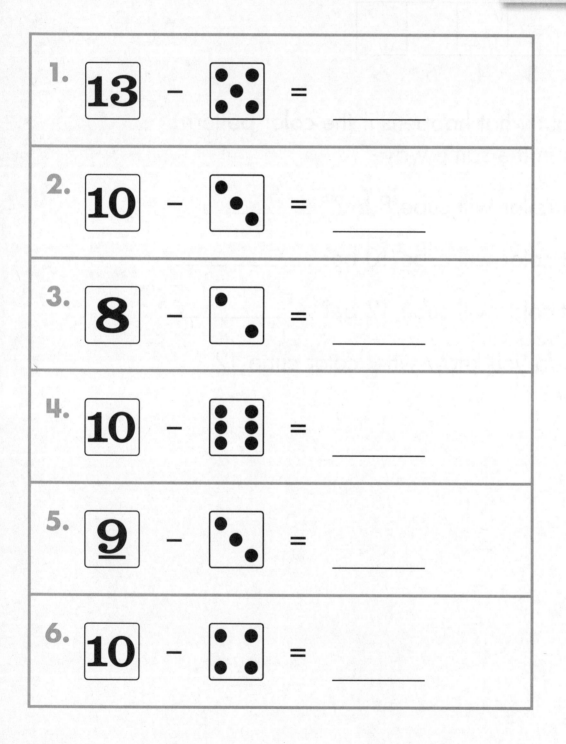

1. 13 - [:: 5 dots] = _____

2. 10 - [: 3 dots] = _____

3. 8 - [:. 2 dots] = _____

4. 10 - [::: 6 dots] = _____

5. 9 - [:. 3 dots] = _____

6. 10 - [:: 4 dots] = _____

Repeating Patterns

NOTE Students practice making repeating patterns, using colors and body movements.

SMH 53–57

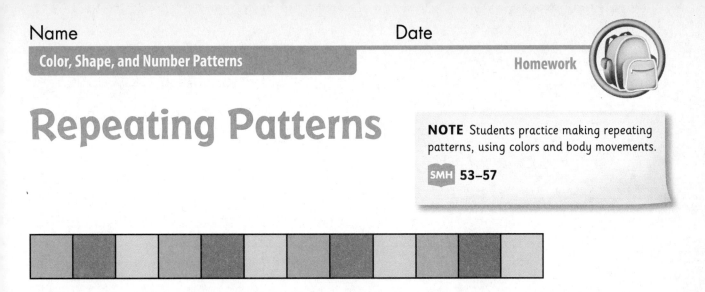

Decide on a body movement pattern that matches this color pattern. Write your code for it below.

Make a different color pattern that matches these patterns.

8 Unit 7

Break a Train

1. Color your pattern.

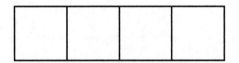

Color your unit.

2. Color your pattern.

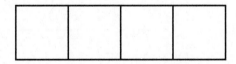

Color your unit.

What's Missing?

Fill in the missing numbers.

NOTE Students practice writing and sequencing numbers 1 to 100.

SMH 27–29

1			4			7		9	10
	12	13		15	16	17		19	
21		23	24				28	29	30
	32			35	36				40
	42		44		46		48		50
51	52	53		55		57		59	
	62		64			67		69	
	73		75	76		78			80
81			84		86		88	89	
	92		94			97			100

Fourths

NOTE Students solve problems about fourths.

Draw lines that cut each shape into fourths.
Color one fourth of each shape.

1.

2.

3. Circle the pizza that shows fourths.

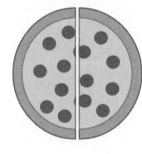
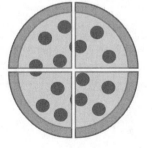
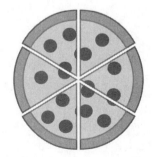

What Comes Here? Part 2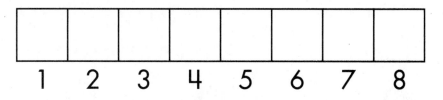

Choose a cube train. Color it in here.

1	2	3	4	5	6	7	8

Think about what happens if the color pattern continues in the same way.

1. What color will cube 10 be? _____

2. What color will cube 12 be? _____

3. What color will cube 16 be? _____

4. What color will cube 19 be? _____

5. How do you know what color cube 19 will be?

All Kinds of Patterns

Color the boxes to make a **color** pattern that matches the **movement** pattern.

NOTE Students work with different kinds of repeating patterns. They match a color pattern to a movement pattern.

SMH 53–57

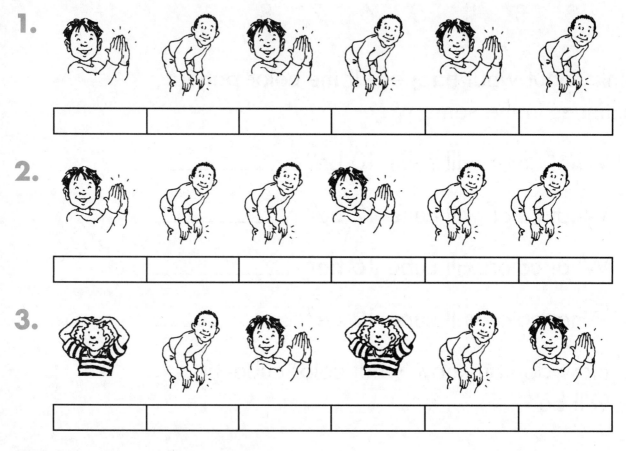

1.

2.

3.

Ongoing Review

4. Which pattern block has 6 sides?

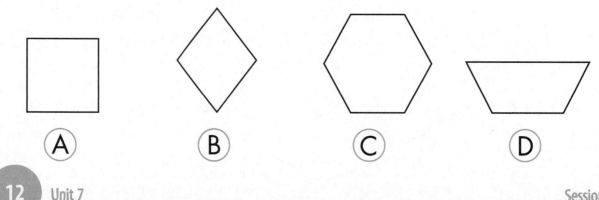

Ⓐ   Ⓑ   Ⓒ   Ⓓ

Kim's Ladybugs

NOTE Students combine two quantities to solve a story problem.

SMH 33–37

Kim saw two ladybugs on a tree. She counted 11 spots on one ladybug and 7 spots on the other ladybug. How many spots did Kim count in all?

Solve the problem. Show your work.

Ongoing Review

Which block is used the most in this design?

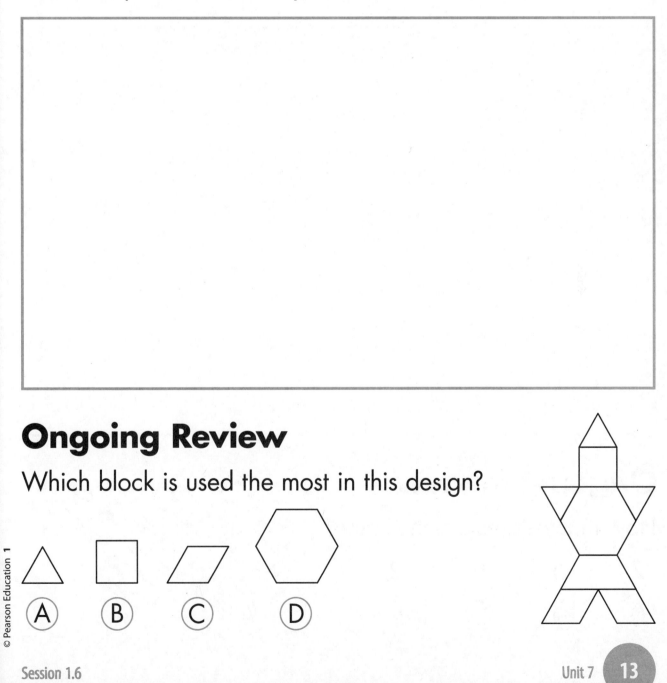

Ⓐ   Ⓑ   Ⓒ   Ⓓ

How Many Baseballs?

Kim's baseball team had 17 baseballs. They let Sam's baseball team borrow 9 of their baseballs. How many baseballs does Kim's team have left?

Solve the problem. Show your work.

NOTE Students subtract one quantity from another to solve a story problem.

SMH **38–42**

Ongoing Review

How many shoes are the same?

7   5   4   2

Ⓐ   Ⓑ   Ⓒ   Ⓓ

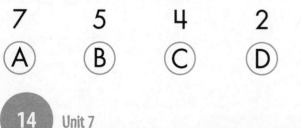

A Calendar

Here is a calendar for you. Fill in the month and dates. Then, find a place to hang it at home.

NOTE Students practice recording dates and creating, reading, and using a calendar as a tool for keeping track of time.

SMH 17, 18, 19

Name of Month

Sunday	Monday	Tuesday	Wednesday	Thursday	Friday	Saturday

Special days this month

What Comes Here?
Part 3

These patterns continue repeating in the same way.

NOTE Students extend a repeating pattern to solve a problem. In each problem, enough of the pattern is shown so that the student can see how it repeats.

SMH **59, 60**

1.

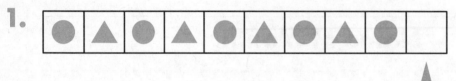

Draw the shape that would come above the arrow. _____

2.

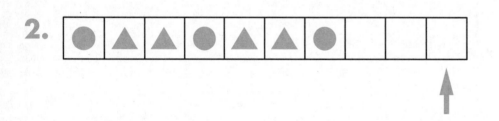

Draw the shape that would come above the arrow. _____

3.

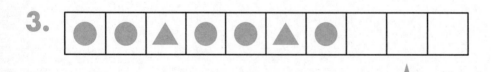

Draw the shape that would come above the arrow. _____

Half Hours

Read each clock, and write the time.

NOTE Students practice telling time to the half hour.

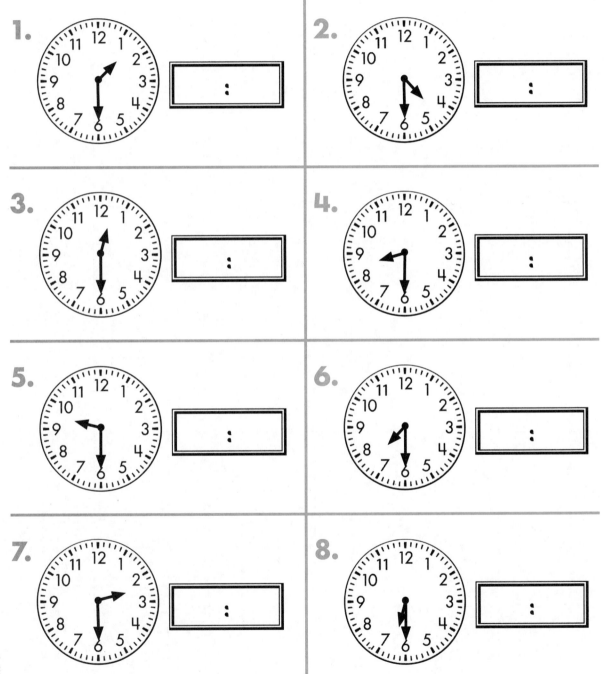

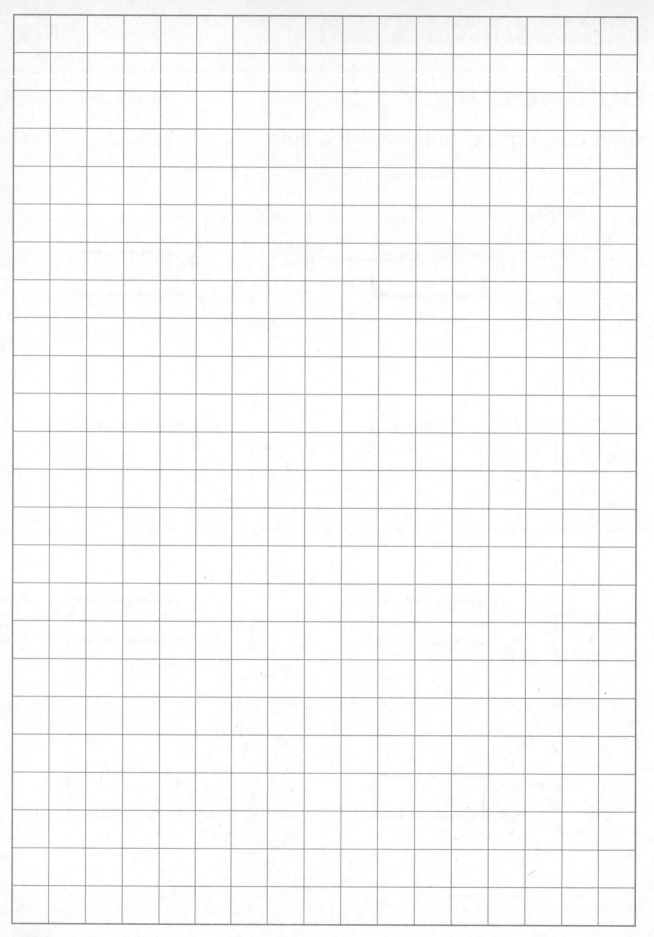

Penny Jar Problems A

© Pearson Education 1

Draw the start number in the jar. Write how
many pennies are in the jar each day.

1. Number to add each day: __2__

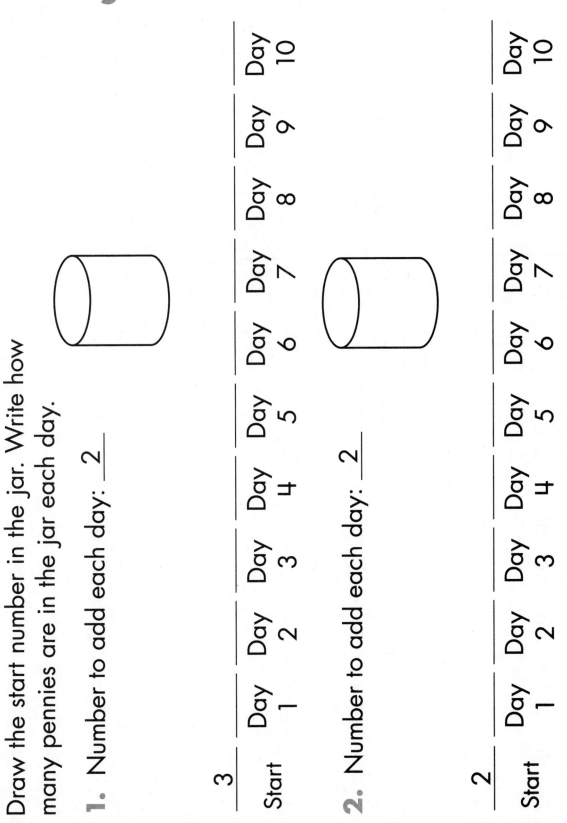

Start	Day 1	Day 2	Day 3	Day 4	Day 5	Day 6	Day 7	Day 8	Day 9	Day 10
3										

2. Number to add each day: __2__

Start	Day 1	Day 2	Day 3	Day 4	Day 5	Day 6	Day 7	Day 8	Day 9	Day 10
2										

Penny Jar Problems B

Draw the start number in the jar. Write how many pennies are in the jar each day.

1. Number to add each day: __3__

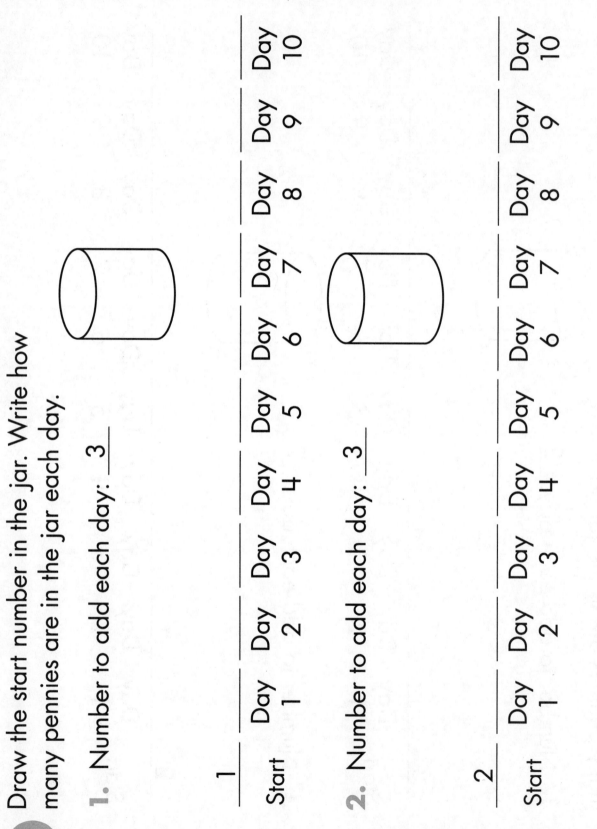

1	Day 1	Day 2	Day 3	Day 4	Day 5	Day 6	Day 7	Day 8	Day 9	Day 10
Start										

2. Number to add each day: __3__

2	Day 1	Day 2	Day 3	Day 4	Day 5	Day 6	Day 7	Day 8	Day 9	Day 10
Start										

Throwing Snowballs

NOTE Students combine three quantities to solve a story problem.

SMH **33–37**

Max was having a snowball fight with his friends. Max threw 6 snowballs at Rosa. He threw 4 snowballs at Sam and 7 snowballs at Kim. How many snowballs did Max throw?

Solve the problem. Show your work.

Ongoing Review

Which group shows one more than the number of marbles?

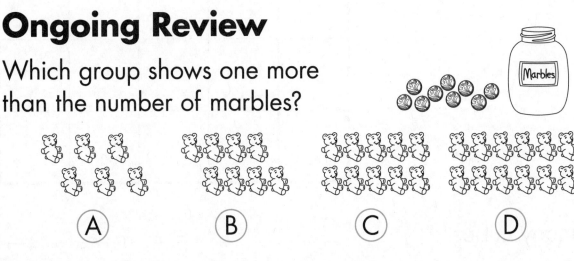

A   B   C   D

Name Date

Staircase Towers A

Start with: ________

Step up: ________

Color in your staircase tower.

How many cubes?

_____ _____ _____ _____ _____

Color, Shape, and Number Patterns

Staircase Towers B

Start with: _____2_____

Step up: _____2_____

Color in your staircase tower.

How many cubes? _____ _____ _____ _____ _____

© Pearson Education 1

Heads and Tails (page 1 of 2)

Imagine that you are playing *Heads and Tails.* Fill in the chart for each game.

NOTE Students practice counting and breaking a number into two parts (e.g., $7 = 3 + 4$).

SMH G13

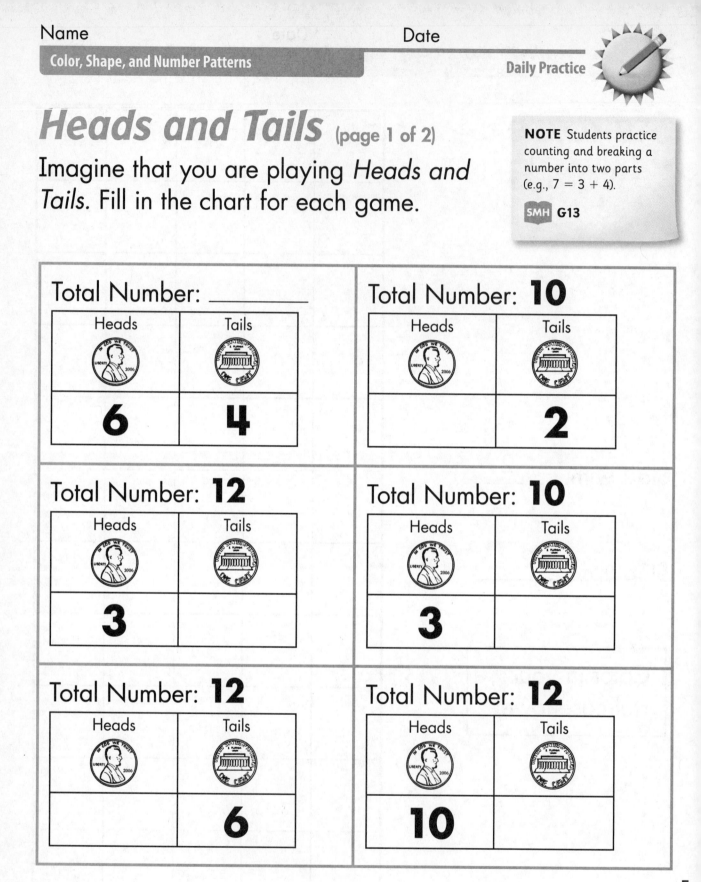

Total Number: _____	
Heads	Tails
6	4

Total Number: **10**	
Heads	Tails
	2

Total Number: **12**	
Heads	Tails
3	

Total Number: **10**	
Heads	Tails
3	

Total Number: **12**	
Heads	Tails
	6

Total Number: **12**	
Heads	Tails
10	

Heads and Tails (page 2 of 2)

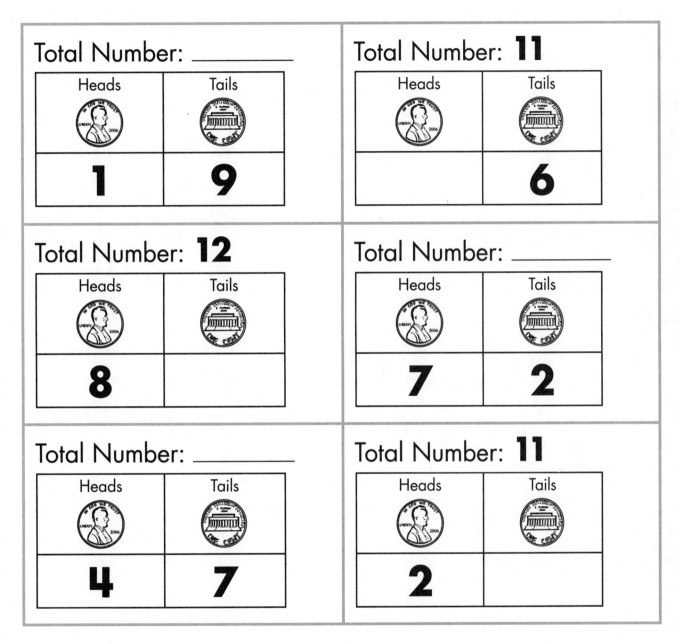

Total Number: _____

Heads	Tails
1	9

Total Number: 11

Heads	Tails
	6

Total Number: 12

Heads	Tails
8	

Total Number: _____

Heads	Tails
7	2

Total Number: _____

Heads	Tails
4	7

Total Number: 11

Heads	Tails
2	

Unknown Numbers

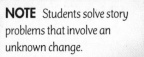

NOTE Students solve story problems that involve an unknown change.

Rosa is helping Max set the table for dinner. 8 people are eating. They each need a napkin and a fork.

1. Max placed 5 napkins on the table. How many napkins does Rosa need to place on the table so that there are 8?

2. Rosa placed 3 forks on the table. How many forks does Max need to place on the table so that there are 8?

Penny Jar Problems C

Draw the start number in the jar. Write how
many pennies are in the jar each day.

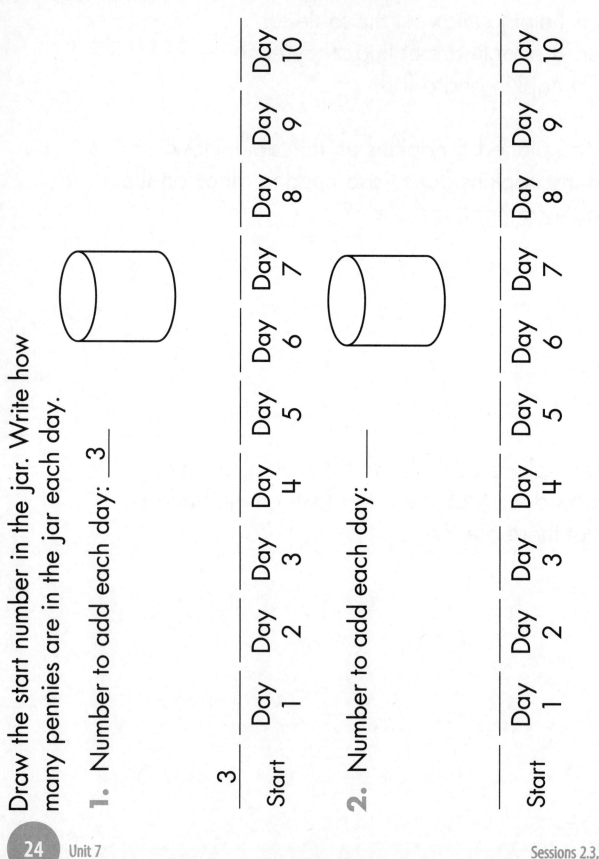

1. Number to add each day: __3__

3									
Start	Day 1	Day 2	Day 3	Day 4	Day 5	Day 6	Day 7	Day 8	Day 9	Day 10

2. Number to add each day: ____

Start	Day 1	Day 2	Day 3	Day 4	Day 5	Day 6	Day 7	Day 8	Day 9	Day 10

Penny Jar Problems D

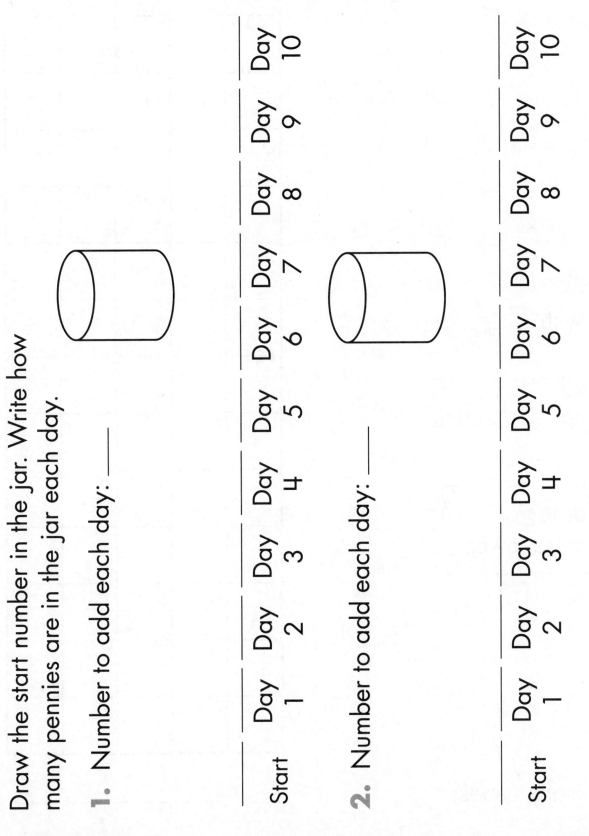

Draw the start number in the jar. Write how many pennies are in the jar each day.

1. Number to add each day: _____

Start	Day 1	Day 2	Day 3	Day 4	Day 5	Day 6	Day 7	Day 8	Day 9	Day 10

2. Number to add each day: _____

Start	Day 1	Day 2	Day 3	Day 4	Day 5	Day 6	Day 7	Day 8	Day 9	Day 10

Color, Shape, and Number Patterns

Staircase Towers C

Start with: _____1_____

Step up: _____3_____

Color in your
staircase tower.

How many cubes? _____ _____ _____ _____

Staircase Towers D

Start with: _____2_____

Step up: _____3_____

| Color in your staircase tower. |

How many cubes? _____

Staircase Towers E

Start with: _____3_____

Step up: _____3_____

Color in your
staircase tower.

How many cubes?

More Penny Jar Problems

NOTE Students record number sequences as they solve penny jar problems. A certain number of pennies is in the jar at the beginning. The same number of pennies is added each day. For the second problem, students decide on their own start number and the number to add each day.

SMH **61–63**

Draw the start number in the jar. Write how many pennies are in the jar each day.

1. Number to add each day: __2__

Start	Day 1	Day 2	Day 3	Day 4	Day 5	Day 6	Day 7	Day 8	Day 9	Day 10
10										

2. Number to add each day: _____

Start	Day 1	Day 2	Day 3	Day 4	Day 5	Day 6	Day 7	Day 8	Day 9	Day 10

Two Shapes (page 1 of 2)

Make a pattern on the number strip with two kinds of shapes.

Glue your pattern here.

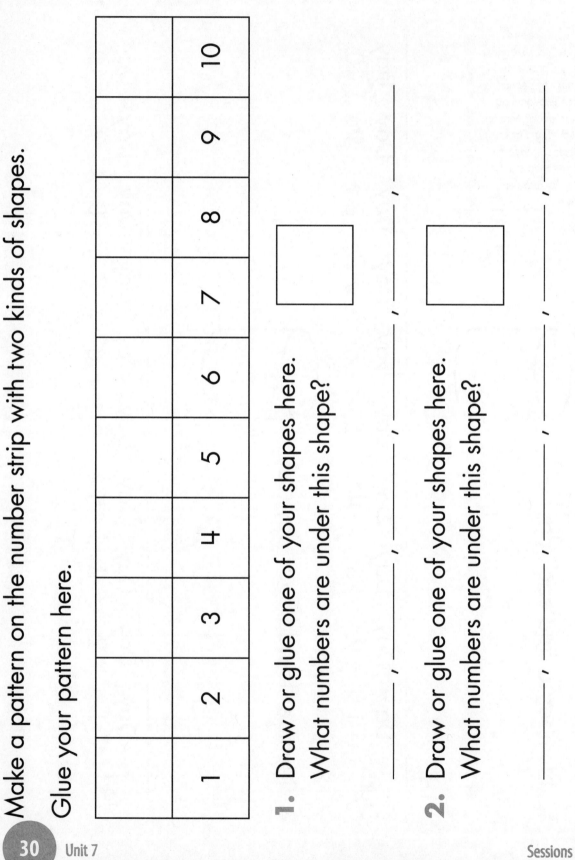

	1	2	3	4	5	6	7	8	9	10

1. Draw or glue one of your shapes here.
   What numbers are under this shape?

2. Draw or glue one of your shapes here.
   What numbers are under this shape?

Two Shapes (page 2 of 2)

If the pattern keeps going:

3. What shape will be in the 13th box?

4. What shape will be in the 14th box?

How do you know?

5. What shape will be in the 17th box?

How Many Chickens?

There were 16 chickens in the farmyard. All of a sudden, 8 of the chickens ran into the barn. How many chickens were left in the farmyard?

Solve the problem. Show your work.

NOTE Students subtract one quantity from another to solve a story problem.

SMH 38–42

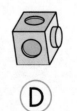

Ongoing Review

What comes next?

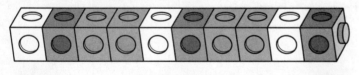

A   B   C   D

Rosa's Penny Jar

Rosa started with 2 pennies in her penny jar.

She puts 2 more pennies in her penny jar every day.

How many pennies will she have on Day 5?

Solve the problem. Show your work.

NOTE Students solve a problem about a situation in which a quantity is increasing at a constant rate over time. Students solve the problem and record their work.

SMH 61–63

Start   Day 1   Day 2

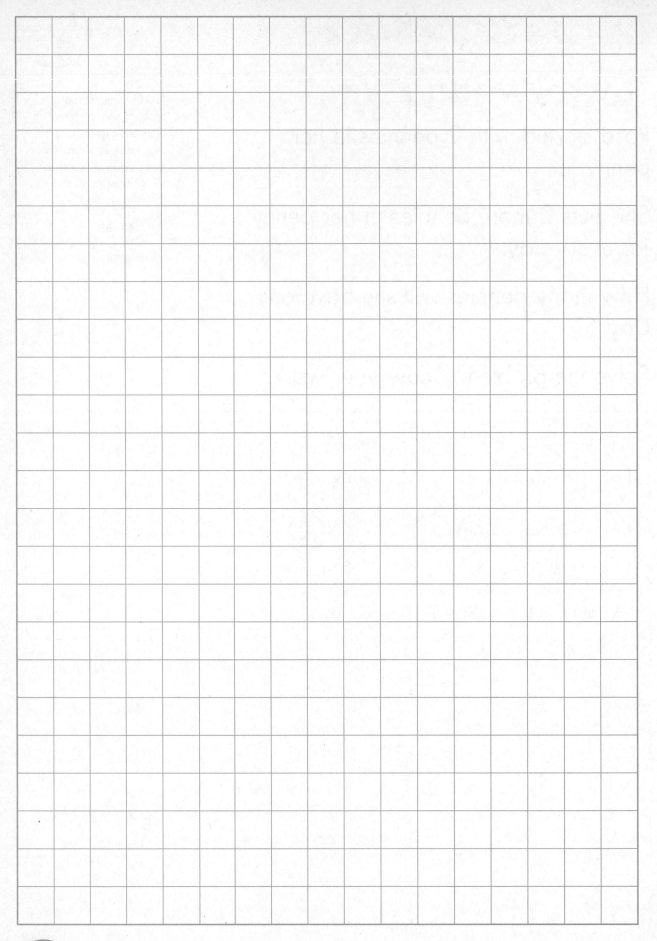

Three Shapes (page 1 of 2)

Make a pattern on the number strip with three kinds of shapes.

Glue your pattern here.

1	2	3	4	5	6	7	8	9	10

1. Draw or glue one of your shapes here.
   What numbers are under this shape?
   _____ , _____ , _____ , _____

2. Draw or glue one of your shapes here.
   What numbers are under this shape?
   _____ , _____ , _____ , _____

3. Draw or glue your third shape here.
   What numbers are under this shape?
   _____ , _____ , _____ , _____

Three Shapes (page 2 of 2) 🖊

If the pattern keeps going:

4. What shape will be in the 12th box?

5. What shape will be in the 16th box?

How do you know?

6. What shape will be in the 20th box?

Lions and Frogs

The teacher has 13 lion stickers and 6 frog stickers. How many stickers does the teacher have?

Solve the problem. Show your work.

NOTE Students combine two quantities to solve a story problem.

SMH 33–37

Ongoing Review

How many children like bananas?

4   12   15   19

(A)   (B)   (C)   (D)

Do you like bananas?

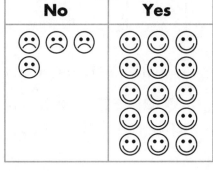

How many children do **not** like bananas?

19   15   5   4

(A)   (B)   (C)   (D)

Repeating Patterns 1

NOTE Students practice working with repeating patterns by determining what shape or letter will be in a later position if the pattern continues in the same way.

SMH **59, 60**

1.

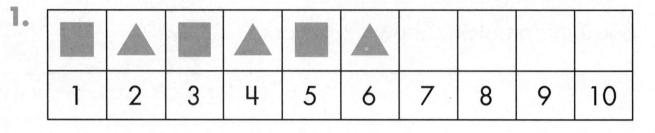

| 1 | 2 | 3 | 4 | 5 | 6 | 7 | 8 | 9 | 10 |

If this pattern continues in the same way,
what shape will be in the 19th box?
How do you know?

2.

A	B	B	A	B	B				
1	2	3	4	5	6	7	8	9	10

If this pattern continues in the same way,
what letter will be in the 18th box?
How do you know?

Repeating Patterns 2

NOTE Students practice working with repeating patterns by determining what shape or letter will be in a later position if the pattern continues in the same way.

SMH 59, 60

1.

○	~	⊥	○	~	⊥				
1	2	3	4	5	6	7	8	9	10

If this pattern continues in the same way,
what shape will be in the 16th box?
How do you know?

2.

R	R	S	S	R	R	S	S		
1	2	3	4	5	6	7	8	9	10

If this pattern continues in the same way,
what letter will be in the 14th box?
How do you know?

Spring Flowers

Carol and Vic are helping to plant a flower garden. Carol has red flowers, pink flowers, and blue flowers. Show one way that Carol can plant her flowers to make a pattern. Describe the pattern.

NOTE Students create their own patterns using three or four elements.

SMH 53–57

Vic has white flowers, yellow flowers, pink flowers, and purple flowers. Show one way that Vic can plant his flowers to make a pattern. Describe the pattern.

Spiral to Infinity Steve Allen

"Fractal images are often made up of small images-within-images, constantly repeating and going smaller and smaller."– **Steve Allen**

Investigations
IN NUMBER, DATA, AND SPACE®

Twos, Fives, and Tens

Investigation 1

Investigation 2

Investigation 3

Investigation 4A

Ten Turns Recording Sheet

Ten Turns

Turn 1   We rolled _____.   Now we have _____.

Turn 2   We rolled _____.   Now we have _____.

Turn 3   We rolled _____.   Now we have _____.

Turn 4   We rolled _____.   Now we have _____.

Turn 5   We rolled _____.   Now we have _____.

Turn 6   We rolled _____.   Now we have _____.

Turn 7   We rolled _____.   Now we have _____.

Turn 8   We rolled _____.   Now we have _____.

Turn 9   We rolled _____.   Now we have _____.

Turn 10   We rolled _____.   Now we have _____.

What's in the Bag?

There are 10 balls in all. Write how many balls are **outside** the bag. Write how many balls are **inside** the bag. Write an equation.

NOTE Students practice finding different combinations of 10.

SMH 48–49

Outside _____6_____

Inside _____4_____

Equation _____$6 + 4 = 10$_____

1.

Outside _____

Inside _____

Equation _____

2.

Outside _____

Inside _____

Equation _____

3.

Outside _____

Inside _____

Equation _____

4.

Outside _____

Inside _____

Equation _____

Missing Numbers Recording Sheet

Round 1: I think these numbers are missing.

_____   _____   _____   _____   _____

Round 2: I think these numbers are missing.

_____   _____   _____   _____   _____

Round 3: I think these numbers are missing.

_____   _____   _____   _____   _____

Round 4: I think these numbers are missing.

_____   _____   _____   _____   _____

Round 5: I think these numbers are missing.

_____   _____   _____   _____   _____

Round 6: I think these numbers are missing.

_____   _____   _____   _____   _____

Twos, Fives, and Tens

Totals and Missing Parts

Write the total number or the missing part.

NOTE Students use addition or subtraction to find the total or the missing addend.

SMH **G19**

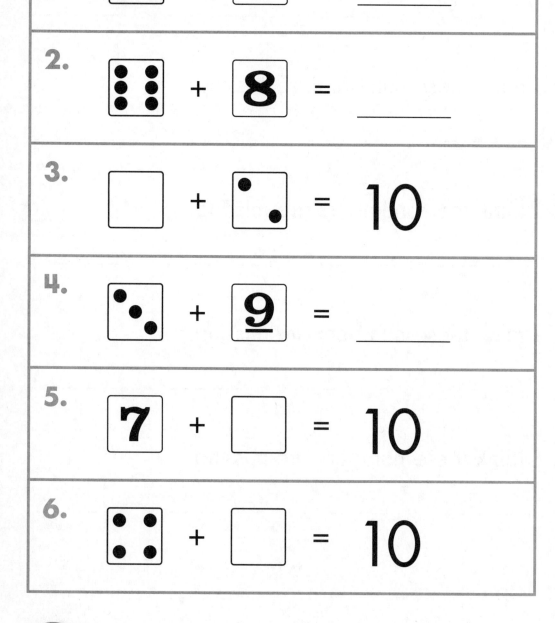

1. ⬜ + **7** = _____

2. ⬜ + **8** = _____

3. ⬜ + ⬜ = **10**

4. ⬜ + **9** = _____

5. **7** + ⬜ = **10**

6. ⬜ + ⬜ = **10**

What's Missing? 1

What are the missing numbers?
Write them on the chart.

1	2	3	4		6	7			
11		13		15			18	19	20
21	22		24		26		28		30
		33		35		37	38	39	40
41		43	44	45	46	47	48	49	
51	52		54	55	56		58	59	60
	62	63	64		66	67	68		70
	72	73	74		76	77	78	79	
81		83		85	86		88	89	
91	92		94	95		97	98		100
	102	103		105		107	108	109	
111		113	114			117		119	120

What's Missing? 2

What are the missing numbers?
Write them on the chart.

1		3		5		7		9	
11		13		15		17		19	
	22		24		26		28		30
	32		34		36		38		40
51	52		54	55		57	58		60
	62		64	65		67	68		70
	72			75			78		
81			84			87			90
91		93		95		97		99	
		103	104			107	108		
111	112			115	116			119	120

What's Missing? 3

What are the missing numbers?
Write them on the chart.

		23		25	26	27	28	29	
	32		34		36		38		
		43		45	46	47		49	
51			54			57	58	59	
	62	63		65		67	68		
									80
	82		84	85		87			
		93			96	97		99	
101	102	103	104				108		
		113		115	116			119	

What's Missing? 4

What are the missing numbers?
Write them on the chart.

						7			
						17			
						27			
31	32	33	34	35	36	37	38	39	40
						47			
						57			
						67			
						77			
						87			
						97			
						107			
						117			

What's Missing? 5

What are the missing numbers?
Write them on the chart.

						17			
		23							
			34						
				45					
								69	
							78		
						87			
	92								
		103							
			114						

Ten in All

There are 10 counters in all. Write how many are **on** the paper. Write how many are **off** the paper. Write an equation.

NOTE Students practice finding different combinations of 10.

SMH 48–49

On ___4___   Off ___6___

Equation ___4 + 6 = 10___

1.

On _____   Off _____

Equation _____

2.

On _____   Off _____

Equation _____

3.

On _____   Off _____

Equation _____

4.

On _____   Off _____

Equation _____

5.

On _____   Off _____

Equation _____

6.

On _____   Off _____

Equation _____

Counting Strips at Home

Write the missing numbers
on the counting strips.

NOTE For this homework,
students practice writing and
sequencing numbers.

SMH 21–23

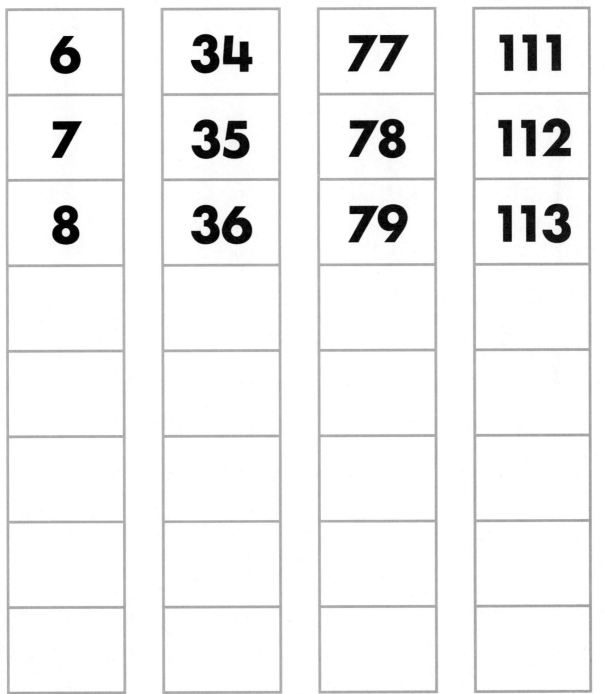

6	34	77	111
7	35	78	112
8	36	79	113

What's Missing? 1

What are the missing numbers?
Write them on the chart.

1	2	3	4		6	7			
11		13		15			18	19	20
21	22		24		26		28		30
	33		35		37	38	39	40	
41		43	44	45	46	47	48	49	
51	52		54	55	56		58	59	60
	62	63	64		66	67	68		70
	72	73	74		76	77	78	79	
81		83		85	86		88	89	
91	92		94	95		97	98		100

What's Missing? 2

What are the missing numbers?
Write them on the chart.

1		3		5		7		9	
11		13		15		17		19	
	22		24		26		28		30
	32		34		36		38		40
51	52		54	55		57	58		60
	62		64	65		67	68		70
	72			75			78		
81			84			87			90
91		93		95		97		99	

What's Missing? 3

What are the missing numbers?
Write them on the chart.

	23		25	26	27	28	29		
	32		34		36		38		
	43		45	46	47		49		
51			54			57	58	59	
	62	63		65		67	68		
									80
	82		84	85		87			
		93			96	97		99	

What's Missing? 4

What are the missing numbers?
Write them on the chart.

						7			
						17			
						27			
31	32	33	34	35	36	37	38	39	40
						47			
						57			
						67			
						77			
						87			
						97			

What's Missing? 5

What are the missing numbers?
Write them on the chart.

						17			
	23								
		34							
			45						
							69		
						78			
					87				
92									

Ten in All

There are 10 counters in all. Write how many are **on** the paper. Write how many are **off** the paper. Write an equation.

NOTE Students practice finding different combinations of 10.

SMH **48–49**

On ___4___ Off ___6___

Equation ___4 + 6 = 10___

1.

On _____ Off _____

Equation _____

2.

On _____ Off _____

Equation _____

3.

On _____ Off _____

Equation _____

4.

On _____ Off _____

Equation _____

5.

On _____ Off _____

Equation _____

6.

On _____ Off _____

Equation _____

Counting Strips at Home

Write the missing numbers
on the counting strips.

NOTE For this homework,
students practice writing
and sequencing numbers.

SMH 21–23

6	**34**	**77**
7	**35**	**78**
8	**36**	**79**

Twos, Fives, and Tens

Daily Practice

Counting to 100

Fill in the missing numbers.

NOTE Students practice writing numbers and working with number order 1–100.

SMH 27–29

1	2	3	4	5		7	8	9	10
11		13	14	15	16		18	19	20
21	22	23			26	27	28		30
31	32	33	34	35		37	38	39	
41		43	44	45	46	47	48	49	50
	52	53	54	55	56		58		60
61			64		66	67	68	69	
71	72	73		75		77		79	80
	82		84	85	86	87		89	90
91			94		96		98	99	

How Many Hands?

Solve the problem. Show your work.

How many hands are there in a group
of 8 children?

Pairs of Things

Write how many are in each group.

NOTE Students practice counting by groups of 2s.

SMH 24–25

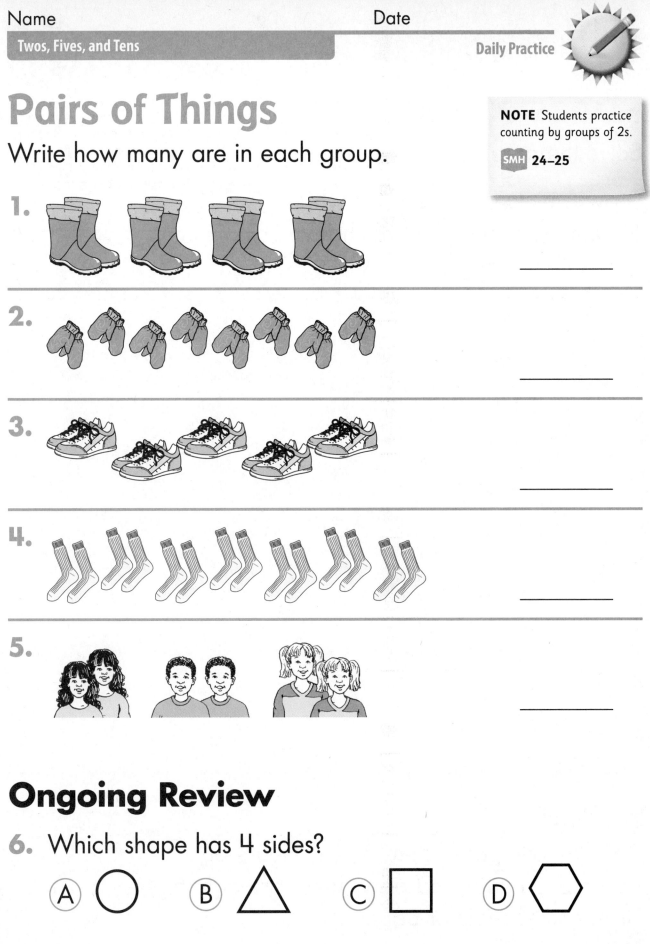

1. _____

2. _____

3. _____

4. _____

5. _____

Ongoing Review

6. Which shape has 4 sides?

Ⓐ ◯   Ⓑ △   Ⓒ ▢   Ⓓ ⬡

Hands at Home

Solve the problem. Show your work.

Draw a picture of everyone who lives at home with you. Find out how many hands there are.

NOTE Students use what they know about groups of 2s to figure out the total number of hands at home, based on the total number of people who live at home.

SMH 24–25

Try this!

Do you have pets? Then try this. Figure out how many hands and paws there are at home. Use another sheet of paper.

© Pearson Education 1

Problems About Eyes, Ears, and Elbows (page 1 of 4)

Solve each problem. Show your work.

1. How many eyes are there in a group of 5 people?

2. How many eyes are there in a group of 10 people?

Problems About Eyes, Ears, and Elbows (page 2 of 4)

Solve each problem. Show your work.

3. How many ears are there in a group of 7 people?

4. How many ears are there in a group of 8 people?

Problems About Eyes, Ears, and Elbows (page 3 of 4)

5. How many elbows are there in a group of 7 people?

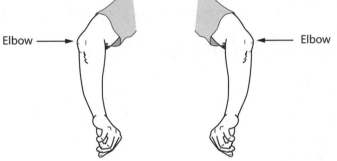

Elbow →   ← Elbow

6. How many elbows are there in a group of 14 people?

Problems About Eyes, Ears, and Elbows (page 4 of 4)

Solve each problem. Show your work.

7. How many eyes are there in a group of 6 people?

8. How many elbows are there in a group of 12 people?

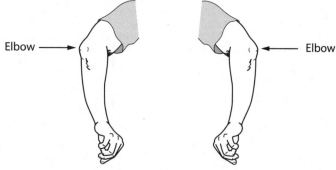

Elbow →   ← Elbow

Tens Go Fish

Imagine that you are playing *Tens Go Fish.*
What card would you ask for to make a
total of 10? Draw a picture of the card.

NOTE Students are
given one number and
determine what number
they need to add to
make a total of 10.

SMH **48–49, G23**

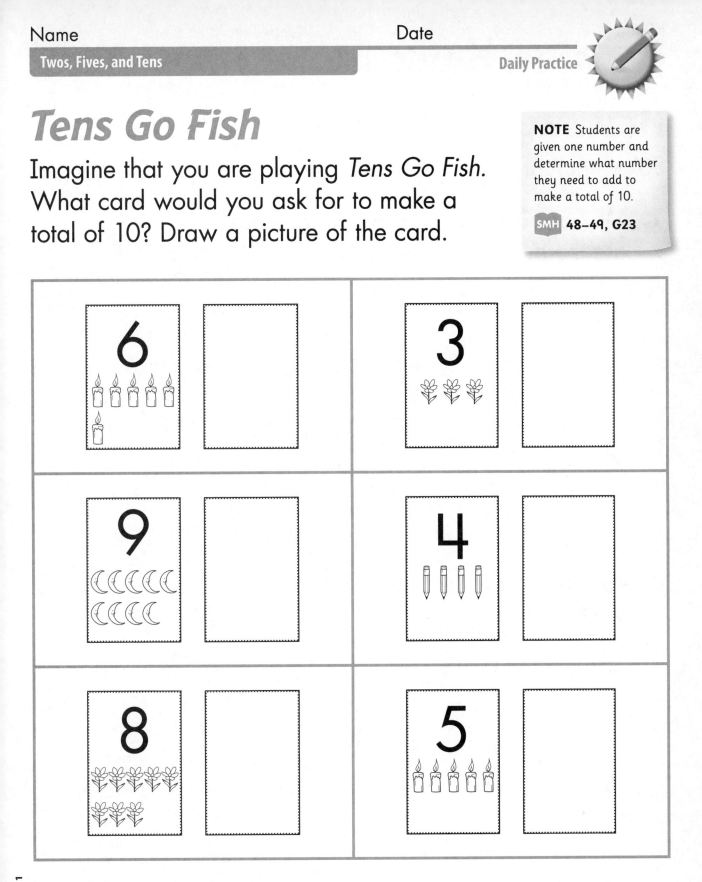

How Many Wheels?

Solve each problem. Show your work.

1. Max has 3 toy cars. How many wheels are there?

2. Rosa has 6 toy cars. How many wheels are there?

How Many Do I See?

Solve each riddle. Record your work.

NOTE Students practice counting and combining things that come in groups of 2s and 4s.

SMH 24–25

1. I see 4 boys.
How many eyes
do I see?

_____

2. I see 3 horses.
How many legs
do I see?

_____

3. I see 6 birds.
How many legs
do I see?

_____

4. I see 4 puppies.
How many ears
do I see?

_____

5. I see 2 cats.
How many legs
do I see?

_____

6. I see 4 girls.
How many eyes
do I see?

_____

Ongoing Review

7. How many days
are in April?

(A) 1

(B) 23

(C) 30

(D) 31

APRIL						
S	M	T	W	T	F	S
				1	2	3
4	5	6	7	8	9	10
11	12	13	14	15	16	17
18	19	20	21	22	23	24
25	26	27	28	29	30	

Cats and Paws

Solve each problem. Show your work.

NOTE Students use what they know about groups of 4s to figure out the total number of paws based on a number of cats.

SMH 24–25

1. There are 4 cats in the yard. How many paws are there?

2. There are 5 cats in the yard. How many paws are there?

Twos, Fives, and Tens

How Many Fingers? 1 (page 1 of 2)

Solve each problem. Show your work.

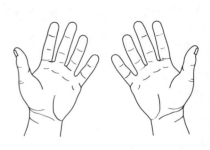

1. How many fingers are there on 4 hands?

2. How many fingers are there on 8 hands?

How Many Fingers? 1 (page 2 of 2)

Try these challenge problems. Solve
each problem. Show your work.

CHALLENGE

The three-toed sloth is an animal
that has 4 feet.

This animal has 3 claws on each foot.

---

1. How many claws does 1 three-toed sloth
   have in all?

2. How many claws do 6 three-toed sloths
   have in all?

Subtraction Problems

Subtract. Write the missing numbers.

NOTE Students subtract one amount from another.

SMH G20

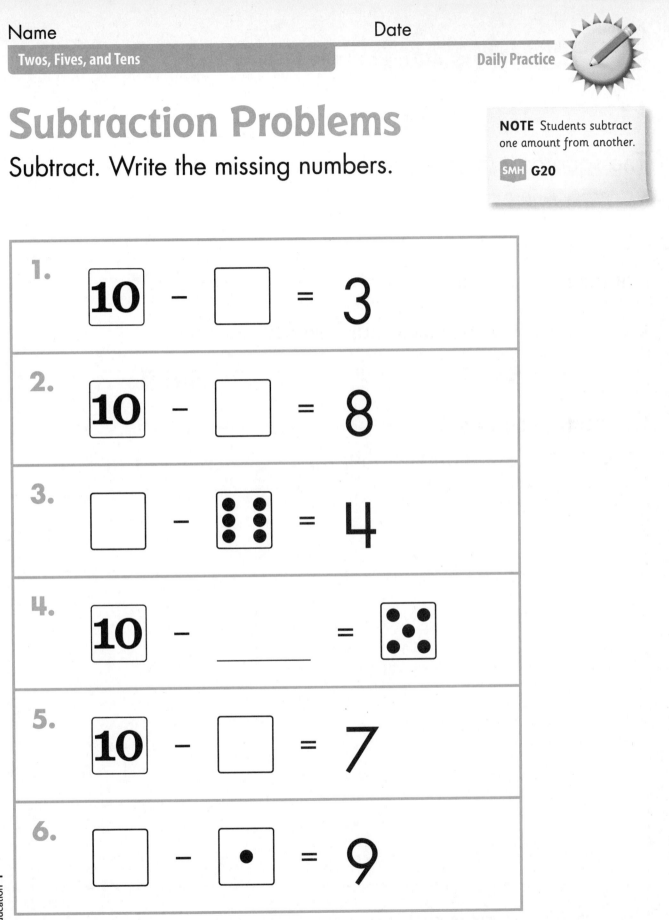

1. **10** – ☐ = **3**

2. **10** – ☐ = **8**

3. ☐ – [dice: 6] = **4**

4. **10** – _____ = [dice: 5]

5. **10** – ☐ = **7**

6. ☐ – [dice: 1] = **9**

Twos, Fives, and Tens

How Many Squares? (page 1 of 2)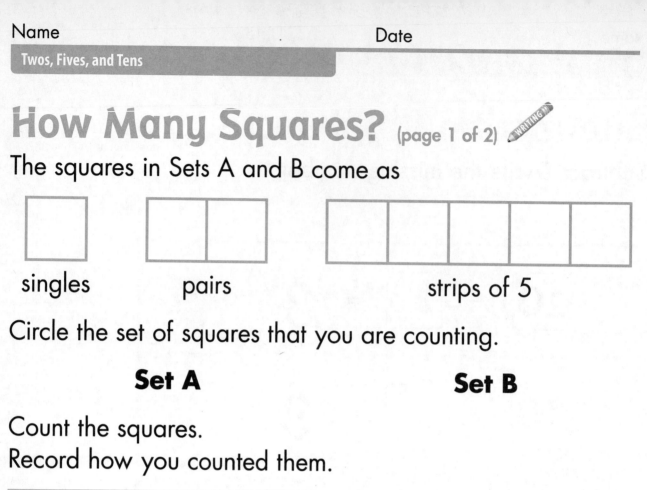

The squares in Sets A and B come as

singles   pairs   strips of 5

Circle the set of squares that you are counting.

Set A   ## Set B

Count the squares.
Record how you counted them.

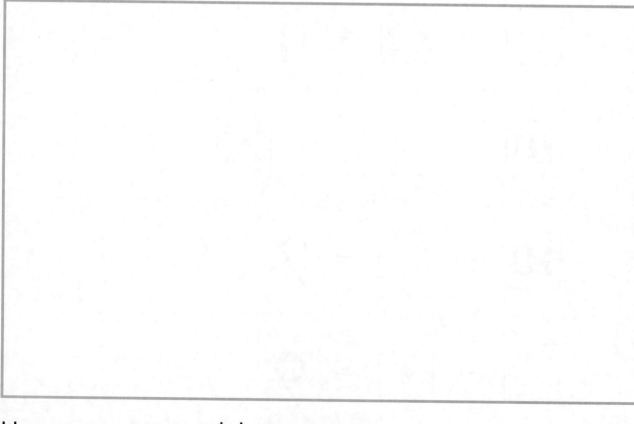

How many squares did you count? _____

How Many Squares? (page 2 of 2)

The squares in Sets A and B come as

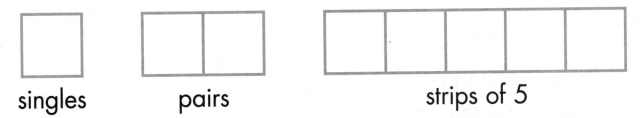

singles   pairs   strips of 5

Circle the set of squares that you are counting.

Set A   ### Set B

Count the squares.
Record how you counted them.

How many squares did you count? _____

Problems About
2s, 4s, and 5s (page 1 of 4) ✏️WRITING

Solve each problem. Show your work.

1. There are 7 people in my family.
   How many feet are there?

2. There are 9 children at the bus stop.
   How many feet are there?

Problems About 2s, 4s, and 5s (page 2 of 4)

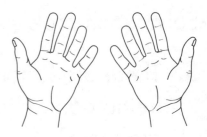

Solve each problem. Show your work.

3. There are 2 children in the kitchen. How many fingers are there?

4. There are 4 children in the house. How many fingers are there?

Problems About
2s, 4s, and 5s (page 3 of 4) WRITING

Solve each problem. Show your work.

5. There are 2 horses and 2 people in the barn. How many legs are there?

6. There are 2 horses, 2 dogs, and 2 people in the barn. How many legs are there?

Problems About
2s, 4s, and 5s (page 4 of 4) ✎ WRITING

Solve each problem. Show your work.

7. There are 2 dogs and 4 people at the park. How many legs are there?

8. There are 3 dogs and 2 people on the sidewalk. How many legs are there?

Using a Calendar

Here is a calendar for you. Fill in the month and dates. Then find a place to hang it at home.

NOTE Students practice recording dates and creating, reading, and using a calendar as a tool for keeping track of time.

SMH 17, 18, 19

Name of Month
_____

Sunday	Monday	Tuesday	Wednesday	Thursday	Friday	Saturday

Special Days _____

_____

_____

More True or False?

Circle the word to show whether the equation is true or false.

NOTE Students determine whether equations are true or false and complete equations to make them true.

SMH 44

1. $10 = 7 + 3$ True   False

2. $10 - 3 = 7$ True   False

3. $10 = 7 - 3$ True   False

Write a number that makes the equation true.

4. $8 + 3 = 1 + \underline{\hspace{1cm}}$

5. $6 + 2 = 10 - \boxed{}$

6. $9 - 5 = \underline{\hspace{1cm}} + 3$

Counting Strips

Write the missing numbers on the
counting strips.

NOTE Students practice counting,
writing, and sequencing numbers.

SMH 21–23

6	17	25	43
7	18	26	44
8	19	27	45

Counting Squares

Write how many squares are in each group.

> **NOTE** Students practice counting and combining things that come in groups of 1s, 2s, and 5s.
>
> **SMH** 24–25

1.

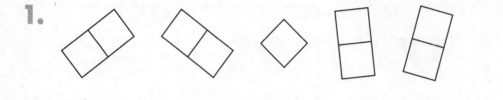

_____

2.

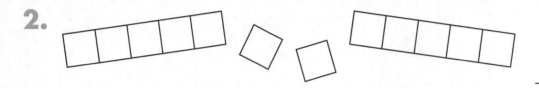

_____

3.

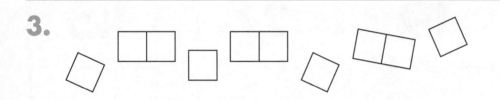

_____

4.

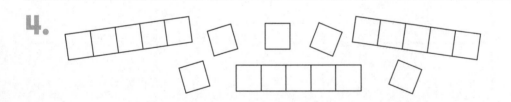

_____

Ongoing Review

5. Which dot cubes show a combination of 10?

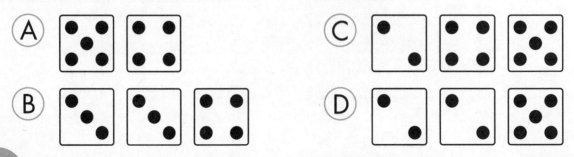

How Many Feet?

Solve the problem. Show your work.

NOTE Students use what they know about groups of 2s and 4s to solve a story problem.

SMH **24–25**

1. There are 3 people and 3 dogs at the park. How many feet are there?

Ongoing Review

2. There are 7 frogs on a log. Then 5 more hop on. How many frogs are on the log now?

Ⓐ 14   Ⓑ 13   Ⓒ 12   Ⓓ 11

More *Tens Go Fish*

Imagine that you are playing *Tens Go Fish*. What card would you ask for to make a total of 10? Draw a picture of the card.

NOTE Students practice finding combinations that make 10.

SMH 48–49, G23

Ongoing Review

Which pair of cards has the largest total?

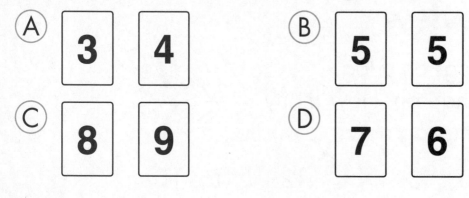

A 3 4

B 5 5

C 8 9

D 7 6

Hours and Half Hours
Read each clock, and write the time.

NOTE Students practice telling time to the hour and half hour.

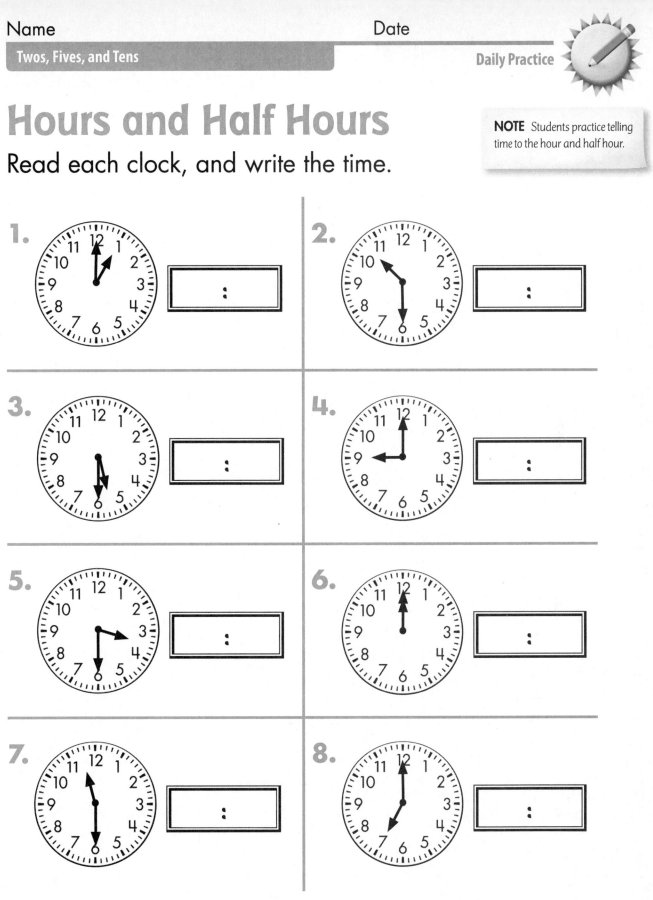

1.

2.

3.

4.

5.

6.

7.

8.

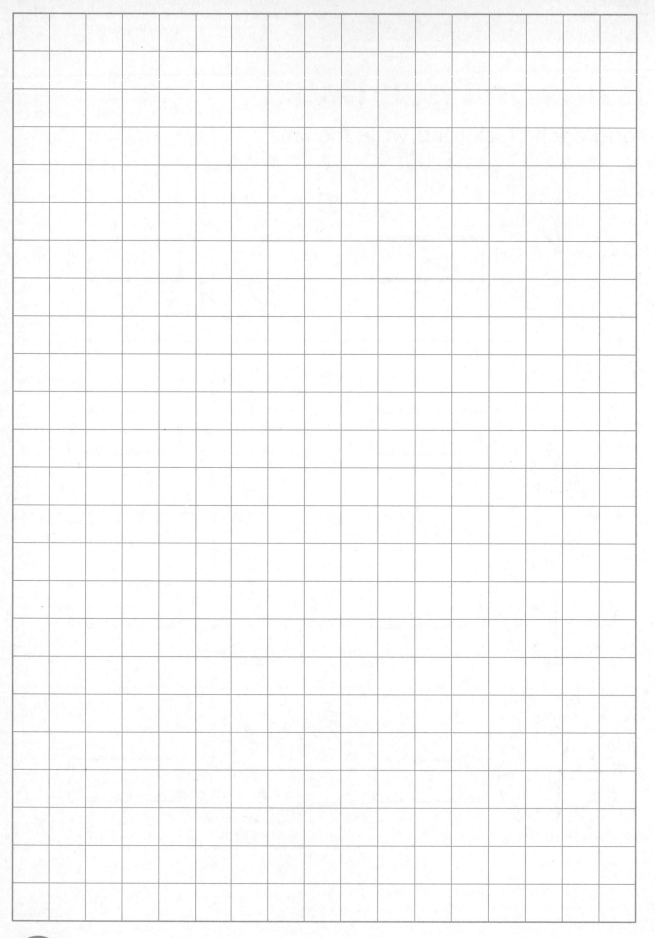

More Counting Strips

Write the missing numbers on the
counting strips.

NOTE Students practice
counting, writing, and
sequencing numbers.

SMH 21–23

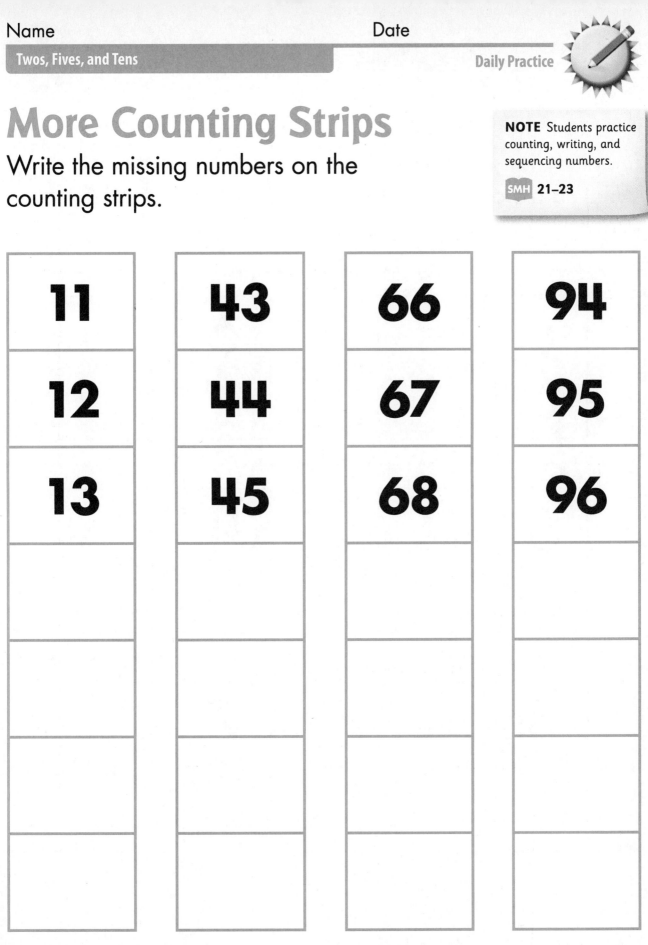

11	43	66	94
12	44	67	95
13	45	68	96

Tens Go Fish at Home

Imagine that you are playing *Tens Go Fish*. What card would you ask for to make a total of 10? Draw a picture of the card.

NOTE Students practice finding combinations that make a total of 10.

SMH **48–49, G23**

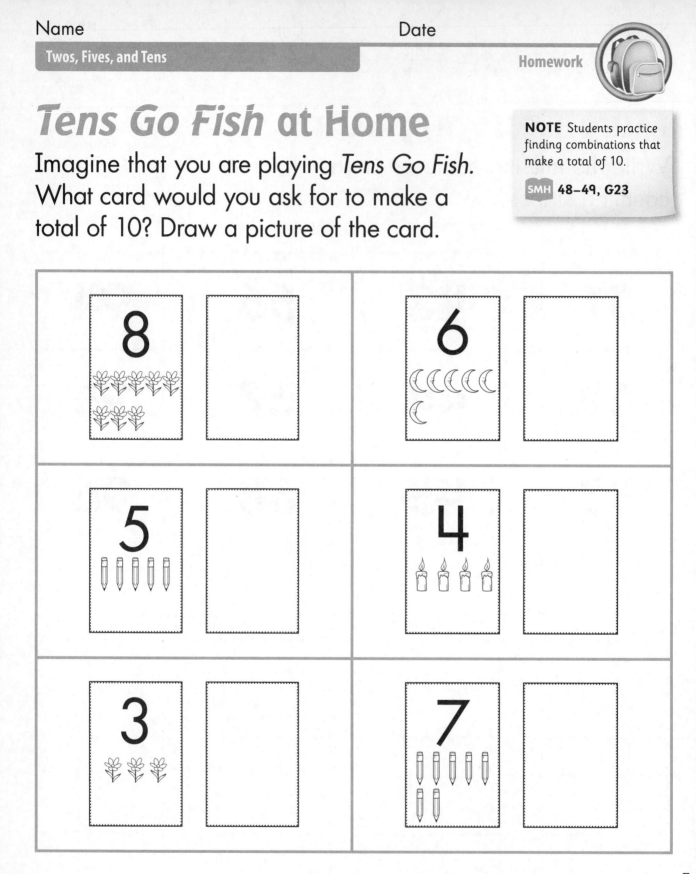

What's Missing?

Write the missing numbers on the chart.

NOTE Students practice writing numbers and work with number order 1–100.

SMH 27–29

		3		5					10
					16		18		
21			25					29	
	32				37		39		
41		43		45					50
51				56		58			
	62	63						69	
	73	74			77				80
			85			88			
91	92				96			99	

Ongoing Review

There are 10 counters in all. How many counters are under the cup?

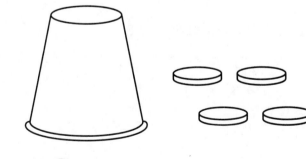

(A) 4   (B) 5   (C) 6   (D) 7

Heads and Tails

Imagine that you are playing *Heads and Tails.* Fill in the chart for each game.

NOTE Students practice counting and breaking a number into two parts (7 = 3 + 4).

SMH G13

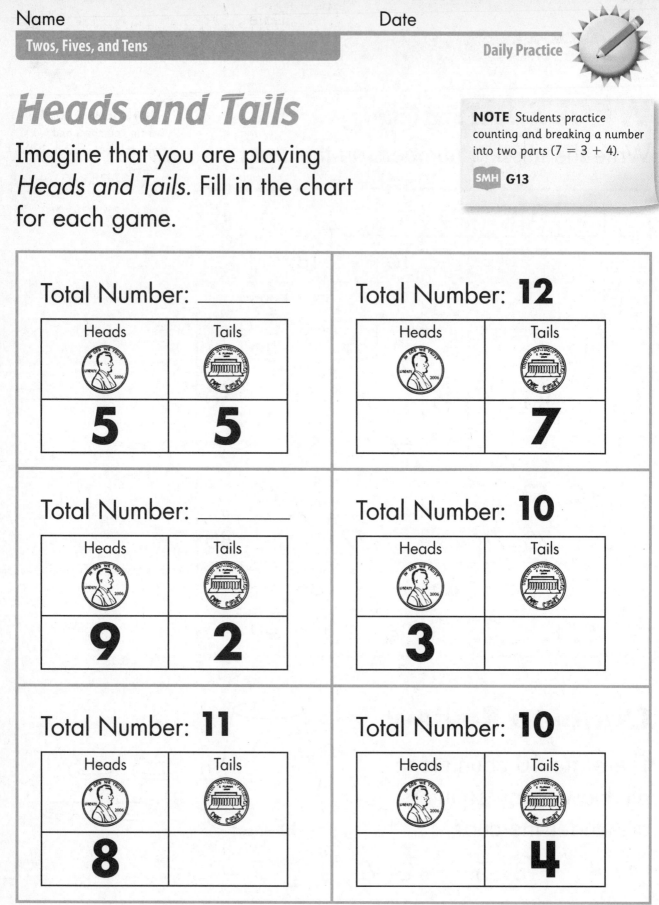

Total Number: _____

Heads	Tails
5	5

Total Number: **12**

Heads	Tails
	7

Total Number: _____

Heads	Tails
9	2

Total Number: **10**

Heads	Tails
3	

Total Number: **11**

Heads	Tails
8	

Total Number: **10**

Heads	Tails
	4

Story Problems with Missing Parts

NOTE Students solve story problems that involve an unknown change.

Solve each problem. Show your work.

1. Kim picked 8 apples.
   On her way home, she ate some apples.
   When she got home, there were 6 apples.
   How many apples did she eat?

2. Max picked some oranges.
   He used 6 oranges to make juice.
   He had 2 oranges left to eat.
   How many oranges did Max pick?

How Many Fingers? 2

Solve the problem. Show your work.

NOTE Students use what they know about groups of 10s to solve a story problem.

SMH 24–25

1. There are 4 children in the kitchen. How many fingers are there?

Ongoing Review

2. There are 11 ducks on the pond. 4 fly away. How many ducks are still on the pond?

(A) 4   (B) 5   (C) 6   (D) 7

Poster Fun! (page 1 of 2)

Imagine that your class is making a poster. Your teacher has some supplies for you and your classmates.

NOTE Students solve real world problems.

SMH 24–25

1. There are 5 paintbrushes in a box. He has 4 boxes. How many paintbrushes does he have?

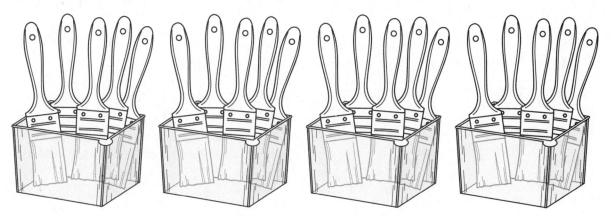

2. There are 2 jars of paint in a box. He has 10 boxes. How many jars of paint does he have?

Poster Fun! (page 2 of 2)

3. There are 10 scissors in a box. He has 2 boxes of scissors. How many scissors does he have?

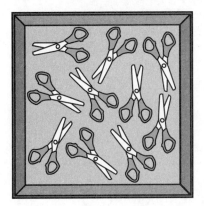 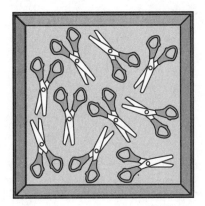

4. There are 5 bottles of glue in a box. He has 5 boxes of glue. How many bottles of glue does he have?

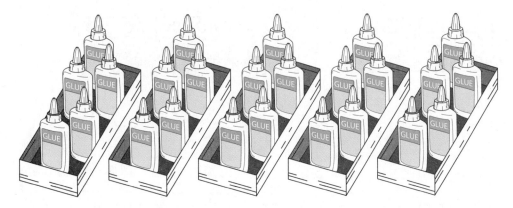

Twos, Fives, and Tens

How Many Cubes? (page 1 of 4)

Write the number of cubes on each 30 mat.

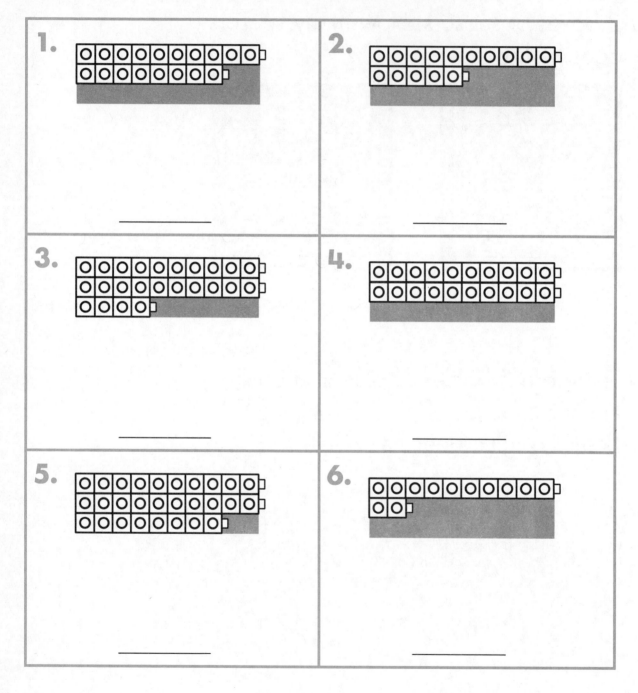

1. _____

2. _____

3. _____

4. _____

5. _____

6. _____

How Many Cubes? (page 2 of 4)

Write the number of cubes on each 50 mat.

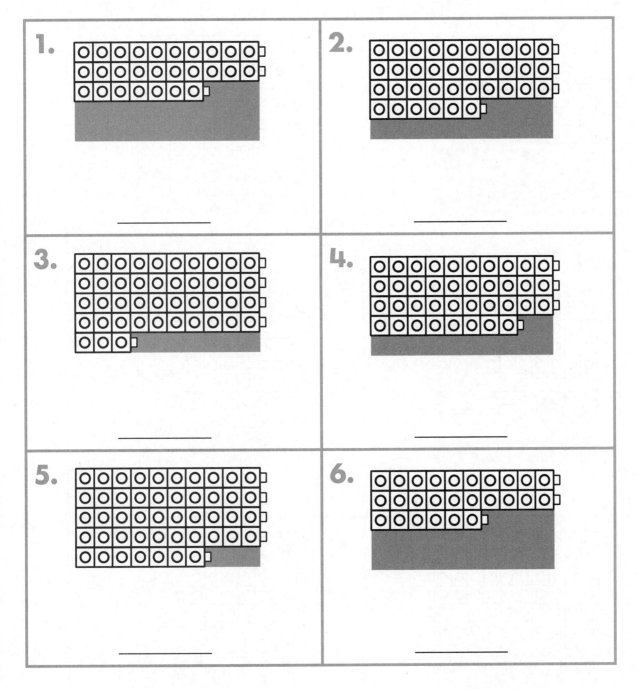

1. _____

2. _____

3. _____

4. _____

5. _____

6. _____

How Many Cubes? (page 3 of 4)

Write the number of cubes on each 100 mat.

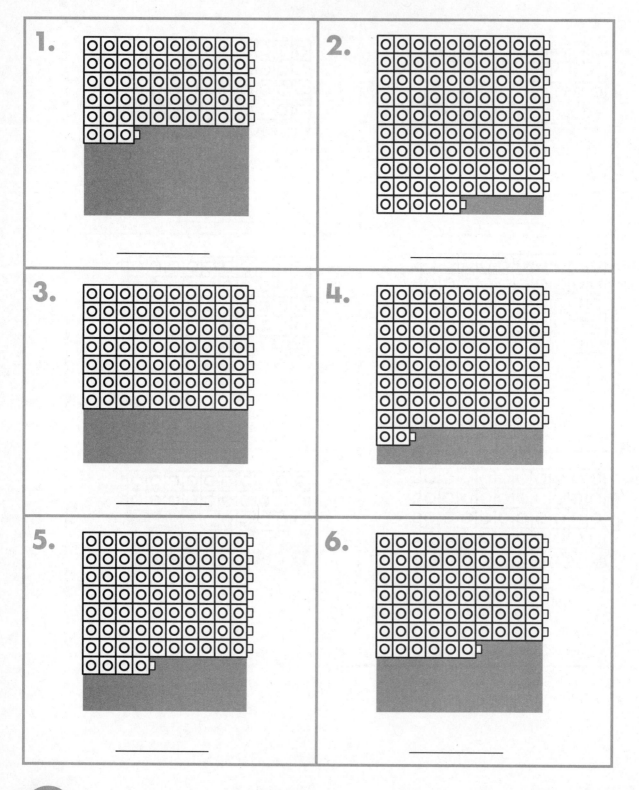

1.

_____

2.

_____

3.

_____

4.

_____

5.

_____

6.

_____

Session 4A.1

Twos, Fives, and Tens

How Many Cubes? (page 4 of 4)

Write the number of cubes.

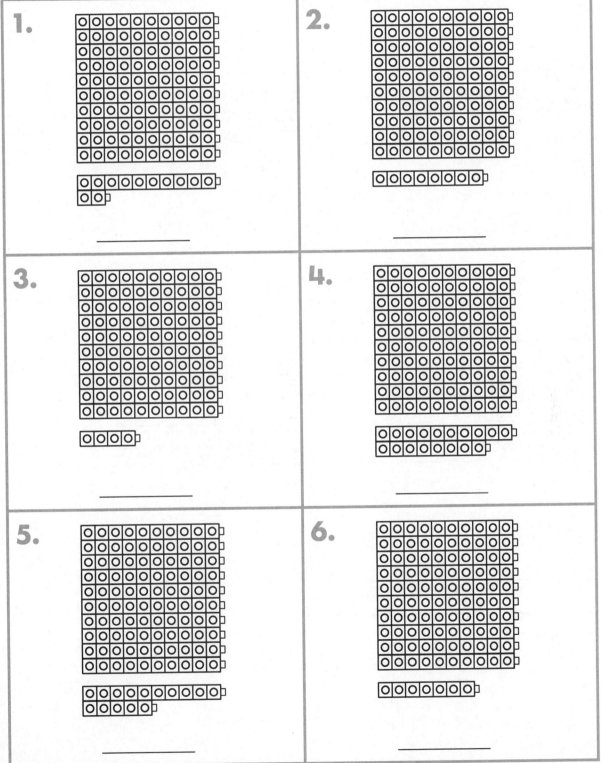

How Many Cubes?

Write the number of cubes. Circle the correct symbol to compare the groups.

NOTE Students represent a quantity of cubes with a written numeral and compare the quantities.

SMH 24–25, 43

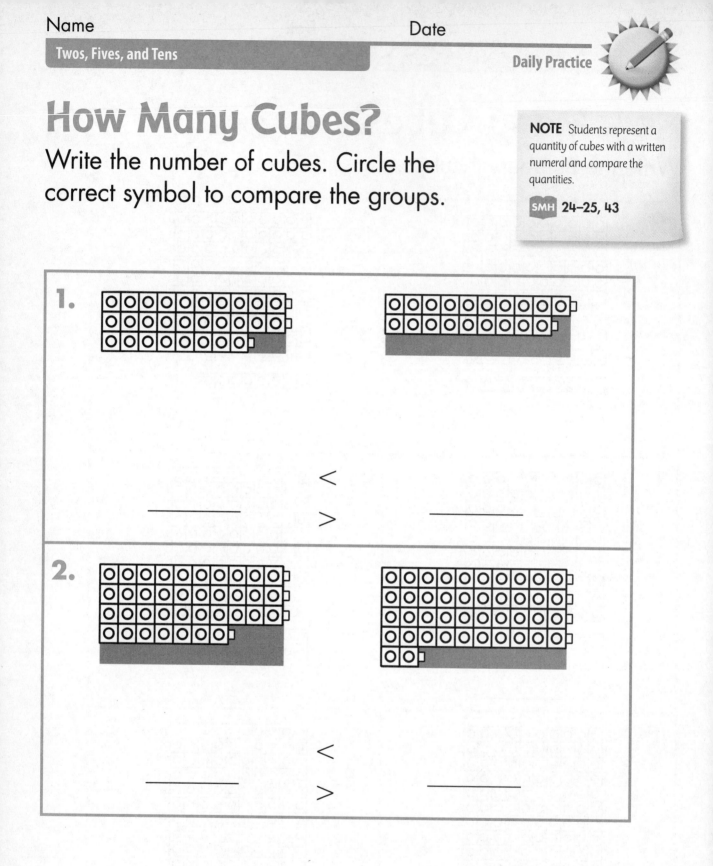

1. _____ < _____

   >

2. _____ < _____

   >

Plus or Minus 10 Recording Sheet

Plus 10	Minus 10
Example: $25 + 10 = 35$	Example: $35 - 10 = 25$

What's Missing? Plus or Minus 10

NOTE Students add 10 to or subtract 10 from two-digit numbers.

Solve these problems. Fill in the numbers on the 100 chart.

32 + 10 = _____   43 − 10 = _____

67 − 10 = _____   16 + 10 = _____

58 + 10 = _____   82 − 10 = _____

18 − 10 = _____   74 + 10 = _____

29 − 10 = _____

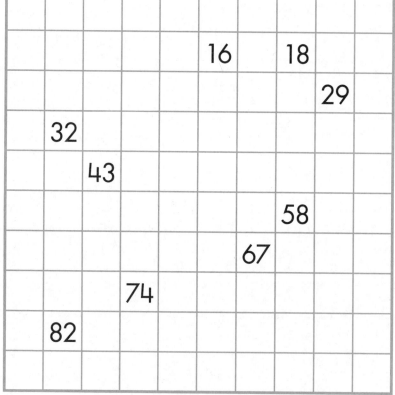

Challenge:

38 + 10 − 10 = _____   61 − 10 + 10 = _____

77 + 10 + 10 = _____   44 − 10 − 10 = _____

Addition Recording Sheet

Write the equation.

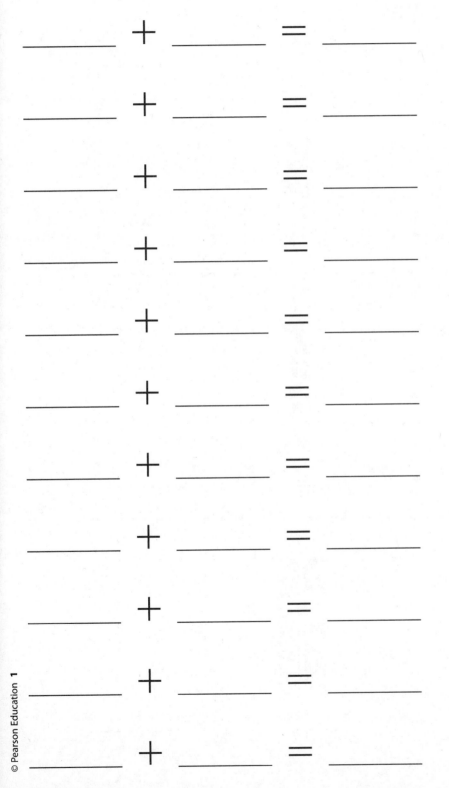

_____ + _____ = _____

_____ + _____ = _____

_____ + _____ = _____

_____ + _____ = _____

_____ + _____ = _____

_____ + _____ = _____

_____ + _____ = _____

_____ + _____ = _____

_____ + _____ = _____

_____ + _____ = _____

_____ + _____ = _____

Practice Adding with Cubes

NOTE Students add a one-digit number or a multiple of 10 to a two-digit number.

Write the number of cubes. Add.

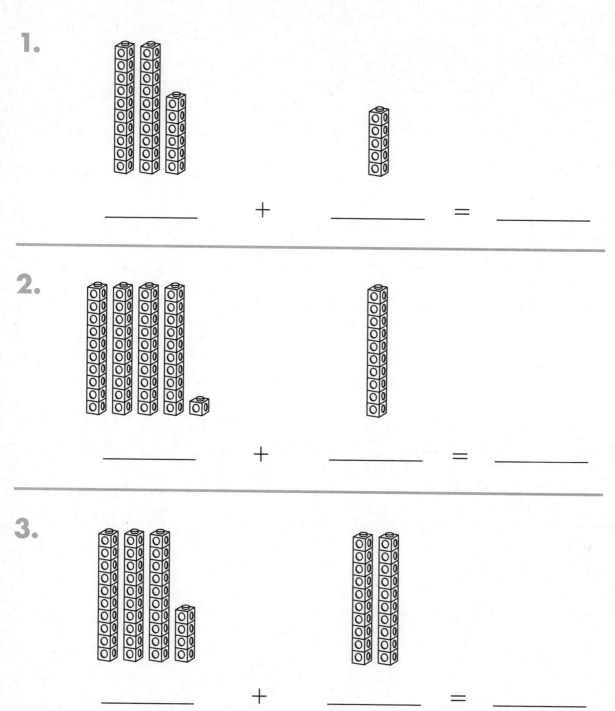

1.

_____ + _____ = _____

2.

_____ + _____ = _____

3.

_____ + _____ = _____

Session 4A.3

Build and Remove

Solve the problems.

1. Build 20.
   Remove 10.
   How many are left?

   ____ – ____ = ____

2. Build 40.
   Remove 20.
   How many are left?

   ____ – ____ = ____

3. Build 30.
   Remove 30.
   How many are left?

   ____ – ____ = ____

4. Build 50.
   Remove 20.
   How many are left?

   ____ – ____ = ____

5. Build 40.
   Remove 10.
   How many are left?

   ____ – ____ = ____

6. Build 50.
   Remove 30.
   How many are left?

   ____ – ____ = ____

Build and Remove 2

Solve the problems.

1. Build 60.
Remove 20.
How many are left?

____ − ____ = ____

2. Build 70.
Remove 30.
How many are left?

____ − ____ = ____

3. Build 80.
Remove 40.
How many are left?

____ − ____ = ____

4. Build 60.
Remove 30.
How many are left?

____ − ____ = ____

5. Build 70.
Remove 20.
How many are left?

____ − ____ = ____

6. Build 90.
Remove 40.
How many are left?

____ − ____ = ____

Subtraction Recording Sheet

Write the equation.

_____ − _____ = _____

_____ − _____ = _____

_____ − _____ = _____

_____ − _____ = _____

_____ − _____ = _____

_____ − _____ = _____

_____ − _____ = _____

_____ − _____ = _____

_____ − _____ = _____

_____ − _____ = _____

Twos, Fives, and Tens

How Many Now?

Write the number of cubes. Subtract.

1.

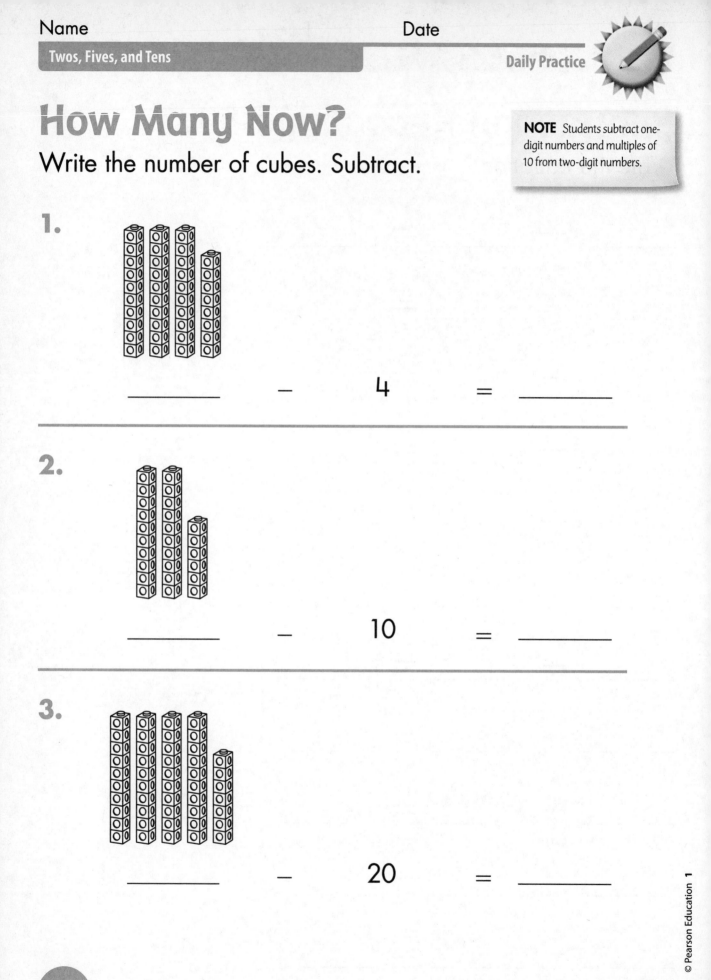

_____ – 4 = _____

2.

_____ – 10 = _____

3.

_____ – 20 = _____

Adding and Subtracting

Solve the problems.

NOTE Students add 10 to and subtract 10 from two-digit numbers.

1. How many cubes?

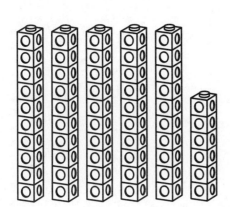

_____

Add 10 more cubes.
How many cubes?

_____

2. How many cubes?

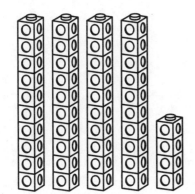

_____

Take away 10 cubes.
How many cubes?

_____

Spiral to Infinity Steve Allen

"Fractal images are often made up of small images-within-images, constantly repeating and going smaller and smaller."– **Steve Allen**

Investigations
IN NUMBER, DATA, AND SPACE®

Blocks and Boxes

Subtraction Practice

Fill in the blank.

NOTE Students subtract one amount from another.

SMH **G20**

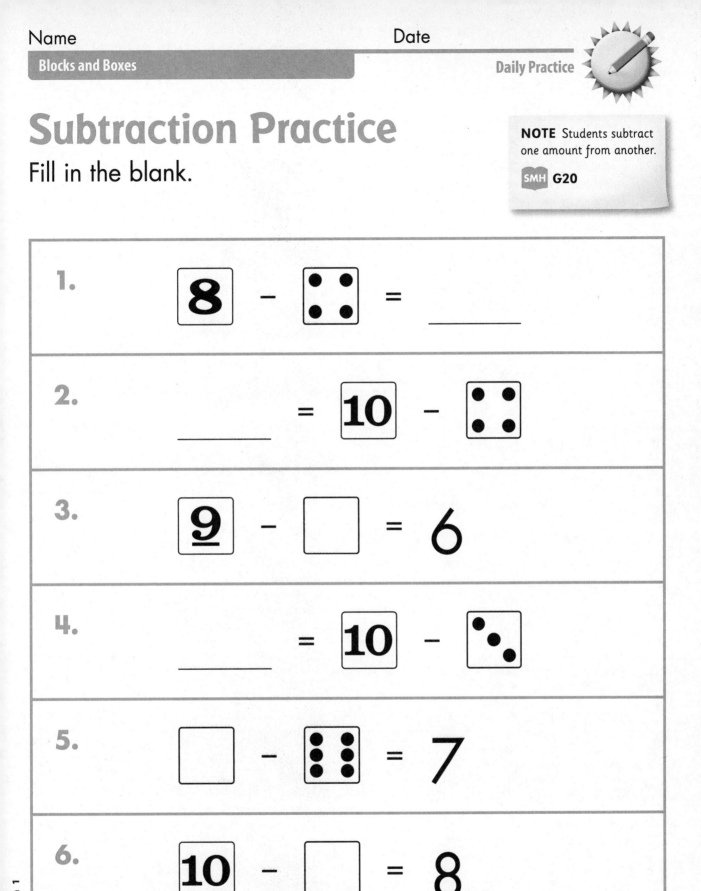

1. $\boxed{\textbf{8}} - \boxed{::} = \underline{\qquad}$

2. $\underline{\qquad} = \boxed{\textbf{10}} - \boxed{::}$

3. $\boxed{\underline{\textbf{9}}} - \boxed{} = 6$

4. $\underline{\qquad} = \boxed{\textbf{10}} - \boxed{\cdot\cdot\cdot}$

5. $\boxed{} - \boxed{:::} = 7$

6. $\boxed{\textbf{10}} - \boxed{} = 8$

More True or False?

Circle the word to show whether the equation is true or false.

NOTE Students determine whether equations are true or false and complete equations to make them true.

SMH 44

1. $8 = 5 + 3$ True   False

2. $7 + 2 = 5$ True   False

3. $10 - 4 = 7 - 1$ True   False

Write a number that makes the equation true.

4. $4 + 2 = \boxed{} + 5$

5. $1 + 6 = 3 + \underline{}$

6. $7 + 2 = 10 - \boxed{}$

Calendar

Here is a calendar for you. Fill in the month and dates. Then find a place to hang it at home.

NOTE Students practice recording dates and creating, reading, and using a calendar as a tool to keep track of time.

SMH 17, 18, 19

Name of Month

Sunday	Monday	Tuesday	Wednesday	Thursday	Friday	Saturday

Special Days _____

_____

More Halves and Fourths

NOTE Students solve problems about halves and fourths.

1. Draw a line to cut the square in half.

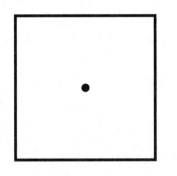

2. Draw lines to cut the circle in fourths.

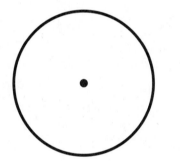

3. Circle the squares that show halves.

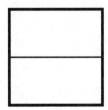 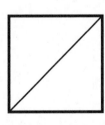 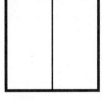 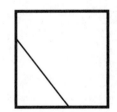

4. Circle the squares that show fourths.

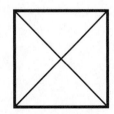 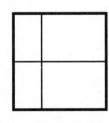 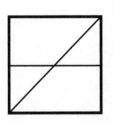

Mystery Footprints

Find one or two things at home that have a special shape. Draw the "footprint" (or outline) of each shape by tracing around it. Bring your drawings to school.

Do not write the names of your objects on your drawings. The class will try to guess what your objects are.

NOTE Students learn about the attributes of a 3-D object by tracing a 2-D outline of one of its faces.

SMH 89

Adding and Subtracting 10

NOTE Students add 10 to and subtract 10 from two-digit numbers.

Solve the problems.

1. How many cubes?

Add 10 more cubes.
How many cubes?

_____

_____

2. How many cubes?

Take away 10 cubes.
How many cubes?

_____

_____

More Mystery Footprints

Write the mystery object for each
mystery footprint.

NOTE Students match
2-D outlines to 3-D objects.

SMH 89

1.

_____

2.

_____

3.

_____

Ongoing Review

People	Chairs
12	10

4. How many more chairs are needed?

Ⓐ 12   Ⓒ 3

Ⓑ 10   Ⓓ 2

Count the Feet

Sam's family went for a walk. There were 5 people and 2 dogs on the walk. How many feet were there?

Solve the problem. Show your work.

NOTE Students use what they know about groups of 2s and 4s to solve a story problem.

SMH 24–25

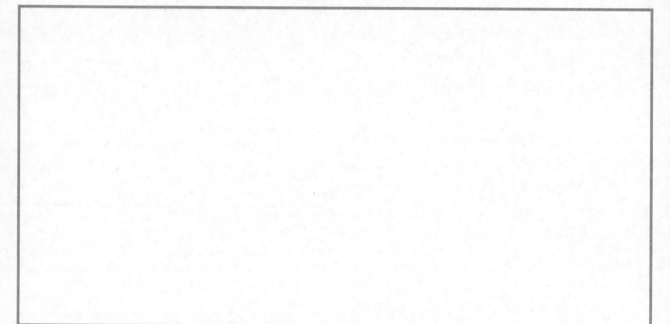

Ongoing Review

There are some beads in the counting jar. There are more than 10 beads. How many beads could be in the jar?

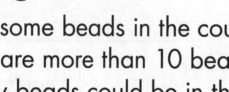

(A) 13   (C) 9

(B) 10   (D) 5

Counting Jar

Unknown Numbers

Solve each problem. Show your work.

NOTE Students solve story problems that involve an unknown change.

Sam and Rosa are going on a Number Hunt.
They are hunting for numbers that have a sum of 9.

1. Sam finds the number 6. What number
must Rosa find to make a sum of 9?

2. Rosa finds the number 3. What number
must Sam find to make a sum of 9?

Find That Shape
(page 1 of 2)

Look at each Geoblock. Circle the object that has the same shape as the Geoblock.

NOTE Students think about the shape of real-life objects and how they compare to the Geoblocks we've been working with in school. Also, please help your child find and wrap a Mystery Box to bring in for an upcoming math activity.

SMH 83, 85

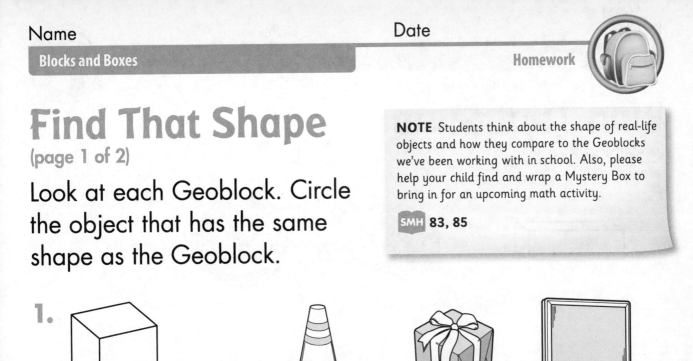

1.

2.

Find That Shape
(page 2 of 2)

3.

4.

5.

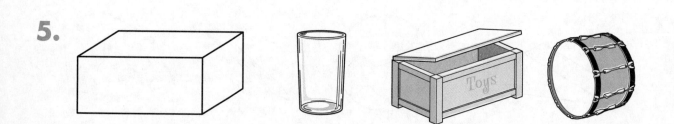

Is It a Match?

Does the picture match the sentence?
If it **does,** circle the picture.
If it **does not,** cross out the picture.

NOTE Students match 2-D shapes to the faces (or sides) of 3-D Geoblocks.

SMH 86

1. I have a side shaped like a **triangle.**

2. I have a side shaped like a **rectangle.**

3. I have a side shaped like a **square.**

Ongoing Review

4. Which group below shows more beans than this group?

(A)

(B)

(C)

(D)

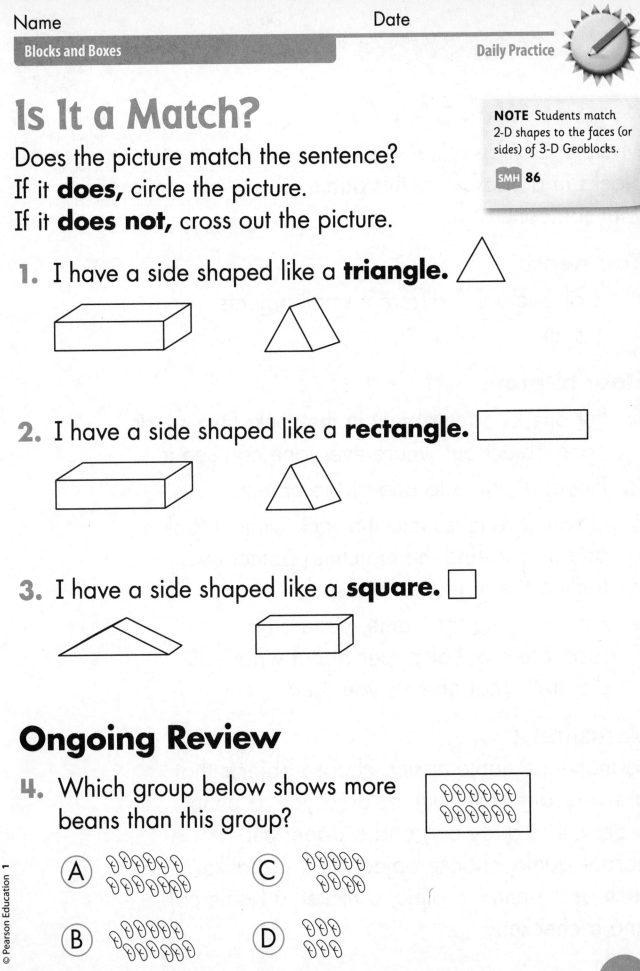

Mystery Objects ✎

Mystery Objects is just like Blocks in a Sock. Play this game with someone at home.

NOTE Students practice identifying 3-D objects by touch by paying attention to important features of 3-D objects, such as size and shape. Also, please help your child find and wrap a Mystery Box to bring in for an upcoming math activity!

SMH 86, 87, 88

You need:

- 2 of each of 5 different small objects
- 1 sock

How to play:

1. Put one of each object in the sock. Put one of each object out where everyone can see it.

2. Player 1 points to one of the objects.

3. Player 2 reaches into the sock without looking and tries to find the matching object by feeling the objects in the sock.

4. After playing the game, write on a separate sheet of paper about what you did. Tell what objects you used.

Variations:

To make the game easier, choose objects that are very different, such as a crayon, a penny, a dot cube, a toy car, and a paper clip. For a harder game, choose objects that are alike, such as a penny, a dime, a nickel, a bottle cap, and a checker.

More Adding with Cubes

Write the number of cubes. Add.

NOTE Students add a one-digit number to a two-digit number.

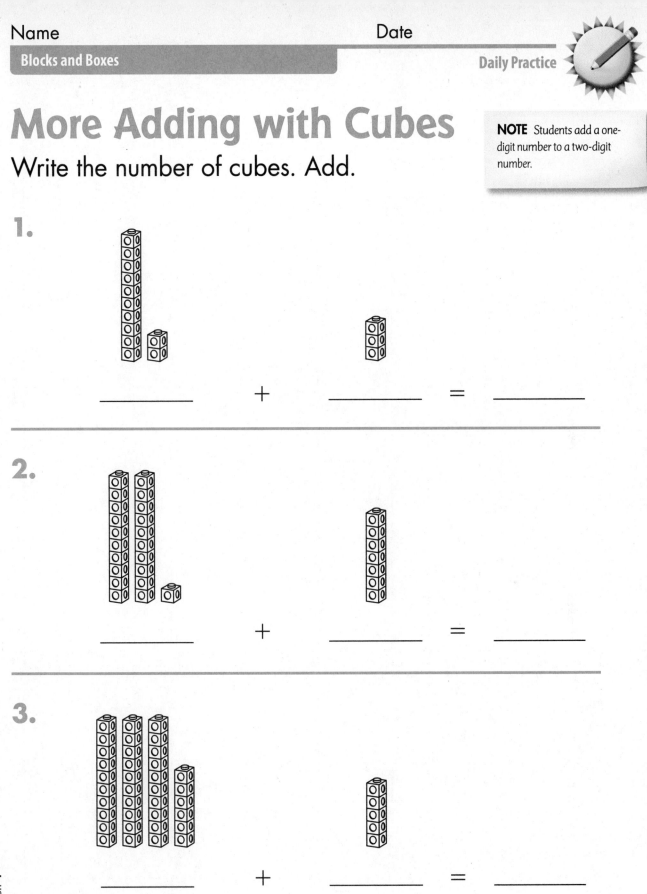

1.

_____ + _____ = _____

2.

_____ + _____ = _____

3.

_____ + _____ = _____

Heads and Tails

Imagine that you are playing *Heads and Tails*. Fill in the blank or chart for each game.

NOTE Students practice counting and breaking a number into 2 parts (7 = 3 + 4).

SMH G13

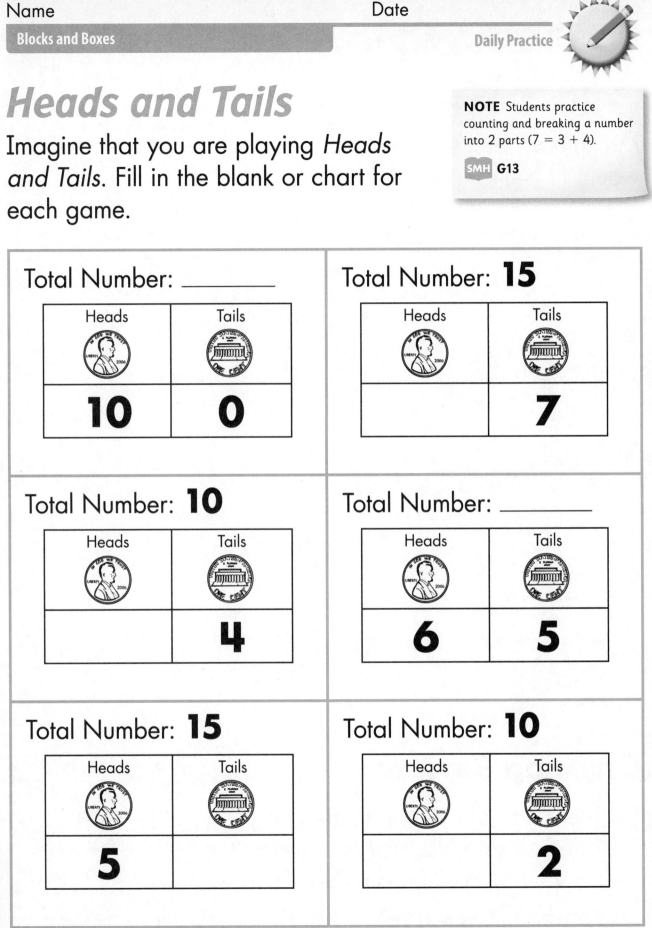

Total Number: _____

Heads	Tails
10	0

Total Number: **15**

Heads	Tails
	7

Total Number: **10**

Heads	Tails
	4

Total Number: _____

Heads	Tails
6	5

Total Number: **15**

Heads	Tails
5	

Total Number: **10**

Heads	Tails
	2

Cube Boxes

Match each box with the object that
would fit **best** inside the box.

NOTE Students compare and relate
the size and shape of 3-D objects to
the size and shape of various boxes.

SMH **83**

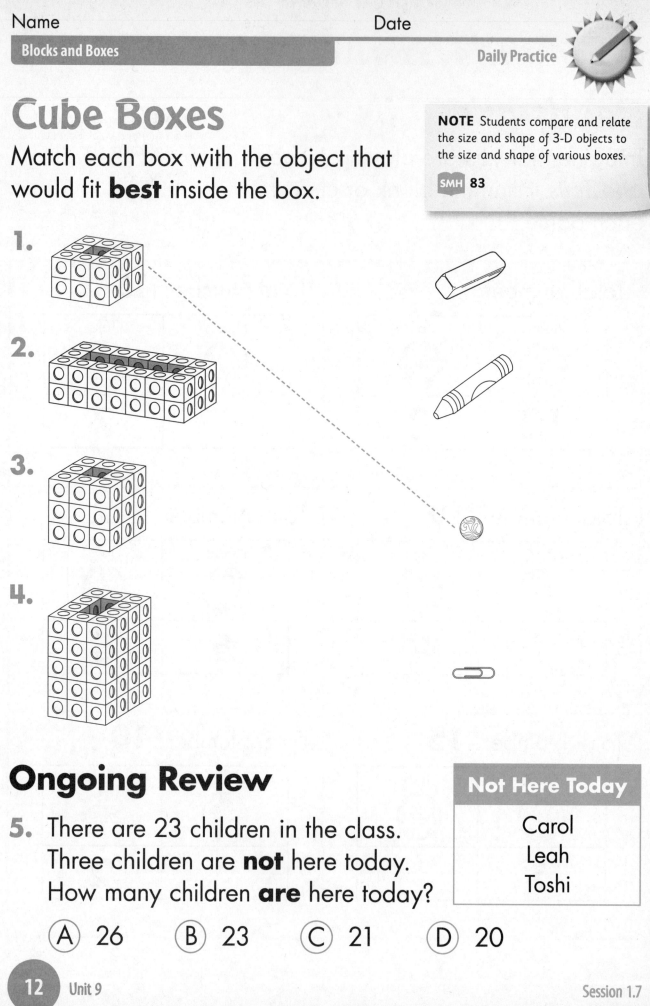

1.

2.

3.

4.

Ongoing Review

5. There are 23 children in the class.
Three children are **not** here today.
How many children **are** here today?

Ⓐ 26   Ⓑ 23   Ⓒ 21   Ⓓ 20

Not Here Today

Carol
Leah
Toshi

© Pearson Education 1

Missing Numbers 1

Write the missing numbers on the counting strips.

NOTE Students practice counting, writing, and sequencing numbers.

SMH **21–23**

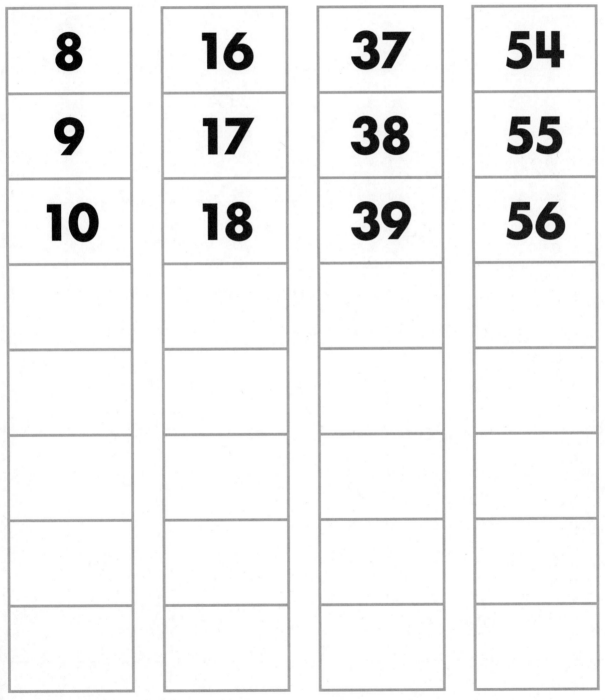

8	16	37	54
9	17	38	55
10	18	39	56

What's Missing?

Fill in the missing numbers.

NOTE Students practice writing numbers and sequencing numbers from 1 to 100.

SMH 27–29

1			4					9	
	13					17			
	22			26					30
31		34					38		
				46	47			49	
	52		55					59	60
61		64							
	73		75				78		
	82					87		89	
	93	94				97	98		

Draw a Building

NOTE Students identify shapes in real-life situations and draw a picture of them.

SMH **83, 84, 85**

Think of a building that you have seen. It may be a building near where you live, or it may be a building you saw somewhere else.

Try to think of a building that has an interesting shape. Draw a picture of the building. If you have a picture of the building, you can paste it on this sheet instead of drawing.

Write one or two sentences about the building.

_____

_____

_____

_____

Adding Tens with Cubes

Write the number of cubes. Add.

NOTE Students practice adding a multiple of 10 to a two-digit number.

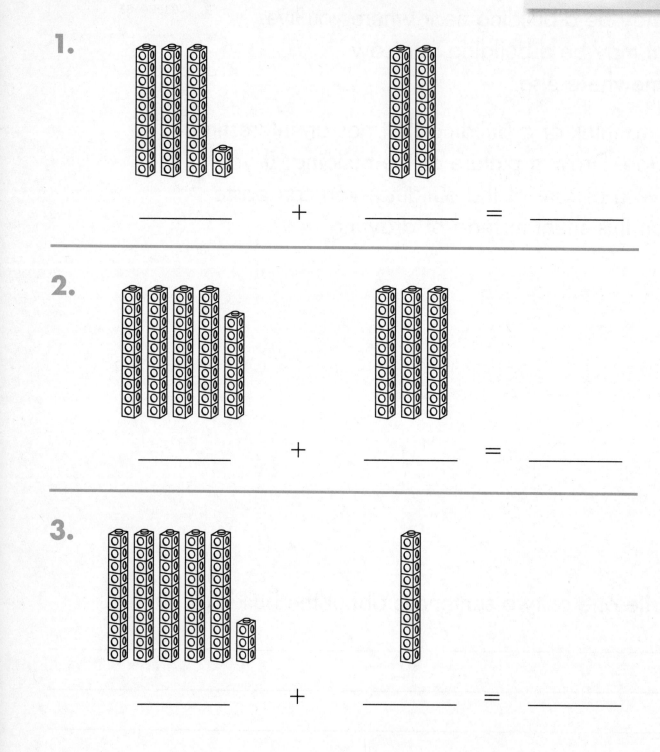

1.

_____ + _____ = _____

2.

_____ + _____ = _____

3.

_____ + _____ = _____

Add to 10

Imagine that you are playing the card game *Tens Go Fish*. What card would you ask for?

NOTE Students are given one number and determine what number they need to add to make a total of 10.

SMH 48–49, G23

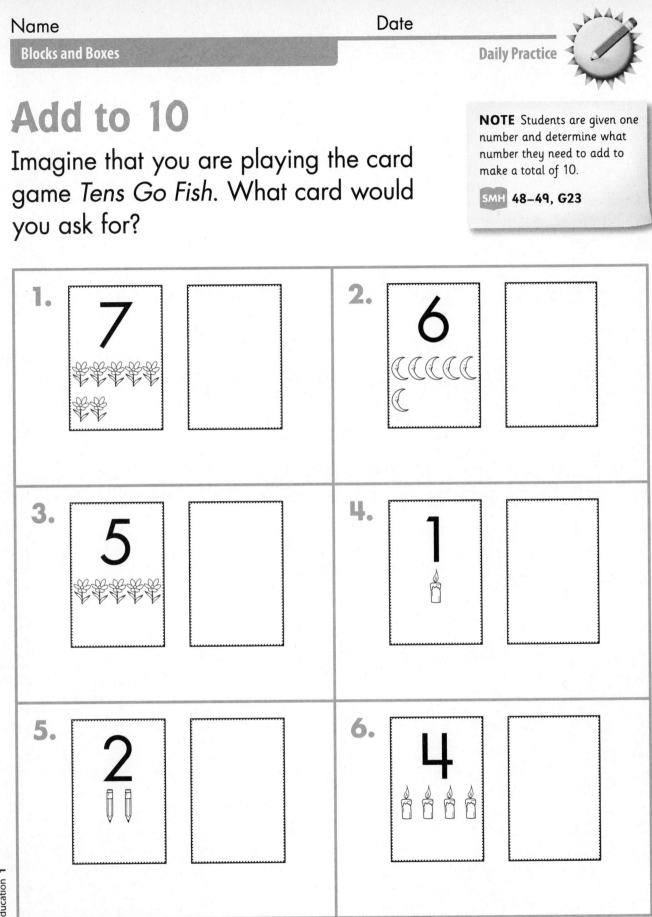

1.   7

2.   6

3.   5

4.   1

5.   2

6.   4

18A Unit 9

How Many Are Left?

Write the number of cubes. Subtract.

NOTE Students practice subtracting a multiple of 10 from a two-digit number.

1.

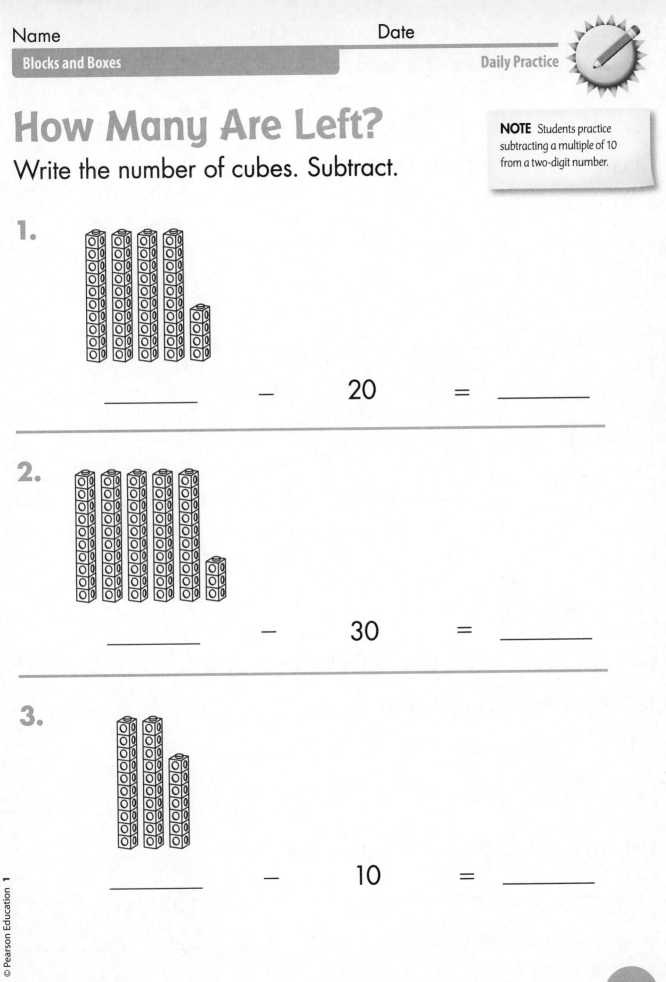

_____ − 20 = _____

2.

_____ − 30 = _____

3.

_____ − 10 = _____

Comparing Cones and Cylinders

Draw a cone and a cylinder.

Tell ways the 2 shapes are alike.

_____

_____

Tell ways the 2 shapes are not alike.

_____

_____

3-D Shape Riddles

Draw a line to connect the riddle to its shape.

NOTE Students match the clues to the 3-D shapes.

SMH 83, 85, 88

Riddle

Shape

1. I'm a box for shoes, and cereal, too.

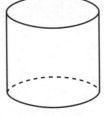

cylinder

2. Kids use me to play games with bats and bases. I'm a shape with no faces!

cone

3. I'll hold your ice cream for you. You can wear me as a party hat, too.

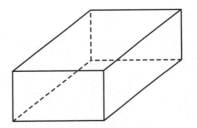

rectangular prism

4. Inside me are sauces. Soup I can hold. Or, think about a paper towel roll.

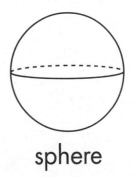

sphere

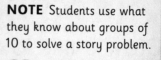

Groups of 10
Story Problem

NOTE Students use what
they know about groups of
10 to solve a story problem.

SMH 24–25

There are 7 people in the classroom.
How many toes are there?

Solve the problem. Show your work.

Missing Numbers 2

Write the missing numbers on the counting strips.

NOTE Students practice counting, writing, and sequencing numbers.

SMH 21–23

15	23	75	97
16	24	76	98
17	25	77	99

Addition and Subtraction Practice

Fill in the blank.

NOTE Students use addition or subtraction to find the total or the missing addend.

SMH **G19**

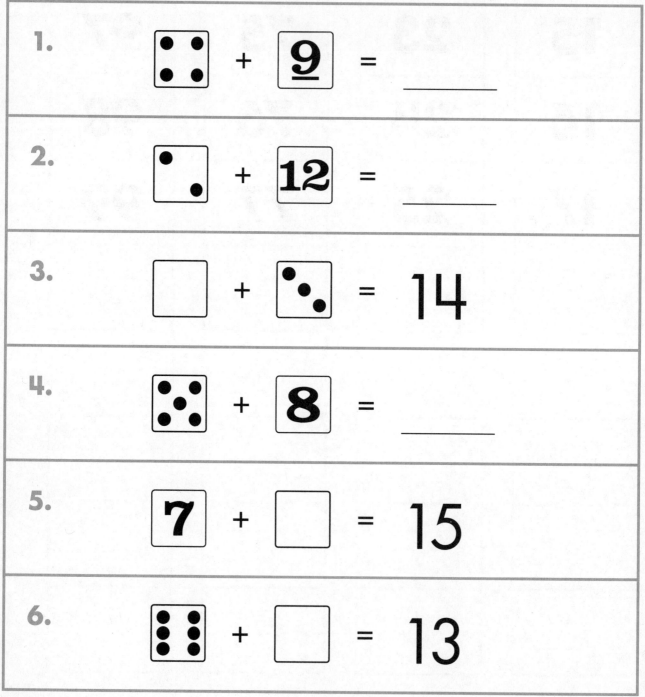

1. [⚃ 4] + [**9**] = _____

2. [⚁ 2] + [**12**] = _____

3. [ ] + [⚂ 3] = **14**

4. [⚄ 5] + [**8**] = _____

5. [**7**] + [ ] = **15**

6. [⚅ 6] + [ ] = **13**

More Footprints

Look at the footprint. Circle the
Geoblock that makes that footprint.

NOTE Students find blocks that
have faces (sides) that match the
given outlines (footprints).

SMH **90**

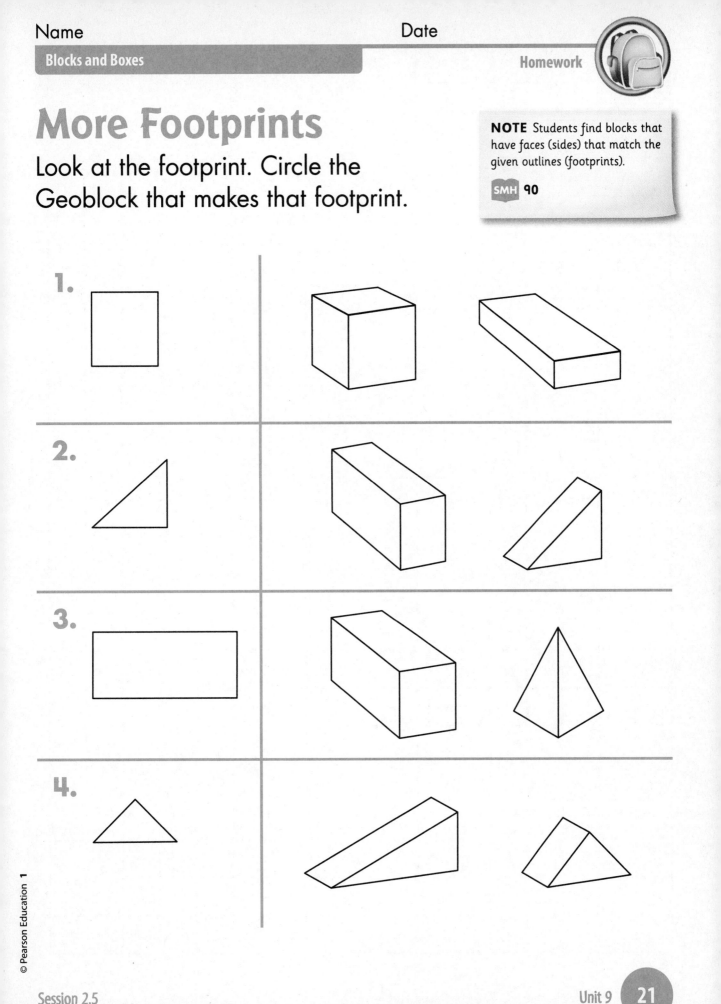

Following Directions

NOTE Students practice following directions and making turns to follow a particular path. Students also practice the counting sequence from 1 to 25.

SMH 21–23

1. Jack and Jill are going to play baseball. Help them follow the directions to the field.

Directions: Start counting at 1. Count to 25. Draw Jack and Jill's path.

1----2	11	6	20	8	17	12
12	3	4	2	19	23	5	1
5	15	5	1	9	10	18	15
10	12	6	7	8	11	24	6
22	3	19	14	13	12	2	14
7	21	16	15	6	21	22	23
16	13	17	18	19	20	9	24
9	4	7	5	11	8	10	25

Ongoing Review

2. Which cards are in order from **least** to **greatest**?

3	5	4		7	5	3		6	8	10		2	4	1
	Ⓐ				Ⓑ				Ⓒ				Ⓓ	

Where Are You? (page 1 of 4)

Use this map to answer the questions on the next page.

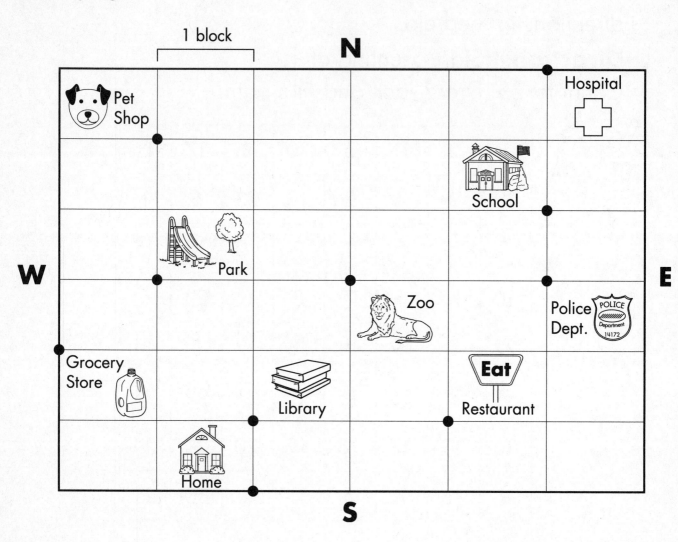

Where Are You? (page 2 of 4)

1. Start at the pet shop. Turn east. Go forward 4 blocks. Turn south. Go forward 1 block. Where are you?

   _____

2. Start at the library. Turn north. Go forward 2 blocks. Turn west. Go forward 1 block. Where are you?

   _____

3. Start at the hospital. Turn south. Go forward 3 blocks. Turn west. Go forward 5 blocks. Turn south. Go forward 1 block. Where are you?

   _____

4. Start at the school. Turn west. Go forward 3 blocks. Turn south. Go forward 4 blocks. Where are you?

   _____

Where Are You? (page 3 of 4)

Use this map to answer the questions on the next page.

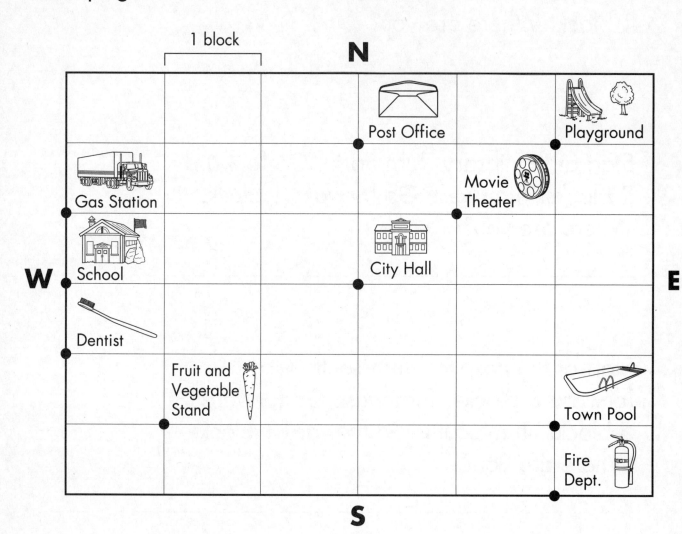

Where Are You? (page 4 of 4)

1. Start at City Hall. Turn west. Go forward
3 blocks. Turn south. Go forward 1 block.
Where are you?

_____

2. Start at the movie theater. Turn south. Go
forward 3 blocks. Turn east. Go forward
1 block. Where are you?

_____

3. Start at the fire department. Turn north. Go
forward 5 blocks. Turn west. Go forward 2
blocks. Where are you?

_____

4. Start at the fruit and vegetable stand. Turn
east. Go forward 2 blocks. Turn north. Go
forward 4 blocks. Turn east. Go forward
2 blocks. Where are you?

_____

Giving Directions

Use the map to write the directions from one place to another.

NOTE Students determine and record how to get from one location to another by counting blocks and turning in particular directions.

SMH 92

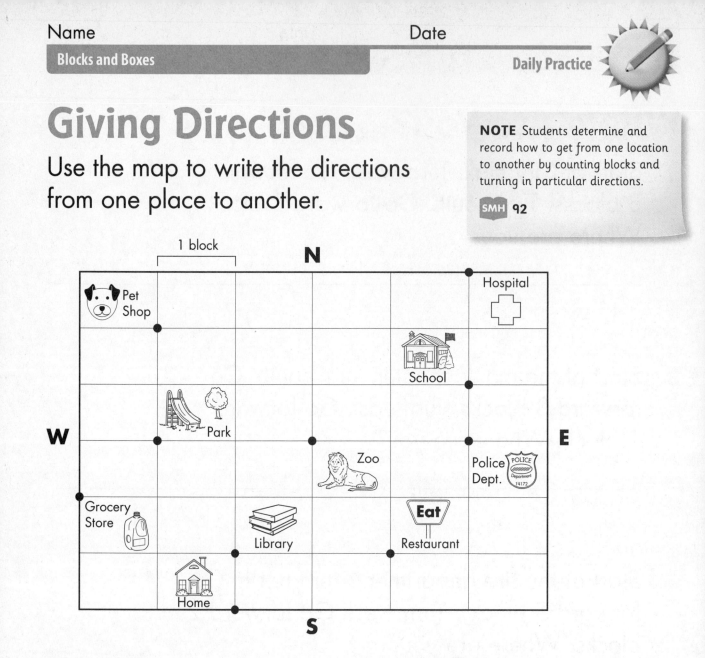

Example: To get from the pet shop to the police department: Start at the pet shop. Turn east. Go forward 4 blocks. Turn south. Go forward 2 blocks.

1. Give directions from the library to the school.

_____

2. Give directions from the home to the zoo.

_____

Robot Paces

> **NOTE** Ask your child to explain how we did this in class. Then do Robot Paces together.
>
> **SMH** 92

This activity takes two people. One person gives directions. The other person is a robot who walks a path from one place to another.

Choose a starting point and an ending point. These can be inside or outside your house. For example, you could start at the table and end up at the front door.

The robot can do only two things—walk straight ahead for so many paces or turn. A robot can follow directions like these: Walk 4 paces. Walk 5 paces. Turn toward the table. Walk 6 paces. Turn toward the front door. Walk 8 paces.

A pace is a normal walking step.

Try this several times. Always choose a starting point and an ending point before you begin. Take turns being the robot.

Write a few sentences about one of your paths.

_____

_____

_____

Mystery Boxes

Match each set of box pieces to the box they could make.

NOTE Students relate the size and shape of 2-D faces to the size and shape of rectangular prisms.

SMH **89, 90**

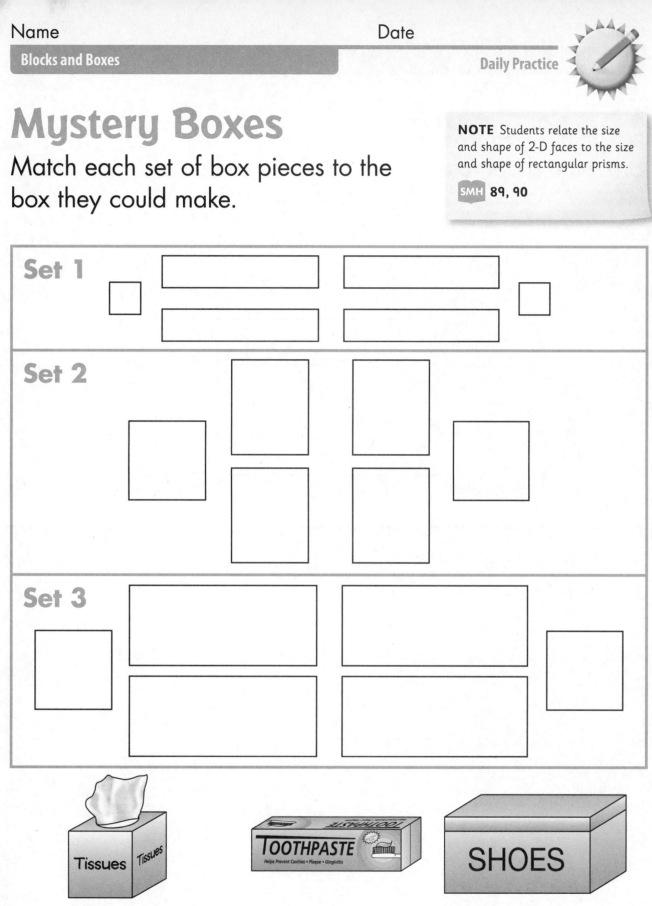

Shape Castle

Draw the shape castle.

NOTE Students draw a three-dimensional building.

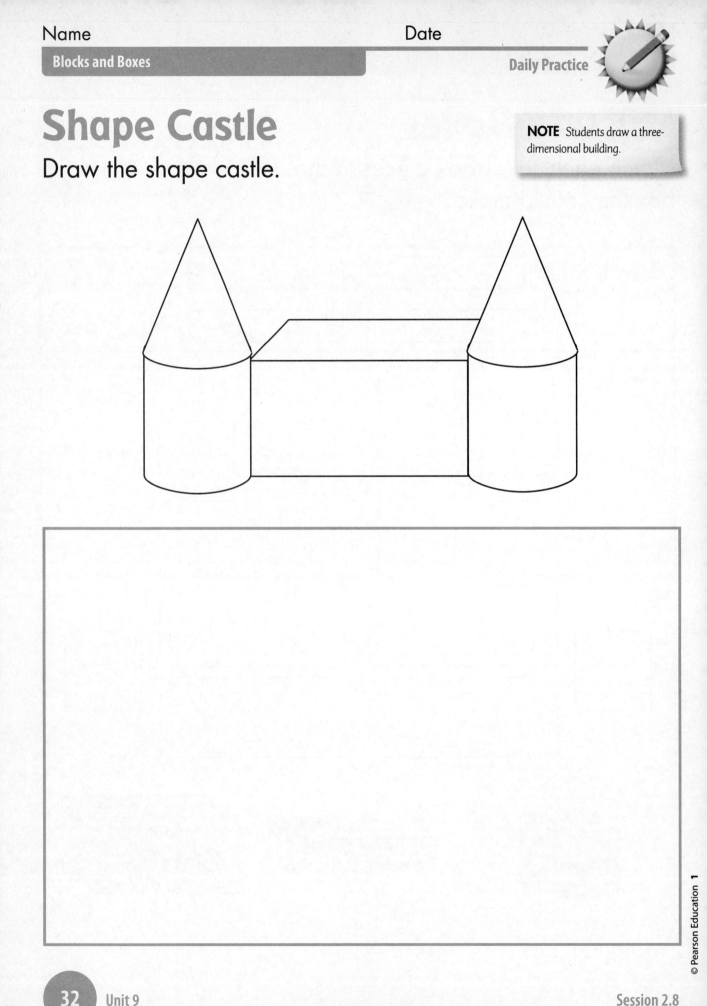